Caesar's Gallic Triumph

'But near Alesia such achievements were effected as it was scarcely for man to attempt, and for little less than a deity to accomplish.'
Paterculus, *History of Rome*, II. XL. VII

Campaign Chronicles

Caesar's Gallic Triumph

The Battle of Alesia 52BC

Peter A. Inker

Campaign Chronicles
Series Editor

Christopher Summerville

Pen & Sword
MILITARY

First published in Great Britain in 2008 by
Pen & Sword Military
an imprint of
Pen & Sword Books Ltd
47 Church Street
Barnsley
South Yorkshire S70 2AS

ISBN 978 1 84415 675 7

A CIP catalogue record for this book is
available from the British Library.

Printed and bound in England by
Biddles Ltd.

Pen & Sword Books Ltd incorporates the imprints of Pen & Sword Aviation,
Pen & Sword Maritime, Pen & Sword Military, Wharncliffe Local History,
Pen & Sword Select, Pen & Sword Military Classics and Leo Cooper.

For a complete list of Pen & Sword titles please contact
PEN & SWORD BOOKS LIMITED
47 Church Street, Barnsley, South Yorkshire, S70 2AS, England
E-mail: enquiries@pen-and-sword.co.uk
Website: www.pen-and-sword.co.uk

Contents

List of Plates
and Maps

Maps

Maps

Caesar's Gallic Triumph

TRIBES OF GAUL

0   100 km

GERMANY

Morini
Nervii
Belgae
Atrebates
Ambiani
Bellovaci
Lexovii
Aremorican Tribes
Veliocasses
Mediomatrices
Suessiones
Osismi
Curiosolites
Aulerci
PARIS
Lingones
Veneti
Parisii
Sequani
Redones
Mandubii
CENABUM
ALESIA
Rauraci
Andes
Senones
Carnutes
Helvetii
Pictones
Turones
BOURGES
Bituriges
BIBRACTE
Santoni
Aedui
Arverni
GERGOVIA
Allobroges
Lemovices
Helvii
Nitiobriges
Gabali
TRANSALPINE
GAUL
Cadurci
Ruteni
THE PROVINCE
Aquitani

SPAIN

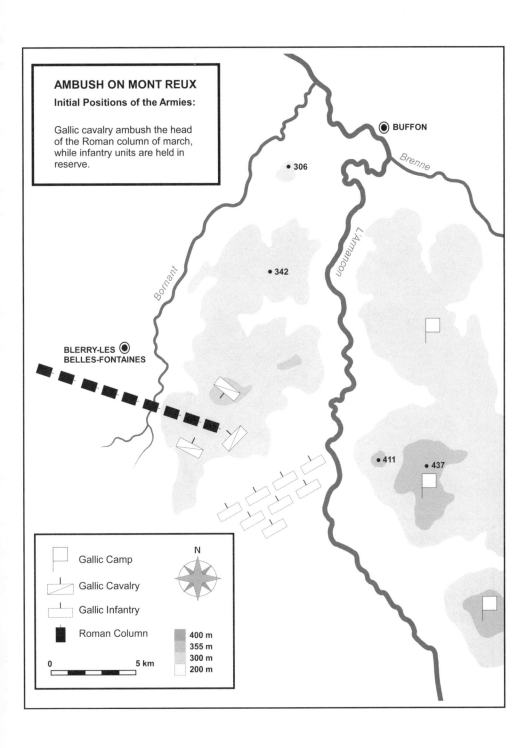

AMBUSH ON MONT REUX

Initial Positions of the Armies:

Gallic cavalry ambush the head of the Roman column of march, while infantry units are held in reserve.

BUFFON

Brenne

• 306

L'Armancon

• 342

Bornant

BLERRY-LES BELLES-FONTAINES

• 411   • 437

Gallic Camp

N

Gallic Cavalry

Gallic Infantry

Roman Column

400 m
355 m
300 m
200 m

0   5 km

Caesar's Gallic Triumph

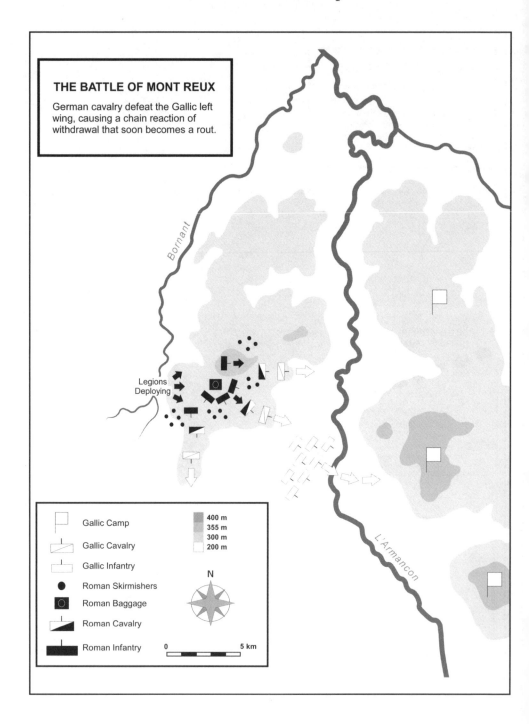

THE BATTLE OF MONT REUX

German cavalry defeat the Gallic left wing, causing a chain reaction of withdrawal that soon becomes a rout.

Bornant

Legions Deploying

L'Armancon

Gallic Camp

Gallic Cavalry

Gallic Infantry

Roman Skirmishers

Roman Baggage

Roman Cavalry

Roman Infantry

400 m
355 m
300 m
200 m

N

0   5 km

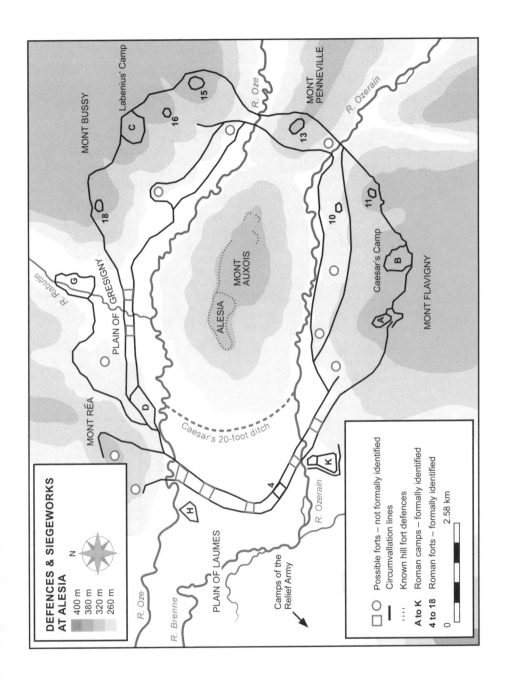

DEFENCES & SIEGEWORKS AT ALESIA

400 m
380 m
320 m
260 m

N

Legend:
□ ○ Possible forts – not formally identified
— Circumvallation lines
⋯⋯ Known hill fort defences
A to K Roman camps – formally identified
4 to 18 Roman forts – formally identified

0 — 2.58 km

MONT BUSSY
Labenius' Camp
MONT PENNEVILLE
R. Oze
R. Ozerain
R. Rabutin
PLAIN OF GRESIGNY
MONT RÉA
ALESIA
MONT AUXOIS
Caesar's Camp
MONT FLAVIGNY
Caesar's 20-foot ditch
PLAIN OF LAUMES
R. Oze
R. Brenne
R. Ozerain
Camps of the Relief Army

C
15
16
18
13
11
10
G
D
A
B
K
H
4

xiii

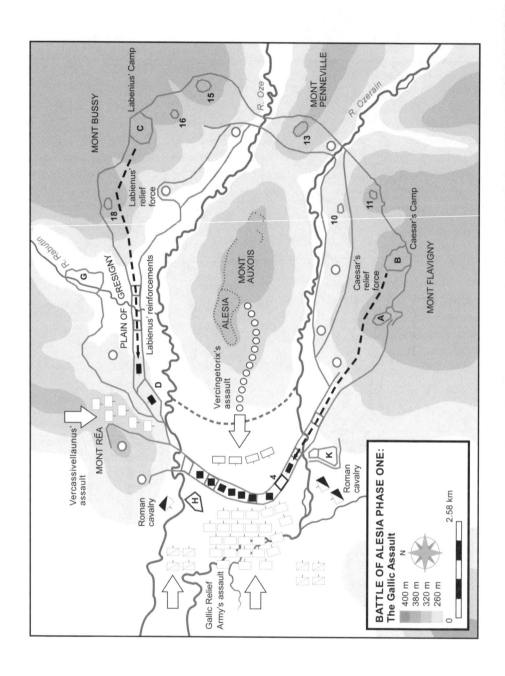

BATTLE OF ALESIA PHASE ONE:
The Gallic Assault

N

0   2.58 km

400 m
380 m
320 m
260 m

MONT BUSSY

Labenius' Camp

15

16

C

R. Oze

MONT PENNEVILLE

R. Ozerain

13

18

Labenius' relief force

11

Caesar's Camp

R. Rabutin

G

PLAIN OF GRESIGNY

Labenius' reinforcements

10

Caesar's relief force

B

MONT AUXOIS

ALESIA

Vercingetorix's assault

A

MONT FLAVIGNY

D

MONT RÉA

Vercassivellaunus' assault

K

4

Roman cavalry

Roman cavalry

H

Gallic Relief Army's assault

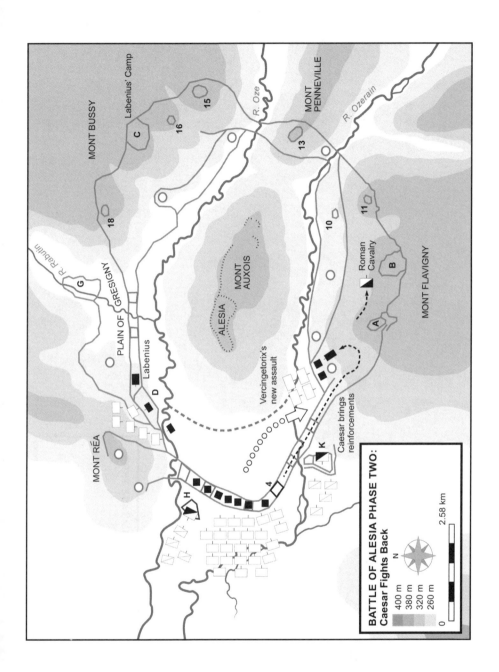

BATTLE OF ALESIA PHASE TWO:
Caesar Fights Back

400 m
380 m
320 m
260 m

0   2.58 km

MONT BUSSY

Labenius' Camp

C

15

16

R. Oze

MONT
PENNEVILLE

R. Ozerain

13

18

11

10

R. Rabutin

G

PLAIN OF GRESIGNY

MONT
AUXOIS

ALESIA

MONT FLAVIGNY

B

A

Roman
Cavalry

MONT RÉA

Labenius

D

Vercingetorix's
new assault

Caesar brings
reinforcements

K

4

H

N

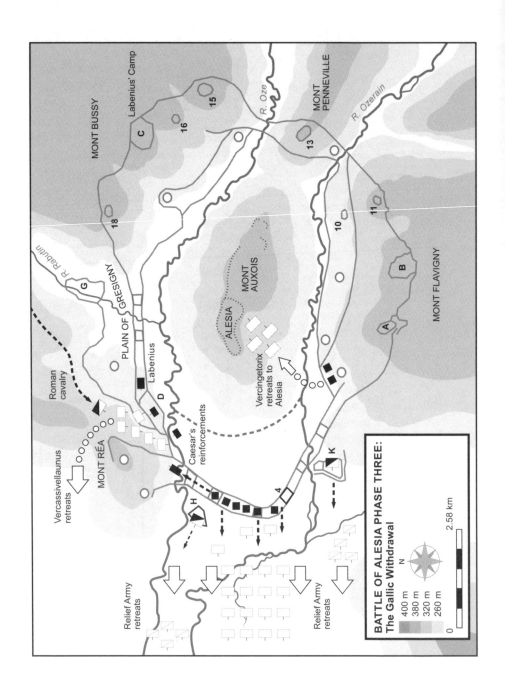

BATTLE OF ALESIA PHASE THREE:
The Gallic Withdrawal

Background

'Heracles, then . . . passing into Celtica and traversing the length and breadth of it, he put an end to the lawlessness and murdering of strangers to which the people had become addicted; and since a great multitude of men from every tribe flocked to his army of their own accord, he founded a great city which was named Alesia after the "wandering" on his campaign.'

[Diodorus Siculus, *Library*, IV. 19. 1]

The Alesia Campaign occurred at a time when significant changes were taking place in both Rome and Gaul. For Gaul the country was evolving, changing from an unformed conglomeration of rural tribal villages controlled by monarchies, to larger confederations of tribes with elected assemblies. For Rome the process of change was different. The Republic had fallen into a state of stagnation; Caesar was rising at a time when 'big men' were beginning to take charge of Roman affairs, a prelude to the total change that took place with the imposition of an emperor and imperial system after Caesar's death. By the end of the Gallic Wars, Gaul became a province and Caesar had extended the territory of Rome from its maritime empire limited to the edges of the Mediterranean, to an empire that was beginning to spread through the heartland of Europe. Caesar chronicled these events in his work *Commentarii de Bello Gallico*, more commonly known as *The Gallic War*. The climax of the war was the Alesia Campaign and the climax of the campaign was the Siege of Alesia itself. There have been many sieges throughout history; some were important in their time but are forgotten by the majority of people today – the Athenian Siege of Syracuse during the Peloponnesian War (414–3BC) and Alexander's Siege of Tyre (332BC) to name but two. Other sieges, however, hold a romantic appeal that sparks the imagination and makes them memorable. It is to this category – along with Troy and Massada – that the Siege of Alesia belongs. The events of 52BC involve large personalities with temperaments that embody the characteristics of the competing forces and cultures of the time.

1

Caesar's Gallic Triumph

Sourcing Alesia

'But Heracles also mingled among the citizens of the city [Alesia], and since these surpassed the others in multitude, it came to pass that the inhabitants as a whole were barbarised. The Celts up to the present time hold this city in honour, looking upon it as the hearth and mother-city of all Celtica. And for the entire period from the days of Heracles this city remained free and was never sacked until our own time; but at last Gaius Caesar, who had been pronounced a god because of the magnitude of his deeds, took it by storm and made it and the other Celts subjects of the Romans.'

[Diodorus Siculus, *Library*, IV. 19. 2]

For the most part, only short extracts survive from ancient documents that describe the history and events surrounding the Alesia Campaign, although there may have been many more that are lost to us. A surprising number of authors mention the events of 52BC, such as Cassius Dio, Diodorus, Florus, Strabo, Suetonius, Polybius, Plutarch and Velleius Paterculus. Whilst some of these accounts don't always provide us with the information we would like, the quantity as a whole proves invaluable. Most take a similar form to that from Velleius Paterculus, briskly dealing with the story:

'During this period . . . more than 400,000 of the enemy were slain by Gaius Caesar and a greater number were taken prisoners. Many times had he fought in pitched battles, many times on the march, many times as besieger or besieged. Twice he penetrated into Britain, and in all his nine campaigns there was scarcely one which was not fully deserving of a Triumph. His feats about Alesia were of a kind that a mere man would scarcely venture to undertake, and scarcely anyone but a god could carry through.'

[Velleius Paterculus, *Roman History*, II. 47]

While interesting, the account offers little to help us understand the battle and so we must rely on three sources to provide detailed information of the events: Julius Caesar, Cassius Dio and Plutarch. The most complete and compelling of these accounts is that from Julius Caesar himself. As one of the combatants, the words of a commander writing shortly after the actual events are of course undeniably significant. Fortunately, Caesar was a consummate writer who had a command of the action that is as absorbing as it is informative. Caesar was a master of the literary art and a seasoned panegyrist, and on face value the *Commentarii de Bello Gallico* is simply a commander's account of his actions, literally his 'notes on the war in Gaul'. In this regard, the real heroes of Caesar's work are his men. Caesar,

Background

ever aware of Roman convention, places the brave Roman soldier at the heart of all his actions. This is somewhat ironic, given that in the late Republic the Roman soldier was changing from the Roman Republican ideal. The Roman myth of the warrior farmer protecting his homelands against the invading barbarian had already been lost, the professional soldier with allegiances only to his officers and fellows becoming the reality.

Some authors suggest that *The Gallic War* was written over the winter of 52–51BC at Bibracte, but recent analysis of the changes in writing style indicate it was written annually, with instalments being sent to Rome for consumption. In contrast, the last instalment of the book (VIII 51–50BC) was written by Aulus Hirtius after Caesar's death, but as this section refers to events after the Alesia Campaign it need not be referred to in detail. *The Gallic War* was written to be read in public by orators, in central places such as theatres or piazzas, and its clear prose would have appealed to all rather than specifically to an elite audience. Although popular in the ancient world, by the Middle Ages Caesar's great work was all but lost. In AD 836 a French Abbot, Loup de Ferrières, rediscovered the work. During a visit to the Abbey of Fulda, Loup de Ferrières made copies of *The Gallic War* and these were passed to the monks resident in the Abbey of Flavigny near Alesia. They made the connection between the Alesia referred to by Caesar and Mont Auxois, mentioned in the text as the *oppidum Alesiense*. From this period forward, the identification of Alise-Sainte-Reine with Caesar's Alesia was common, although there were other contenders.

More recently, at the beginning of the eighteenth century, attempts were made to fit Caesar's descriptions of his battles with the topography in France. In the nineteenth century Napoleon III, the leader of France and nephew of the Emperor Napoleon, systematically set out to identify the key locations in Caesar's *Gallic War*. Napoleon III recorded these heroic events of France's past in his seminal work *Histoire de Jules César*. This work included the archaeological excavations that were undertaken in Gaul in 1866 by Colonel Stoffel on behalf of Napoleon III. The archaeological excavations were able to identify ditches associated with Caesar's initial barrier built to block the Helvetii in 58BC. Further work uncovered evidence of Caesar's camps in the Belgic territory in the north of France, and the siegeworks at Gergovia. However, probably most famous of these archaeological discoveries was the identification of the works at Alesia. Although these excavations were based on actual evidence, when we scrutinize Stoffel's map of Alesia, it becomes clear that many of his conclusions are hypothetical. The main route of the circumvallation was partially identified by archaeological excavation and dated by the recovery of weapons and equipment from the time. Archaeological research was an immature science at the time, and many of the attributions of artefacts coming from the excavations are now seen as erroneous. On the whole, Stoffel's excavations were typical for the nineteenth century, although they still provide us with the bulk of the evidence and material from the site. Nowadays it is still not a simple matter to define where these camps were. Misidentification of archaeological features has taken place in the past and in order to understand the process of development of the siegeworks, we have to look at the way in which the evidence has been built up over time. Ultimately, our understanding of the Battle of Alesia is still derived almost entirely from the works of Caesar.

> 'But you, Roman, must remember that you have to guide the nations by your authority, for this is to be your skill, to graft tradition onto peace, to show mercy to the conquered, and to wage war until the haughty are laid low.'

[Virgil, *Aeneid*, VI]

Caesar's work tells us little of the mundane, preferring to focus on the momentum built up through his actions. His descriptions are clearly biased towards his victories and they were plainly used by him to further his own political manoeuvrings. The invasion of Britain for instance, seems to have served no real purpose, apart from furthering his image and providing him a political foothold in the region. In the Senate, dissent was voiced about the requirements for such undertakings. Nonetheless, the discontent of his enemies was overshadowed by the retelling of his exploits, and of his journeys to the little-known island on the edge of the world were received with almost as much interest as Columbus' ventures to the New World 1,500 years later. Caesar was continuing a long tradition of Roman progression towards its perceived destiny, a route that began with the mythic Aeneas. For Caesar, this journey was all the more real because Caesar's name *Iulius*, claimed descent from the son of the legendary Aeneas. In Roman history, Aeneas was a Trojan soldier whose mother, the goddess Venus, led him in the wake of the Trojan defeat to Italy. Here he founded Rome, and in Caesar's mind he was the inheritor of this lineage. As he set forth to conquer Gaul, Caesar would have felt that he was fulfilling his destiny, a mythic destiny that had already been set by his divine ancestors.

Gauls or Celts?

> 'Those who inhabit the inland parts beyond Marseilles, and about the Alps, and on this side the Pyrenees mountains, are called Celts;

Background

but those that inhabit below this part called Celtica, southward to the ocean and the mountain Hyrcinus, and all as far as Scythia, are called Gauls. But the Romans call all these people generally by one and the same name, Gauls.'

[Diodorus Siculus, *Historical Library*, II]

In the beginning of *The Gallic War* Caesar goes out of his way to define the character of the land of Gaul, and a note on the use of the terminology is worth revisiting here. There is often confusion surrounding the terms Celtic and Gallic and usually they are used interchangeably. The difference between these two words is simple, yet over the years has developed many deviations in meaning. The etymology of the words is quite straightforward. The term Celtic comes from the Greek *Keltoi*, whereas the term Gallic or Gaul comes from the Latin *Galli*. Both terms apply to the various neighbouring tribes of the Greeks and Romans who shared much in common with their culture termed 'La Tène', but do not necessarily relate to the same ethnic people or the same geographic area. Similarly, the term German – *Germani* – related to anyone from a tribe occupying the vast territory north and east of the Rhine and Danube, clearly a huge area that includes many different ethnic and cultural groups. Caesar was the first to really define the limits of Gaul and provide a description of its constituent tribes. Caesar mentions there were three parts to Gaul, which he divided into the Belgae, Aquitani and the Gauls. The Belgae, he says, lived in the north of France around the Marne and Seine, the Aquitani lived in the south of France by the River Garonne and the Gauls lived between the two, through the central part of France. Caesar referred to Gaul like we refer to the Middle East or Africa, denoting a continent of states. He pointed out that the three distinct peoples within Gaul had their own languages, customs and laws – what today we might call separate 'ethnic identities'. Within these ethnic identities, separate groups were identified by tribal appellations and these are the tribal names that are passed down to us in Caesar's *Gallic War*. Whilst Caesar comments that the Gauls call themselves Celts in their own language, the modern term Celtic is now fraught with a complexity of ethnic meaning developed over the intervening two millennia. These distinctions deserve a book of their own and therefore will be avoided here. Therefore in this book the term Gallic will be used rather than Celtic, as it reflects the modern reference to the peoples specifically of France. Where 'Celtic' is used it will refer to the wider La Tène cultural group that lived on the borders of the non-Roman world of Western Europe.

Caesar's Gallic Triumph

Roman Motivations

Romans established connections with Gaul over a century before Caesar's invasion, both economic and political, and particularly with the Aedui tribe. The Gauls saw Roman goods as exotic and precious; in fact Gallic money even came to imitate Mediterranean forms. Eventually, the Gallic aristocracy became reliant on Roman luxury goods, using them to demonstrate their power. In return, Rome was becoming reliant on Gallic wealth, in terms of gold and slaves. In fact, the Gauls were using gold coinage, unlike the Romans, who had restricted access to the metal. Recent evidence shows that Gaul had many gold mines, the gold being used not only for coins, but neck-torcs, armbands, brooches and rings. There is still debate as to the extent to which the Gauls were influenced by Roman pressure before the Gallic War, although reliance on Roman assistance seems well entrenched before Caesar's invasion.

The catalyst that changed the political character of Gaul and its relationship to Rome was Caesar's intervention in the migration of tribes from modern-day Switzerland (the Helvetii) into Gaul. Over the course of the war, pro-Roman Gallic leaders gradually lost their positions, partially because Rome was unwilling to help them and partially because when the Romans imposed their will, Gallic leaders became identified with Roman oppression. Roman intervention at the beginning of the war was not solely aimed at stopping the migration of the Helvetii; it was also aimed at restoring pro-Roman governments in Gaul and extending Rome's influence. But it is hard to believe that Caesar was more interested in political intrigues of people he saw as barbarians than he was in Gallic gold. On the eve of the invasion Caesar was facing ruin and judicial investigation. After the invasion, all these matters became moot, and over the course of six years Caesar's activities subdued the Gallic condition to a state where it had become yet another Roman province. Caesar's pockets had become lined with Gaul's wealth. His fortunes changed so dramatically that he was able to mount an attempt to become the supreme ruler of Rome. Ironically, Caesar's invasion was both a disaster and a gift to Gaul. It began the process that coalesced the discrete tribes and cultures of the land into a unified whole, something no Gaul, not even Vercingetorix, had been able to do.

The Commanders
and Their Armies

<hr>

Caesar

In July 100BC Gaius Julius Caesar was born into an old aristocratic and wealthy family; his formative years saw some of the most important changes in Roman history to date. At the age of eleven he would have witnessed the Social Wars – the rebellion of Rome's allies against the Roman city-state, until it capitulated and gave citizenship to all the peoples of Italy. In his teens Caesar became head of the family after his father's death. He also witnessed the political intrigues that took place in Rome in the run-up to a vicious civil war between Marius (to whom Caesar was related) and Sulla. In his twenties, he was captured by pirates and on his release experienced the fear engendered in Roman society by the Spartican Slave Revolt. In his thirties, he married Sulla's daughter Pompeia, and watched as Pompey used his political skills to gain power over the Senate. Caesar now engaged himself wholeheartedly in politics and by the time he was forty, Caesar had allied himself with Pompey, becoming part of the first Triumvirate, along with Crassus.

From this time onwards Caesar vied for power with his two associates, using all the skills he had developed over the previous years. This was a significant time for Rome, after 450 years the Republic was beginning to fall apart. During the course of the previous century, the assemblies and magistracies that characterized Republican politics were found to be wanting. Corruption and manipulation of the voting populace was increasingly problematic. Wealthy individuals were enticed by the lure of power to gain sole rule – a practice that led to a series of bloody civil wars. Power was being held in fewer hands and the addition of wealth from conquered lands only enhanced this process. Increasingly, wealthy families used their position as military leaders for their own benefit, utilizing their armies in their political manoeuvrings. After spending all his money to become *consul* Caesar was in deep debt and by the time his term in office had finished he was being investigated for irregularities whilst in office. Obtaining a governorship of Transalpine Gaul, Caesar saw his opportunity

Caesar's Gallic Triumph

to recoup some of his losses while avoiding the attentions of the Senate.

'out of all the numerous provinces he made the Gauls his choice, as the most likely to enrich him and furnish suitable material for Triumphs.'

[Suetonius, *Lives of the Twelve Caesars*, 22]

In 59BC, along with the control of two provinces, Caesar inherited four legions: three in Cisalpine Gaul (the Seventh, Eighth and Ninth) and one in Transalpine Gaul (the Tenth). Even though he turned out to be a born general, he was a politician first and foremost. Caesar's primary motivation was his own personal and political improvement, and so he saw these armies as a tool for political manoeuvring, therefore he engaged himself wholeheartedly in military affairs. He felt that if he could move into the Gallic sphere of influence he would be seen as reducing the threat to Rome. Engagement in Gallic affairs would not only increase opportunities for him to improve his position with the Senate, but also to capitalize on Gaul's wealth.

In the spring of 58BC Caesar had found a pretext to intervene militarily in Gaul, and the great 'Battle for Gaul' was set in motion. As a catalyst for this invasion, the Germanic *Helvetii* were migrating from the eastern region of Switzerland towards the Gallic *oppidum* of the *Allobroges*, at Geneva. There were tribes who saw Caesar's entry into Gaul as an invasion, a major threat that would only increase. This last point was made all the more central when Caesar's political interests were thrown into sharp relief by an unprovoked campaign against the Belgae the year after his initial invasion (57BC). Alternatively, Caesar's crossing into Gaul was taken by other Gallic tribes as a helpful event that would further their own political ambitions. Many Gallic tribes felt that siding with Caesar was in their interests and the larger tribal groups, who aimed to benefit from his activities, supported Caesar's actions. Rome imposed allegiances upon them and demands that were pro-Roman. Caesar took hostages to enforce the connection between the Gallic tribes and Rome. He also used the allied tribes as a recruiting base to increase the number of troops in his army, thereby boosting control over the region. But Gallic tribes were also able to use Caesar to protect their interests against tribes that would harm them, and also wage war against enemy tribes in the name of Rome. In this way Caesar created tribal allegiances and was able to open Gallic markets for Roman trade and exploitation. Wealthy Roman businessmen made money by supporting the production of military equipment, from swords to ships, which facilitated the war.

For Caesar the Gallic war was also an economic war, opening up the whole of northern Europe for economic exploitation by Rome. By 52BC, the effects of six years of constant war and exploitation in Gaul had the effect of mobilizing warriors from every region of Gaul. During Vercingetorix's revolt, the Alesia Campaign finally galvanized Gaul against Rome's expansionist tendencies. Luckily for Caesar, at the time he was campaigning in Gaul there was no corresponding revolt in any of the bordering provinces, which would have drawn his forces elsewhere. Before the decade was out, the process Caesar had begun in Gaul had gathered enough momentum that any threat had been expunged, so much so that Rome's control of Gaul's wealth continued for the next 500 years, until the Germanic invasions and Rome's defeat by the Franks at the Battle of Soissons in AD48.

'He was highly skilled in arms and horsemanship, and of incredible powers of endurance. On the march he headed his army, sometimes on horseback, but more often on foot, bareheaded both in the heat of the sun and in rain. He covered great distances with incredible speed, making 100 miles a day in a hired carriage and with little baggage, swimming the rivers which barred his path or crossing them on inflated skins, and very often arriving before the messengers sent to announce his coming.'

[Suetonius, *Lives of the Twelve Caesars*, 57]

Caesar's success in Gaul was based squarely on his personal characteristics and empathy with the regular soldier. Although he had no formal training, Caesar was an instinctive leader who was aggressive and decisive, with an ability to turn situations to his advantage. This natural leadership was enhanced by his ability to engender loyalty in the ordinary soldier. These advantages could have their drawbacks: Caesar's aggressiveness could manifest itself in actions that were impulsive or not thought through. His concentration on achievement meant he had little time for the complexities of logistics, which often led him to become overstretched and undersupplied. The Alesia Campaign seems to be the prime example of this. After splitting his forces and overstretching himself in central Gaul, Caesar was forced to withdraw to The Province. After being ambushed on the journey, Caesar's genius was his ability to extract his army from this dire situation to his own benefit by turning the tables on Vercingetorix. Like all wars, Alesia was a contest of wills, and as Pyrrus and Hannibal had already found out, one could defeat individual Roman armies, but their tenacity meant that they would fight on until they ultimately won.

'He valued his soldiers neither for their personal character nor for their fortune, but solely for their prowess, and he treated them with equal strictness and indulgence; for he did not curb them everywhere and at all times, but only in the presence of the enemy. Then he required the strictest discipline, not announcing the time of a march or a battle, but keeping them ready and alert to be led on at any sudden moment wheresoever he might wish. He often called them out even when there was no occasion for it, especially on rainy days and holidays. And warning them every now and then that they must keep close watch on him, he would steal away suddenly by day or night and make a longer march than usual, to tire out those who were tardy in following.'

[Suetonius, *Lives of the Twelve Caesars*, 65]

While he was writing *The Gallic War*, Caesar goes out of his way to build up the tension in the reader, building it to a point where only his presence can alleviate the pressure. Caesar clearly presents himself as the military genius, which no doubt he was, but beneath the surface some of his personal flaws can also be observed. For instance, Caesar was not averse to using tricks, both material and political, even though he disdained this behaviour in others. He was also not averse to the deliberate use of terror to wage war and, while somewhat acceptable in the period, he doesn't accept the policy when it comes from his enemies. While pointing to the failures of others, Caesar regularly masks his own mistakes with a veneer of purposeful action. Although his recollections seem to lead Caesar inexorably to victory, he was clearly not working in isolation. In reality, Caesar was facing a highly motivated and clever enemy, and at their head was Vercingetorix, a leader with the capability to defeat Caesar.

Caesar's Army

The Republican period ran from a traditional start date established after the last King of Rome in 509BC and ended after Caesar was assassinated and Augustus became supreme ruler in 31BC. Detailed archaeological and historical evidence for this period of Roman military history is somewhat elusive, but we do have three authors who provide us with some evidence of the structure and behaviour of the early Roman army: Livy, Polybius and, of course, Caesar himself. Their descriptions are good as far as they go, but provide us with only a narrow view of the army of the late Republic. The authors, excepting Caesar, do not provide a contemporary view of Caesar's army and tend to focus only on an idealized image of the legions, with little or no attention given to other units such as allies or mercenaries. The case is not much better with regard to the archaeological evidence. Here we can find some suitable contemporary evidence for the

Caesar's Army

Roman army of the late Republic, but it is extremely limited, focusing on a few camps in Spain and naturally Alesia. Unfortunately, as most of this data was unearthed over a century ago, even this evidence is patchy. Our understanding of Caesar's army, therefore, is built from a mix of contemporary and not so contemporary sources, scholarly research and debate.

Clearly Caesar's legions did not simply spring to life fully formed. While they were raised as complete units, this arrangement came about as part of an inherited system of behaviour. To understand the character of the Caesarean legion it is worth taking a brief look at how the legions developed from their foundation. In reviewing the development of the legion as a whole, some of the relationships between Gaul and Rome will become apparent. The legion, as we understand it, was the consequence of a long period of changes absorbed in the wake of military defeat. Although the Roman legion is now seen as the epitome of military genius, the reality was somewhat different; in fact, Rome's success as a military power seems to have been due more to its ability to learn from its mistakes. Rome's brilliance was that it could accept its weaknesses and adopt the successful elements of its enemies, whilst all the time placing these within a structured military system. In due course, the legion developed from the propertied man's annual obligation to fight to protect his land during the summer months, to the requirement for all males to fight lengthy warfare for a campaigning season (usually March to October) and finally to professional soldiers paid to fight constantly over prolonged periods of many years. This transformation was concurrent with the expansion of Roman territory and the change from the protection of the local community to the requirements for a standing army to protect a vast and diverse Empire.

The armies of early Italy were little more than war-bands of infantry and cavalry, raised by local tribes or princes when required, and fighting when the seasons allowed. Charismatic and powerful men led these bands, the best of which could provide protection for the individual and an opportunity for advancement. It could be argued that these traits were enshrined in the system from this early date, as the patronage of wealthy and powerful leaders can be seen in the armies of Rome throughout its history. Caesar was certainly a general who instilled in his legions personal devotion to him. Finally, the early system of ad hoc recruitment became more standardized, in order to provide a more regular and predictable turnout of men. The first Roman armies consisted of around 3,000 men and were organized on the basis of tribal groups, called a *legio* or a 'levying'. Each tribe contributed 100 men towards the total force – the origin of the 'century' of Caesar's legion. The wealthy elites in the tribe were relied upon to supply the cavalry for the army, as only they could afford expensive equipment and horses. This group, the *equites* or knights, survived as a social group long after their original function had vanished, serving as officers in Caesar's army. In essence these early armies fought in similar ways to most early European armies of the period. Warrior bands would fight under the command of their local leader in unstructured groupings, while commanders would range around the battle, urging them on to fight and selecting suitable enemy leaders for combat. It is interesting to consider that the Gallic armies Caesar faced were very much on a par with these early Roman armies.

After the Roman Republic began in 509BC, the Roman army became far more formalized, along the hierarchical lines society was taking. Greek-style Hoplite warfare was the most advanced military tradition at the time and represented a significant advancement on earlier military tactics. In Hoplite warfare, troops fought as a densely packed line of heavily armed spearmen. Cohesion was the key to this style of fighting and so the hierarchical nature of Roman society was replicated in the legion. Only those men with property were allowed to fight, giving the men a sense of duty and an interest in preserving the State. It is worth noting here that Roman citizens were providing the entire range of troop types in the army – a situation that was not to last. As Rome expanded the areas coming under its domination, there also came a necessity for an expanded army. The increased wealth of Rome meant that the number of infantry and cavalry centuries could also be increased.

By the fourth century BC, Rome's experiences of fighting with the Latin and Gallic tribes had revealed serious weaknesses in the Hoplite form of warfare. The more flexible fighting styles of the Gauls and Samnites often highlighted the sluggish and formulaic nature of Hoplite warfare. To counteract this problem the Romans began to adopt less dense formations, which in turn required a revision of their tactics and equipment. The Roman phalanx was reorganized into fighting formations called *maniples* – literally 'handfuls'. The overall result was slowly changing the legions from the rigid defensive formation of the phalanx into a cohesive collection of flexible offensive fighting units. The fourth century BC saw the entire Italian peninsula come under the control of Rome and as the sphere of influence increased, so did the embracing of allied Italian peoples into the Roman army. On campaign it became common for allied soldiers to comprise about the same number of troops as the Roman legionaries. Armed like the legionaries, these allied troops formed up either side of the legions in *alae* or wings. From this time on, allied or mercenary units came to be a significant feature of the Roman army.

Caesar's Army

'On the expedition he [Marius] carefully disciplined and trained his army whilst on their way, giving them practice in long marches, and running of every sort, and compelling every man to carry his own baggage and prepare his own victuals; insomuch that thenceforward laborious soldiers, who did their work silently without grumbling, had the name of Marius' mules.'

[Plutarch, *Lives of the Noble Greeks and Romans*, 13]

The turn of the first century BC saw a significant change in the character of the Roman army. This has often been attributed to just one man, Marius, but this may be somewhat overstated and simplistic. Transformations had been taking place over the course of the previous three centuries, therefore Marius' role is most likely to have been as a catalyst for the changes already developing. The army was now spending long periods away from home and it was becoming a genuine career choice with the possibility of gaining wealth and land from the proceeds of victory. Previously, the Roman army had been an organized militia, galvanized with discipline and training. Increasingly, the army was becoming more specialized and developing a core of professional soldiers as Roman society became geared for on-going war. Pragmatism was required in the face of the demands put on the army by the ever-expanding areas of land to be controlled. This also resulted in a relaxation of the prescribed requirements for entry to the army, which had gradually been eroded almost as soon as the legion was developed. The acceptance of elements of the non-land owning populace into the army had only been done in extremis before, but now Marius attempted to increase the strength of the army by changing the property requirements for service. He allowed the recruitment of *proletarii*, the landless citizens of Rome, making the class-based system redundant. The state had for some time been supplying equipment to the army and so standardization was already occurring. Hence by Marius' time, the army was equipped fairly uniformly and the complex strata exhibited in the previous system was removed. Thus Marius was unwittingly responsible for homogenizing both the equipment and structure of the legions, by allowing the process to become formalized.

In accepting the landless into the army, the State also had to accept the responsibility of arming the legions, which, up until then, had been paid for by the soldiers themselves. After their service these landless soldiers were left to fend for themselves, so while they were in the legions they were willing to follow any charismatic leader that promised them land afterwards. Gradually, a subtle difference in the mind-set of the legions emerged, from a landed militia protecting their own Roman lands, to a professional army dominating annexed foreign provinces. Soldiers began to develop greater loyalty to their generals, identifying with their leaders who, like them, sought personal enrichment rather than seeing the maintenance of the structure of the State as the purpose of their fighting. Individual grants of land and money, distributed after military successes and service, were now becoming commonplace. The politics of the late Republic were becoming ever more competitive, hence in the struggle for advancement senators succumbed to more and more aggressive policies and expansionist pressure. This was the world that Caesar made his own.

Caesar leaves out much of the detail of his army because his audience was well informed about the character of the Roman army of the period. Caesar does tell us that he was using a system of cohorts, a simplified version of the previous maniple system. Marius is thought to have been responsible for the change from maniples to cohorts but it is likely that both systems could have been in place together for a period. When Caesar set out on his Gallic adventure in 58BC the cohort system was well established. Manipular legions were made up of three distinct lines of formation, each one equipped differently and socially differentiated. The cohort legion did away with these equipment complexities, replacing them with a flexible body of similarly armed men. It is likely that the system was introduced to deal with the difficult nature of warfare in Spain. Tactics had to be developed to combat both the Spanish guerrilla warfare and the mountainous character of the landscape. The system retained the three-line formation, with a strengthened rear rank as a reserve.

Caesar formed his legions for battle into what is called a *triplex acies* formation, being four cohorts in front, with two lines of three cohorts behind. This formation was something of a compromise between being wide enough to form a broad frontage and deep enough to have reserves. The middle cohorts provided the reserve for the front cohorts, while the rear cohorts could be used for outflanking the enemy or if the legion was attacked in the rear. The basic building blocks of the legion were the eighty-man centuries, each one commanded by a centurion. Caesar depicts the centurions as the fundamental glue of his legion, providing harsh discipline and motivational inspiration in equal measures. Six of these centuries would provide a 400-man cohort: this played the role of an individual tactical unit on the battlefield, ten cohorts together forming the legion.

In the last century of the Roman Republic the command of the army was removed from publicly elected consuls. Only after their period of office could they command – a circumstance that had the effect of further breaking the army's connection to a citizenry. Caesar tells us that most of the legions for his Gallic campaigns were raised during the winter months, when campaigning had ceased. As governor of three provinces, he inherited the four legions that were stationed in them and these could be augmented by further recruitment from the provinces. Initially it seems that Caesar would raise the legion out of his own money, then, after gaining acknowledgment of the unit from Rome, the legion would become the responsibility of the State to maintain. Caesar enlisted troops into the legions of both citizen and part-citizen 'Latin' status, thus continuing the process of blurring the qualifications for entry to the legions. By collecting these diverse groups into unified legions, and by exerting direct personal control over them, Caesar was able to place himself as the main focus of the legion's loyalties, before that of any other – even the State. This meant that his forces were extremely loyal to him: a factor that was to play its role in the subsequent Civil War (49–45BC).

The officers of the legions were not trained. In fact, most received their posts as part of their political career. Six tribunes were placed as middle-ranking officers of the legion and these were generally young and untested men of aristocratic birth, often lacking in initiative or bravery. Caesar chose the tribunes personally, many purely on the basis of political expediency and patronage. Above the tribunes was a *quaestor*, a junior senator who oversaw an entire province and provided Caesar with finances. Overall control of a legion was placed in the hands of a *legatus*. Caesar chose a number of *legati*; usually former tribunes, they were senators from a variety of backgrounds and experiences, but were usually politically motivated choices.

Over the course of the Gallic Campaign, Caesar increased his legions from the four he inherited, to twelve at the height of the fighting for the Alesia Campaign. Thus, Caesar could have had up to 57,600 men at his disposal. However, this number was only the paper strength of the legion, based on around 4,800 men per legion. The actual number would, more likely, be half this amount by the campaigning of late summer 52BC. Battle casualties, infirmity, exhaustion and general wastage from the previous months' campaigning would all have played a part in reducing this tally to less than 30,000 men at Alesia.

The 30 miles of fortifications – making up the circumvallation and contravallation at Alesia – may seem very large, but when one considers that its construction was divided among almost 30,000 available men, each soldier would only have had to dig around 5 feet of trench and rampart in the six weeks it took to prepare. In this light, the defences do not seem such a superhuman task. In fact, when one considers that it was usual for Roman legionaries to build a camp at the end of the day's march, the building of these fortifications seems well within the capabilities of the average soldier. In truth, the greater task would have been the logistics of the operation, including the planning, design, organization, supply and implementation of the construction. However, this is where the Roman military machine came into its own. If the defences at Alesia are exceptional, this is only because the management of the army was exceptional and equal to the Herculean task. Motivation to create such an engineering feat was an important factor in Caesar's army. Infantry training tended to focus on physical ability, including running, jumping, marching and building – clearly necessary for the construction work.

Increasingly, espirit de corps was also encouraged. The legions began to be individualized by number and by name. Added to this, individual legions were picked out by nicknames, often recognizing their exploits, and by use of awards and honours on their banners and standards. This is not to say that the legions were uncritically loyal to their leaders. While the soldiers were made to give oaths of allegiance that imposed legal and religious constraints on them, the Roman army was still prone to revolts and indiscipline was common, mainly over pay or ill treatment. Often rewards would be granted to keep the legionaries content. Caesar would often bestow on his soldiers a promotion as part of the system of rewards, especially for centurions. At Alesia Caesar's handing over of slaves and booty to his soldiers after the defeat of Vercingetorix is a clear example of this. To this was added the spoils of war, along with *donativa*, one-off payments made by the general in gratitude of service. After the Alesia Campaign, Caesar decided to double the pay to ensure the loyalty of his soldiers for the coming civil wars.

The remaining archaeological evidence from Alesia is confined to the siegeworks themselves. Roman weapons of the late Republic are scarce throughout Europe, most coming from siege sites in Spain. At Alesia there is surprisingly little in the way of Roman military equipment and this is likely to be due in part to biases in the excavation of material. In the main, archaeologists have focused their attentions on understanding the form of the Roman defences. This means the results have concentrated upon the character of ditches that bordered the Roman circumvallation and contravallation. These, it has been discovered, were filled with javelins and arrowheads, which make up the predominant proportion of the total weapons discovered at Alesia. While some Roman *pila* (the legionary's offensive missile) have been found, most of the other weapons are likely to be Gallic in origin. If one considers that the ramparts were mainly the focus of incoming missiles from the Gallic army, then outgoing Roman missiles would have been fired into areas further from the ramparts, where little or no excavation has been undertaken. Similarly, all the swords so far discovered seem to be of Gallic origin, and again this may not be unusual, as Roman weapons would have been retrieved after the battle had finished to be used in future campaigns, whereas Gallic ones would only have been recovered if they were considered valuable.

> 'Gaius Sulpicius . . . commanded those who were in the front line to discharge their javelins, and immediately crouch low; then the second, third, and fourth lines to discharge theirs, each crouching in turn so that they should not be struck by the spears thrown from the rear; then when the last line had hurled their javelins, all were to rush forward suddenly with a shout and join battle at close quarters. The hurling of so many missiles, followed by an immediate charge, would throw the enemy into confusion.'

> [Appian, *History of Rome: Gallic Wars*, 1]

Archaeological evidence shows that the panoply of equipment of the Roman soldier differed only in detail from that of the better-equipped Gallic warriors – sword, long shield, helmet, mail armour and spear. Nevertheless, their appearance was different enough for one soldier to comment that soldiers in the distance were not Roman because of their 'Gallic weapons and crests'. The Romans' equipment wasn't the only thing that was different from the Gauls; their fighting techniques varied too. After throwing their pila, the legionaries would engage the enemy adopting a crouching stance and using a juxtaposition of punches with the shield boss and stabs with a sword. It is evident from sculptural and archaeological evidence that the majority of Roman legionaries were equipped to fight in this style, with heavy armour and equipment. A large number of weapons have been found at Alesia, almost 400 in total, 140 of which are either javelins or spears. Unfortunately, these could be either of Roman, Gallic or German origin. Some of the spearheads must be Roman but it is unclear which, as leaf-shaped spearheads were a common form used across Europe at the time. However, using other sources of evidence, we can piece together a picture of Caesar's legionaries. In the late Republic the average legionary would have a decorative tall bronze helmet with a short neck guard and large cheek pieces, a derivative of Gallic styles. The form was called 'Montefortino type' and was sometimes enhanced with horsehair or feather trappings. These decorative helmets were beginning to be replaced by a more easily produced, plain style of helmet called a 'Coolus' or 'Buggenum-type' helmet. It is likely that both types were in use at Alesia. In general, legionaries would wear a mail coat that reached nearly to the knees, which was hitched up with a military belt. Some sculptures suggest that these coats could have further mail reinforcing on the shoulders. Pieces of chest fastenings from these mail coats have been found at Alesia. However, as the Gauls were the inventors of this form of defensive equipment, defining whether these fittings are Gallic or Roman is very difficult. All legionaries would also carry a long curved wooden shield, strengthened by a vertical central spine and which had a small bronze boss covering the handgrip. On a legionary's belt there would have been a stabbing sword on the right hip and a long dagger on the left. Both these weapons seem to be copied from types common in Spain.

> '[Caesar's] . . . soldiers, hurling their javelins from the higher ground, easily broke the enemy's phalanx. That being dispersed, they made a charge on them with drawn swords. It was a great hindrance to the Gauls in fighting, that, when several of their shields had been by one stroke of the pila pierced through and pinned fast together, as the point of the iron had bent itself, they could neither pluck it out, nor, with their left hand entangled, fight with sufficient ease; so that many, after having long tossed their arm about, chose rather to cast away the shield from their hand, and to fight with their person unprotected.'

> [Caesar, *The Gallic War*, I. 25]

The one piece of the legionary's equipment that can be directly attributed to Roman invention was his primary offensive weapon, the pilum. Pila were a form of spear with a long thin metal shaft and a small pointed head. Although pila are a Roman invention, examples of similar types of weapons were also developed in Gallic and German contexts. Among the huge number of missile weapons found at Alesia, pila are the predominant Roman weapons evident. Up until recently, only fragments of pila were discovered, mainly coming from the foot of Mont Réa. But in 1991 a complete example of a Roman pilum was discovered in Fort Eleven. The examples from Alesia are characterized by long thin shanks and points that come in pyramidal, leaf-shaped or lance-shaped forms. There are different ways in which pila were connected to the wooden shaft: some were connected by a socket that fitted over the shaft and was riveted to it; other pila shafts had a wide tongue that was sandwiched between the shaft and riveted in place. A final type had a pointed tang that was driven into the shaft and secured by a collar. Usually, a round shaft was used for the socketed and collared pila, whereas a square shaft was used for the tongued versions. It is likely that the socketed pilum was lighter than the tanged pilum, this is because the tanged pilum was often weighted to provide extra penetration on impact. After his excavations at Alesia, Napoleon III had replica pila made and tested. The results showed that the reconstructed examples could be launched 30m and penetrate wood 3cm thick. Heavier pila were weighted with lead and could have been thrown up to 70m. It is likely, therefore, that pila were thrown at the Gauls before they entered the defences of the circumvallation and contravallation at Alesia.

The equipment available for use by the legionary was extensive and the legionary himself carried much of it. The requirement that legionaries carry all their equipment is attributed to Marius: hence the term 'Marius' mules', although the likelihood is that this is a misattribution. The soldiers had always been required to carry their equipment, a regulation that was regularly flouted. It is likely that Marius simply reinforced a standing regulation in an attempt to make the soldiers more self-reliant and less reliant on a baggage train – part of creating a professional army. Vegetius suggests up to 60 pounds of equipment should be carried during training and Josephus claims each soldier carried a saw, a basket, an axe, a pick, a strap, a billhook, a length of chain and three days' rations. The rest of a soldier's equipment, his tents and so on, were carried with the baggage. Along with this equipment, the Roman army took with it large numbers of servants and slaves, who were usually not armed but had sufficient knowledge of tactics to be of use. Sometimes these groups were added to the regular army to give the impression of a larger force than was actually available, such as at Gergovia, where they were mounted on horses to look like cavalry. Merchants and camp followers would also be part of the train, providing services that would otherwise be unattainable in foreign countries. Large numbers of followers and baggage had the tendency to slow the column on marches and so attempts were made to reduce these numbers. One way of reducing the reliance on camp followers was the local requisition of supplies and the creation of storage bases along the route of march. In Gaul, where Vercingetorix had instigated a scorched earth policy, this was impossible to maintain and so it is likely Caesar had more followers than he would have wished to have.

The legions also took on campaign with them numbers of artillery pieces. These could be used aggressively, either in open battles and sieges to provide preparatory fire, or defensively to protect camps and siegeworks. Roman artillery comprised various sizes of *ballista* (sometimes called a *catapulta* or catapult). The ballista was a torsion catapult that used two twisted skeins of hair or tendons to provide energy for a string that fired projectiles. The ballista was built in various sizes that fired anything from small crossbow-sized bolts to large cannonball-sized stones. Parts of *ballistae* occur occasionally on archaeological sites. At Alesia three bolt heads were discovered, betraying the presence of ballista there. Ballista would allow Caesar to cover most of the regions outside his defences with a combination of fire from the hills surrounding the defences and the ramparts of the circumvallation. The larger engines were probably fixed in place once built and reserved for siege work, whereas the smaller artillery was often broken down and moved on pack mules, but could also be erected on carts or wheels (*carroballista*) to make them mobile on the battlefield.

Caesar's Allies

'It was the practice of the Romans to make foreign friends of any people for whom they wanted to intervene on the score of friendship, without being obliged to defend them as allies.'

[Appian, *History of Rome: Gallic Wars*]

Throughout the Republican period, Rome relied heavily on its allies for additional infantry and cavalry forces to make up for a lack of manpower. In some cases these were specialist fighters recruited on an ad hoc basis and in varying strengths from the locality. More important were the allied light troops who were drawn from Mediterranean regions Rome had long been in contact with and with whom they had the closest relations. These troops were customarily raised for the duration of a campaign, which sometimes led the Romans themselves to questions their allies' quality and commitment. Allied formations were usually under the control of an individual unit's chief, and were armed, equipped and fought in the particular unit's traditional style.

Usually the allied contingent of the Roman army was of equal or larger size than the legionary force and was usually formed along Roman lines. Units regularly seem to have been about 500 or 1,000 strong and broken down into either six or ten centuries. These could be arraigned with the main army in the centre of the Roman line or placed on both wings. Sometimes the more lightly armoured allied contingents were mixed with the heavier armed legionaries to prevent the allies from being picked off. Along with the heavily armed troops, many of the allies provided specialist light infantry troops, such as archers and slingers. These units are likely to have been dressed according to their ethnic origin, although there is no definitive evidence of which units were at Alesia. Over forty arrowheads have been recovered from Alesia and it is thought that some of the Roman forms of arrows with one and two barbs are likely to have been used by allied Roman troops. Roman arrows were manufactured from iron and were up to 7.8cm long and 2.5cm wide. Tests of reconstructed bows suggest they would have had a maximum range of around 300m, and so they would be able to fire at the Gauls beyond even the deepest of Caesar's defences. Slings were also used and a number of examples of slingshot come from Alesia, most notably three with inscriptions on them. Reconstructed slingshots have shown a range of up to 400m, easily enough to provide covering fire from any of the hilltops around Alesia into the valleys below.

Throughout his campaigns in Gaul Caesar does not define the constitution of his cavalry and so we cannot be certain about their number or ethnicity. It is likely that at least some of the cavalry at Alesia were Roman. At the beginning of the conflict, Caesar was also able to call upon friendly Gallic tribes to provide him with Gallic cavalry and these were employed as warriors, as well as scouts, guides, interpreters and messengers. However, Caesar had always considered them unreliable, a belief which was confirmed once Vercingetorix rebelled and Caesar lost the majority of his Gallic troops to his rival. Some must have been retained however, if only in an intelligence role, but by the beginning of the Alesia Campaign Caesar was forced to employ new cavalry in the form of German mercenaries.

'Caesar, as he perceived that the enemy were superior in cavalry, and he himself could receive no aid from The Province or Italy, while all communication was cut off, sends across the Rhine into Germany to those states which he had subdued in the preceding campaigns, and summons from them cavalry and the light-armed infantry, who were accustomed to engage among them. On their arrival, as they were mounted on unserviceable horses, he takes horses from the military tribunes and the rest, nay, even from the Roman knights and veterans, and distributes them among the Germans.'

[Caesar, *The Gallic War*, VII. 65]

Caesar tells us that the bulk of the German mercenaries were cavalrymen. Evidence for Germanic cavalry in the archaeological record at Alesia is slight; this is partially because German weapons are hard to distinguish due to their similarity with Gallic weapons. One shield boss with a central projecting stud is almost certainly German, given its similarities to later German bosses. Bones of horses coming from the ditches discovered at the foot of Mont Réa have been identified as coming from a male horse of no more than three years old. These bones may represent the well-bred young stallions given to the German cavalry. If this is correct, the evidence would conform well to the German cavalry attack on this region. Recent interpretation suggests that these horse remains may have been deliberately buried in the ditches, not simply to cover them up, but in a form of sacrificial burial. It was the Gallic custom to bury sacrifices in the peripheral ditches of sanctuaries. In Gallic eyes, the circumvallation ditch may have been associated with the practice of ritual sacrifice in these periphery ditches after the defeat.

'There is not even any great abundance of iron, as may be inferred from the character of their weapons. Only a very few use swords or lances. The spears that they carry – *framea* is the native word – have short and narrow heads, but are so sharp and easy to handle, that the same weapon serves at need for close or distant fighting.'

[Tacitus, *Germania*, VI]

Along with the cavalry, the Germans are described as using spearmen who mingled with the mounted troops. This tactic may explain the successes of the German cavalry during the Alesia Campaign. Tacitus tells us that German warriors were lightly armed, the cavalry often having only a spear and shield. The infantry were armed in a similar manner, with the addition of a number of small javelins. All the Germans were dressed lightly with few wearing armour or helmets. Some even fought completely naked. In the main, German warriors wore breeches and large cloaks that would be draped over their shoulders in regional style. Their clothing was manufactured in simple colours and patterns, the only ostentatious part of their dress being elaborate knotted hairstyles. These varied from tribe to tribe and so identified each warrior as the member of a particular clan, a practice that had continued for hundreds of years.

'[The Germans are] . . . a people who excelled all others, even the largest men, in size; savage, the bravest of the brave, despising death because they believe they shall live hereafter, bearing heat and cold with equal patience, living on herbs in time of scarcity, and their horses browsing on trees. It seems that they were without patient endurance in their battles, and did not fight in a scientific way or in any regular order, but with a sort of high spirit simply made an onset like wild beasts, for which reason they were overcome by Roman science and endurance.'

[Appian, *History of Rome*, 3]

Caesar tells us that the River Rhine marks the border between the Gallic peoples to the south and the Germans to the north. German warriors were famed for their physique, size and fearlessness – attributes which in Roman eyes made them appear as savages. Like the Gauls, the Romans had a stereotype for the Germans, who were seen as brutish to the point of indifference to death (a recurrent image even up until the present). As ever, the reality was very different; the German peoples had as complex a society as any other of the period. There were close affinities between Celtic peoples and Germans, in art, religion and culture. An innate conservatism meant that German tribes were slow to change and reduced access to resources seems to have meant that their technologies were less advanced than in Gaul. What they lacked in technology the Germans made up for in vigour. It was this trait that so impressed Caesar in his brief excursion across the Rhine into Germany – a trait that was to put to great use during the Alesia Campaign.

Vercingetorix

The key leader of the Gallic army was the now mythic figure, *Vercingetorix*. When Vercingetorix is mentioned in ancient sources, it is usually only in relationship to the Gallic War and Alesia; beyond this we know little. This makes it rather challenging to piece together the small scraps of evidence to produce something of his history. Vercingetorix must have been born sometime between the 80s and 70s BC, and he grew up at Gergovia, the strongly defended oppidum and capital of the *Arverni* tribe. He was the son of a powerful noble of the Arverni, called *Celtius*. Vercingetorix was born into a time of cultural flourishing and social change across Gallic society. The flowering of art and culture is evident in the La Tène art and its products; the metalwork in particular is still a source of inspiration today. At this time, Gallic society was in flux. Urbanization was having the effect of internationalizing trade and developing a money-based economy. Tribes were forming into large alliances that could be seen as prototypes to nation states, and some even had 'senates' along Roman lines. The meaning of Vercingetorix's name – 'great king of heroes' – is interesting in this regard. It appears to be part of a calculated attempt by Celtius, his father, to promote his family's bid for power. If Celtius was attempting to make his position as ruler incontrovertible, it didn't work. After he made an effort to become king, the nobles of the Arverni killed him. Some suggest that Vercingetorix's attempts to unite the tribes of Gaul were a similar attempt to become king, this time of the whole of Gaul. In the protodemocratic environment of the period, Vercingetorix's and his father's efforts to become supreme ruler of Gaul were a reversion to old-fashioned practices of monarchy. Perhaps they can be seen as the last-ditch attempt by some of the nobles within Gaul to revive the archaic system that they favoured. Although some authors attempt to say that Vercingetorix did succeed in unifying Gaul, it is clear that this was not the case. He may have been a leader, but only of a group of tribes with a common enemy rather than with a common philosophy. If Vercingetorix had unified Gaul he would not have had to request allies to send men to his rebellion – they would already have volunteered. The greatest irony connected to these events is that where Vercingetorix and his father failed to unite the Gauls under a single leader, the achievement can perhaps be said to have been accomplished by Caesar.

In the winter of 53–52BC, at the end of six long years of a Roman presence in Gaul, localized gatherings of Gallic chiefs occurred across the land. They met to discuss Rome's sustained presence throughout Gaul and their resentment at Caesar's continued interfering in their interests. The chiefs calculated that with Caesar in Italy at the time, if they could cut him off from his armies it would be possible to launch successful raids against Rome's legions, which would be leaderless and uncoordinated. Vercingetorix was one of the first to rise to the occasion. It is difficult to know whether this was a genuine attempt to defeat Caesar or an attempt to revive his family's grab for power. It is likely to have been both. Dio tells us that Vercingetorix was on friendly terms with Caesar early in the Gallic War. Like many of the powerful chieftains of Gaul, he kept on Rome's side when Caesar's actions served his purposes and particularly when they were at the expense of his enemies. Whatever Vercingetorix's motivations, the leaders of the Arverni tribe were still prepared to side with Rome and so they were not happy with Vercingetorix's move against Caesar. Consequently, Vercingetorix's uncle, *Gobannitio*, along with the leaders of the tribe, confronted Vercingetorix. When they saw Vercingetorix was unwilling to stop his course of action, they expelled him from Gergovia. Undeterred, Vercingetorix gathered what forces he could from the 'beggars and outcasts' of the surrounding territory and with this motley crew he created the core of an army. Following these events, Vercingetorix went on to gather the aggrieved Gallic tribes of Gaul, culminating in a revolt and the Alesia Campaign of 52BC.

> '[Vercingetorix] . . . was a man of enormous energy, strict disciplinarian severity of his punishments compelled any who were hesitating to obey, guilty of crime put to death at stake or tortured. Lesser crimes had ears cut off or a single eye cut out to be a warning. By these savage means he quickly got an army together.'
>
> [Caesar, *The Gallic War*, VII. 4]

Caesar depicts Vercingetorix as having a complex mixture of personality traits. Vercingetorix was clearly highly motivated, but all things considered he had nothing to lose and everything to gain. These factors meant that he was determined to the point of callousness. His widespread use of a scorched earth policy and willingness to eject the civilians of Alesia from the hill fort, even when they invited him in, are symptomatic of his attitude.

Vercingetorix

Even by the standards of the day these were harsh measures. But this does seem to be a character trait of his, as Vercingetorix always took a hard line even from the outset. To some extent contradicting this, he was also willing to hear petitions and at times reduced his strict decisions after particularly convincing appeals. Florus tells us that Vercingetorix was a brave and courageous man who united a terrifying people through force of personality. Vercingetorix's strict disciplinarian attitude may therefore have resulted from the exigencies of the situation – cometh the hour, cometh the man. Certainly, the Gauls were always supportive of Vercingetorix's actions, declaring him as:

'A consummate general, and that they had no doubt of his honour; that the war could not be conducted with greater prudence.'

[Caesar, *The Gallic War*, VII. 21]

Physically Vercingetorix appears to have been tall and imposing. Coins show he did not wear a moustache in characteristic Gallic fashion, although he had a typical mane of wavy hair. Combined with his imposing physical traits, Vercingetorix also seems to have been a good speaker. He is portrayed as often gaining the support of the populace with shrewd, passionate or persuasive arguments, using the required approach depending on the situation. Vercingetorix's fervent conviction in his cause does seem to manifest itself in his consistent belief in the success of the Gallic cause. His passionate belief seems to have motivated the Gauls that followed him to forge ahead through difficult situations. Caesar tells us that defeat of Vercingetorix spurred him on to greater things and actually increased his standing with other Gauls:

'Accordingly, as ill success weakens the authority of other generals, so, on the contrary, his dignity increased daily although a loss was sustained.'

[Caesar, *The Gallic War*, VII. 30]

However eloquent or persuasive Vercingetorix's arguments were, he was still facing a difficult situation in relation to Caesar. In time Caesar states that he had to revert to base bribes or promises to get the support of the less motivated tribes. Vercingetorix was also an intelligent man and he employed gifted and persuasive men like himself to advance his cause with the tribes that were wavering in their loyalties. This approach seems to have been very successful, and Caesar goes out of his way to point to Vercingetorix's successes, although he labels Vercingetorix's behaviour as underhand in this regard.

Vercingetorix was clearly a skilled tactician. His use of a scorched earth

Caesar's Gallic Triumph

policy and destruction of strategic locations such as bridges and oppida show he had a good grasp of the extended nature of Roman warfare, unlike many of his contemporaries. Equally, his use of forced marches and avoidance of pitched battles betray the hand of an astute tactician in the vein of Caesar. Vercingetorix was, therefore, probably the best leader Gaul could produce at the time. His actions over the months prior to Alesia enhanced his position as the head of the Gallic forces, a position that was finally confirmed by a gathering of the general council of Gauls at Bibracte. To his credit, after the defeat at Alesia, when the Gauls were utterly crushed, Vercingetorix showed something of his personal mettle. Whereas many leaders would have attempted to flee or shirk their responsibilities, Vercingetorix told his followers to do with him what they would. In the end they decided to hand him over to Caesar, partly in an attempt to pacify Caesar and partly in an attempt to win Caesar over to his old acquaintance. Caesar was in no mood for compromises though: he dealt brusquely with his adversary, packing Vercingetorix off to Rome to be dealt with at his leisure.

> 'Having ended the wars, he [Caesar] celebrated five Triumphs, four in a single month, but at intervals of a few days, . . . The first and most splendid was the Gallic Triumph . . . as he [Caesar] rode through the Velabrum on the day of his Gallic Triumph, the axle of his chariot broke, and he was all but thrown out; and he mounted the Capitol by torchlight, with forty elephants bearing lamps on his right and his left.'

> [Suetonius, *The Lives of the Twelve Caesars: Julius Caesar*, 37]

Vercingetorix was held in a Roman gaol for nearly six years after the Battle of Alesia. In that time Caesar's fortunes continued to rise. In 46BC Caesar had defeated his greatest enemies, both outside the Empire and within Rome. On the verge of becoming a king, he was able to celebrate his victories of the past years with four great 'Triumphs'. Caesar's Triumphs featured not only Gaul, but also Egypt, Asia, and Africa – countries he had conquered in the intervening years. But the Conquest of Gaul was the event that set him on the road to success and it was only fitting that it was to be the opening celebration. A Triumph was both a civil ceremony and a religious rite, the Senate bestowing on Caesar forty days of public thanksgiving. It was also an opportunity to present Rome's victories in a great propaganda event. The Triumph was an important signifier of the success of an individual. It could not be given without certain criteria being met. The general must have killed a significant number of the enemy, he must be an elected official, he must have brought the army home, thus

Vercingetorix's Army

signifying the end to fighting, and the Senate must approve the event. The affair was predominantly a procession through the gates of Rome, amongst tapestry and flower bedecked streets, houses and temples. Paterculus states that Caesar spent 600 million *sesterces* on the Triumphs, made possible by his selling the spoils of the wars. The procession was led by members of the Senate, followed by trumpeters and carts full of the spoils of battle, weapons, standards and trumpets of the enemy. Then came civil servants, followed by Caesar himself in a two-horse chariot. If, as Suetonius tells us, Caesar's chariot axle *did* break on the way to his Gallic Triumph, it was an ominous occurrence. At the end of the celebrations a white bull was sacrificed, but this wasn't the only sacrifice to the gods. As a climax to the extravaganza Vercingetorix was brought in chains through the streets. After being humiliated in front of the populace of Rome, he was taken away and ritually strangled in the seclusion of a small cell. With Vercingetorix's death, Gaul's hopes for freedom from Rome likewise died. Nevertheless, Caesar's great Triumph was to be short-lived; his fortunes had become intertwined with those of Vercingetorix and within two years Caesar had also been murdered.

Vercingetorix's Army

'In Gaul there are factions not only in all the states, and in all the cantons and their divisions, but almost in each family, and of these factions those are the leaders who are considered according to their judgment to possess the greatest influence, upon whose will and determination the management of all affairs and measures depends. And that seems to have been instituted in ancient times with this view, that no one of the common people should be in want of support against one more powerful; for none [of those leaders] suffers his party to be oppressed and defrauded, and if he do otherwise, he has no influence among his party. This same policy exists throughout the whole of Gaul; for all the states are divided into two factions.'

[Caesar, *The Gallic War*, VI. 11]

When we try to understand the form of Vercingetorix's army, we are faced with a number of problems. Documentary records provide some descriptions, but not even Caesar describes Vercingetorix's army in detail. On the whole, the information sources for Gallic society and warfare are problematic: they mainly come from ancient authors who rarely provide us with the type of perspective we require to place the Gauls correctly in context. Often the sources themselves are not first-hand, being repetitions of other authors or uncritical retellings of travellers' stories. However,

Caesar's Gallic Triumph

Caesar's *Gallic War*, along with other ancient sources, provides us with some useful descriptions of the Gallic peoples, although we must be wary of accepting his descriptions in too unquestioning a manner.

Caesar had his own reasons for writing his works: they promoted his image and presented Roman actions positively. In addition, Caesar gained much of his information on the battlefield or in the political arena – hardly the place to discover the nuances of a nation's culture. And so, like other authors before him, he resorted to using previous works to fill in the gaps of his experience. The physical appearance of 'Celts' given by Caesar matches authors such as Strabo, Diodorus Siculus, and Pliny. These all focus on the remarkable aspects of the Celtic appearance that were unusual to Mediterranean eyes: fair skin, hair and blue eyes. The descriptions of Gauls are often derived from those peoples closest to Roman provinces and show little of the range and complexity of the Celtic societies further away. By portraying the Gauls as 'barbarians', the Romans could focus attention on certain Gallic attributes for their own purposes, sometimes to contrast how well the Romans behaved, sometimes to show how badly. There was a certain contradiction in this, as the Romans sometimes ridiculed behaviour in the Gauls that the Romans themselves engaged in.

> 'These [nobles], when there is occasion and any war occurs (which before Caesar's arrival was for the most part wont to happen every year . . .), are all engaged in war. And those of them most distinguished by birth and resources have the greatest number of vassals and dependants about them. They acknowledge this sort of influence and power only.'

> [Caesar, *The Gallic War*, VI. 15]

Vercingetorix's army was based on the ad hoc accumulation of willing participants organized along tribal lines, in contrast to the Roman army's formal standing armies with strict military structures. One way to understand how Vercingetorix's army functioned, therefore, is to understand the structure of wider Gallic society. A problem when attempting to reconstruct Vercingetorix's army in this context is the fact that Gallic society had little homogeneity. At the time of Caesar's invasion, Gallic culture was still rooted in prehistoric religious and tribal customs, which differed from tribe to tribe. The role of the 'king' is a good example. It sometimes commingled the role of leader with that of high priest. In many tribes, however, attempts were made to keep these two roles separate. Religion still played a dominant role in Gallic life and priests took the role of wise arbitrators seriously, attempting to balance military and civilian leadership by halting the unrestrained power of either. By Caesar's invasion, kingship in some tribes was starting to be replaced by elected positions, much like the process that had happened previously in classical Mediterranean civilizations. The *Aedui* (whose capital at Bibracte was used as the focal point of the Alesia Campaign) seem to have been one of the most advanced along this process, although many other tribes were also developing similar mechanisms. At the time of the Alesia Campaign the Aedui had developed a constitution and had an elected magistrate called a *vergobret*, who functioned in the role of king. Separate from this civilian magistracy there was also a growing military magistracy. In charge of these was a military chieftain – a role that separated the military and political functions of the leaders, thus preventing the concentration of power in a single person's hands. A larger group formed solely from the nobility of the villages formed a 'senate' that would decide the grander fate of the tribe as a whole, such as whether it went to war or the election of magistrates. Nobles tended to come from kin groups with a long history of noble or renowned ancestors and marriage between these noble families helped maintain their status. Vercingetorix's attempt to unify Gaul was therefore seen by some Gauls as an attempt to circumvent the new structures and revive a system of hereditary kings that would place him foremost.

> 'the commonality is held almost in the condition of slaves, and dares to undertake nothing of itself and is admitted to no deliberation. The greater part, when they are pressed either by debt, or the large amount of their tributes, or the oppression of the more powerful, give themselves up in vassalage to the nobles, who possess over them the same rights without exception as masters over their slaves.'

[Caesar, *The Gallic War*, VI. 13]

Although social divisions were clearly demarcated, the struggle for power within these groups was inevitable. Even within noble families, members would compete with each other for support in order to gain supremacy. However, Gallic clientage was where the real social power was held and this was based on how many supporters an individual could accumulate. This system enabled wealthy chieftains to extend their control over large numbers of followers with little regard to social standing, tribal boundaries or definitions. Honour was a major feature of this relationship and this meant commoners had to be protected by their leaders. If they failed, they lost their honour and also their clients. This was a mutually beneficial system whereby wealthy individuals would protect their 'clients' and, in return, would be supported by them. Caesar makes note of this system, describing it as an ancient Gallic custom, but it was also very similar to Roman practice. So long as a leader could guarantee support and protection to his clients he would be maintained as leader. These social distinctions exhibited in the political system were apparent in the military system. At Alesia, the tribal leaders used this relationship to gather bands of warriors, calling upon those who owed them allegiance.

The Gallic tribes, like all 'Celtic' peoples, had a society based on warrior ideals. War was not only seen as destructive, but also productive. The necessary hierarchies required for military combat reinforced the social ties and structures they were formed from. In order to fight, a Gaul had to have achieved puberty and be wealthy enough to own his own arms. This mechanism guaranteed that each warrior had a stake in the successful outcome of the battle. At the top of the social pyramid was the military chieftain, a post that was annually elected and maintained only a controlling position over the 'armed council' that decided matters of warfare. These were made up of the nobility, who held the most prestigious place in battle, due in part to their ability to furnish themselves with both horse and complete panoply of the best quality armour. At the bottom were various levels of commoners who were mainly consigned to the ranks of the infantry, although they were not confined to that status – the possibility was always open to them to improve their position. In times of social upheaval it was not unknown for commoners to be a central part of societal transformation. Commoners retained their rights as freemen, whether they were well off and landed or part of the underclass. On the other hand, slaves were non-citizens with no rights. Often either captured or bought outsiders, their role was servile. Although their position could be changed and their lowly status was not always passed on to their offspring, only in extremis were slaves allowed to fight.

At the outset of hostilities the council called together an assembly of all the warriors, usually at a central place in the tribal region. During the Alesia Campaign, the hill fort at Bibracte was used as the focal centre, not only for the Aedui tribe, but also for the whole of the rebellious tribes of Gaul. With all of the available warriors armed and drawn together, the armed council could assess the state of readiness of the army. These events could also be an opportunity for intertribal competition through the display of prowess and equipment, showing their readiness and willingness for war. Weapons were not only used for war but also could signify an individual's status within society. The type of weapon a warrior had and how elaborate or decorated it was influenced how others interacted with him.

> 'The nation of all the Gauls is extremely devoted to superstitious rites; and on that account they . . . who are engaged in battles and dangers, either sacrifice men as victims, or vow that they will

sacrifice them, and employ the Druids as the performers of those sacrifices; because they think that unless the life of a man be offered for the life of another man the mind of the immortal gods cannot be rendered propitious, and they have sacrifices of that kind ordained for national purposes.'

[Caesar, *The Gallic War*, VI. 16]

Before battle it was not uncommon for rites and rituals to be performed and augurs to divine the fate of the battle. The Gauls had a range of gods forming an organized system of belief, depending on tribal preference. Many of the Gallic gods were directly associated with sky gods, the war god being one of the greatest. Usually the war god also had a male and female appearance and these often had positive and negative characteristics, which manifested as constructive or destructive traits. By the Roman invasion of 58BC, the Roman and Gallic gods were very similar in general terms, showing something of their shared Indo-European origins. After the assimilation of Gaul into the Roman Empire, these shared origins led to the relatively easy incorporation of the Gallic gods within the Roman pantheon.

'Mars presides over wars. To him when they have determined to engage in battle, they commonly vow those things they shall take in war. When they have conquered, they sacrifice whatever captured animals may have survived the conflict, and collect the other things into one place. In many states you may see piles of these things heaped up in their consecrated spots; nor does it often happen that any one, disregarding the sanctity of the case, dares either to secrete in his house things captured, or take away those deposited; and the most severe punishment, with torture, has been established for such a deed.'

[Caesar, *The Gallic War*, VI. 17]

Particularly common war gods were *Teuates*, *Esus* and *Taranis*; these gods usually had a physical manifestation, particularly on the battlefield. War gods also tended to be bloodthirsty and some writers suggest that they were only appeased with human sacrifice. Examples of such sacrifices were the drowning of a man in a tub to appease Teuates, hanging a man from a tree and pulling him to pieces to encourage Esus and encasing several people in a hollow tree and burning them to satisfy Taranis. Rites attributed to war gods often focused on the ritual deposition of war booty and sacrifice of captives.

'According to their natural cruelty, they are impious in the worship of their gods; for malefactors, after that they have been kept close prisoners five years together, they impale upon stakes, in honour to the gods, and then, with many other victims, upon a vast pile of wood, they offer them up as a burnt sacrifice to their deities. In like manner they use their captives also, as sacrifices to the gods. Some of them cut the throats, burn, or otherwise destroy both men and beasts that they have taken in time of war.'

[Diodorus Siculus, *Historical Library*, II]

Gallic gods were worshipped in religious sanctuaries often cut off from the outside world by large walls and ditches filled with ritual offerings. At Beauvais and Amiens, enclosures have been found with 30–50m-long sides surrounded by palisades, ditches and banks. A wooden temple in the centre of the enclosure was decorated with paintings, sculptures and weapons. Caesar and Livy both suggest that temples were used to display human and animal trophies of war until they decomposed and then were ritually destroyed in enclosure ditches. Animal bone and human sacrifice have also been discovered in these enclosure ditches. One of the largest was at Ribemont-sur-Ancre in the Somme, where remnants of over a thousand individuals aged between fifteen and twenty years old were found. They were probably sacrificed, possibly to war gods, and their bones were stacked criss-cross in a pile.

'They [the druids] wish to inculcate this as one of their leading tenets, that souls do not become extinct, but pass after death from one body to another, and they think that men by this tenet are in a great degree excited to valour, the fear of death being disregarded.'

[Caesar, *The Gallic War*, VI. 14]

This treatment was not confined to sacrificial victims. Warriors also were given sacrificial treatment. Community ossuaries are known, where dismembered bodies were laid on the ground and skulls detached and treated ritually. These practices may be connected with cult practices and much of the skeletons show evidence of wounds that do not suggest a natural death. One ancient author, Nicander of Colophon, noted that the Celts practised a form of divination at tombs of dead warriors. In the south of France, a whole range of stone sculptures from sanctuaries reveals that the development of a hero cult was widespread in the centuries before the Roman invasion. Entremont, Roquepertuse and Glanum, all in Provence, are some of the best known Celtic sanctuaries in the world, due mainly to the cult of the head found at these places. Headhunting seems to have occupied a curious place in Gallic religion, and commonly occurs in art as carved stone severed heads with half closed eyes. There are historic accounts of how Gauls collected human heads and hung them from their horse's necks or nailed them up as trophies. An explanation has yet to be found for the practice, although the cult must be linked with the concept of the spirit residing in the head and may even be linked to the ritual wearing of a torc necklace.

'Their hair was of gold, their clothing was of gold and light stripes brightened their cloaks. Their milk-white necks had gold collars around them, a pair of Alpine spears glinted in each warrior's hands, and their bodies were protected by tall shields.'

[Virgil, *Aeneid*, VIII. 659–62]

Certain warriors would wear chunky neck rings called torcs, usually made of gold or bronze and very rarely of silver, and these would reflect the noble status of the individual. Torcs represented the epitome of the Celtic craftsman's skill and are well represented in Gallic and Classical art. After the Gallic Wars, many torcs were taken from the defeated warriors. In the Roman military torcs came to be used as a symbol of rank and achievement, finally being incorporated into the military decorations of the Roman army. Clearly the torc was a significant part of the Gallic warrior's dress. So important, in fact, that some Gallic warriors wore only the torc. For religious reasons these warriors, called *gaesatae*, went to war naked. However, it is unlikely gaesatae were present at Alesia because Caesar would have mentioned them given their specific religious connections and unusual appearance.

'For they [the Gauls] were most excellent fighters on horseback, and were thought to be specially superior as such . . .'

[Plutarch, *The Parallel Lives*, 6]

In ancient sources the Gauls were famed for their excellence as cavalry and the quality of their horses. It is likely that they carried small shields, in either geometric shapes or simply round. Although the cavalry wore no clothing specific to their rank, we can assume that their higher status meant that their equipment was of better quality. Excavation at Alesia has revealed the advanced nature of Gallic horsemanship. Two types of horse bit were found, one a simple snaffle-bit of a common form used across Europe at the time. The other, a complex curb bit, is a form invented by the Celts only a hundred years before the Battle of Alesia and would have given the rider complete command of the horse with one hand. The Gauls were also credited with inventing spurs, although of the six spurs originally discovered at Alesia only two remain, one of iron and one of bronze. The

Caesar's Gallic Triumph

Gauls were also notable for having developed an ingenious form of saddle, one reason for their renowned cavalry skills. Unfortunately no saddle remains have been discovered at Alesia, but contemporary examples show they had four pommels that held the rider on the horse without the need for stirrups.

> 'The Gauls are tall, with moist white flesh; their hair is not only naturally blond, but they also make artificial efforts to lighten its colour by washing it frequently in lime water. They pull it back from the top of the head to the nape of the neck . . . thanks to this treatment their hair thickens until it is just like a horse's mane. Some shave their beards, others let them grow moderately; nobles keep their cheeks clean shaven but let their moustaches grow long until they cover their mouths . . . they wear amazing clothes: tunics dyed in every colour and trousers that they call bracae [breeches]. Their pinstriped clothes in winter and light material in summer, decorated with small, densely packed, multicoloured squares.'

> [Diodorus Siculus, *World History*, V. 28. 30]

This description from a Roman source gives a general likeness of the Gallic men. Some of these characteristic features are mentioned by other authors and so are likely to be applicable to Vercingetorix's army as a whole. Long hair seems to feature strongly, often as a wild swept-back mane or lime washed and drawn into a horse-like mane. Likewise, with this long hair comes a long curving moustache, often covering the mouth and sometimes with a small beard. In the main, the Gallic warrior's dress was similar to peoples across northern Europe at the time, consisting of tight breeches with a long shirt with sleeves, and slits on the sides to help movement. Light cloaks were also worn, sometimes fastened by bronze brooches with elaborate decoration and coral or enamel inlay. Clothing was usually manufactured from woven wool and when different dyed wools were used this would produce attractive multicoloured plaid or striped patterns. This could be enhanced with embroidery and belts with gold and silver ornamentation. In wartime the wealthier members of Gallic society would have worn coats of mail. Unfortunately, not even the smallest scrap of mail has been recovered from Alesia, although a number of mail coat fasteners have been recovered, confirming they were in use, no doubt this was because of their high value.

> 'Meanwhile the King of the Gauls espied him, and judging from his insignia that he was the commander, rode far out in front of the rest and confronted him, shouting challenges and brandishing his spear. His stature exceeded that of the other Gauls, and he was conspicuous

for a suit of armour which was set off with gold and silver and bright colours and all sorts of embroideries; it gleamed like lightning.'

[Plutarch, *The Parallel Lives* 7]

Weapons found at Alesia provide us with excellent examples of late La Tène (first century BC) metalwork. Unfortunately, the location of the weapons recovered from Alesia were not recorded to modern standards, being simple lists attributed to ditches without any complex stratigraphic analysis. However, on the basis of coin dates, from more recent excavation it has been shown that these ditches are contemporary with the Battle of Alesia. Regrettably, only the ironwork from the Gallic warrior's assemblage of equipment survives, as the wood and leather has long since decomposed in the moist soils. Nonetheless, taken as a whole, the weapons provide a useful cross-section of the iron weapons used at Alesia.

'These are the creatures who assail you with such terrible shouts in battle, and clash their arms and shake their long swords and toss their hair.'

[Appian, *History of Rome: Gallic Wars*]

The ideal Gallic warriors were, above all, swordsmen. Their swords were long, often close to a metre in length, and were not used for thrusting but for a slashing style of fighting. The ferocity of these assaults meant that Roman legionaries had to be trained to overcome the fear that these wild charges created. By the late La Tène period swords were becoming shorter than they had been in the past, but swords as long as 0.75m were common. These longer blades have been attributed to the cavalry, but this is not necessarily the case as earlier Gallic swords had much longer blades. The Gallic peoples liked elaborate metalwork, and so swords and scabbards have been found with ornate patterned and inlaid designs. At Alesia, twenty-one swords have been found, in some cases still in their original sheaths. In general, these swords are typical of other European examples from the late La Tène period. The swords have blades with either rounded or pointed tips, with the wider examples having acid-etched decorations on them. Examples of sheaths show they originally had oval U-shaped fittings on one side, for attachment via straps to the belt. There they would be worn on the right hip. These belts could be made of linked iron rings or loops, but more commonly would be simple leather straps. Sword handles were wooden and so now are lost, but their bent W-shaped guards still occur, usually made of iron, but sometimes made of bronze. The parts of twenty-one swords found at Alesia present a broad spectrum of sword evolution, indicating they were in use over a long period of time, perhaps representing their prior use as heirlooms or the desperate use of any weapon available, even if it was old and damaged. Remarkably, two more unusual types of sword were uncovered deliberately intertwined with a sword sheath and buried in a ditch. This behaviour hints at possible ritualistic practices that were carried out after the battle, the ditches of the circumvallation perhaps being seen in Gallic eyes as enclosure ditches around the sanctuary of Alesia, a place where so many Gauls had sacrificed themselves.

> '[The Gauls] . . . wear bronze helmets with large projecting figures which give the wearer the appearance of enormous size. In some cases horns are attached so as to form one piece, in others foreparts of birds or quadrupeds worked in relief.'

> [Diodorus Siculus, *History*, 30.2]

Gallic helmets came in a variety of forms, from simple bronze bowls to elaborately decorated tall bronze helmets with coloured inlays on them. The more simple helmets were plain bronze bowls with short protruding neck guards, called 'Montefortino' or 'Coolus' types, after the place of their original identification. More elaborate versions had decorative edges and domes and cheek pieces decorated with multiple circular bosses. Sometimes the wealthiest individuals would have taller pointed domes to their helmets, enhanced with pink coral or red enamel inlays, ornately decorated horns, statuettes or horsehair plumes. None of these more elaborate helmets were discovered at Alesia, presumably because such expensive items would only be attainable by a few commanders and as such would be too valuable for Roman soldiers to leave behind. A further type of helmet was developed in the late La Tène period, which was made of iron. This 'Agen-Port' form of helmet became the forerunner to the imperial Gallic helmet that was popular in the Roman army for the next 200 years. Agen-Port helmets had corrugated reinforcements and wide strengthening brims. The Gallic helmets found at Alesia are of a very similar form that was widespread in Gaul. Indeed, their importance is such that they were named the 'Alesia' type. The inner domes of the helmets were discovered to have the remains of organic materials still adhering to their sides, indicating that leather or wool was used to pad them out. Twenty cheek pieces, some highly elaborate, suggest that some of the helmets were richly decorated and probably belonged to noble warriors. Only tribal chiefs and cavalrymen are likely to have worn these helmets.

> '[The Cimbri] . . . wore helmets, made to resemble the heads and jaws of wild beasts, and other strange shapes, and heightening these with plumes of feathers, they made themselves appear taller than they

were. They had breastplates of iron, and white glittering shields; and for their offensive arms, every one had two darts, and when they came hand to hand, they used large and heavy swords.'

[Plutarch, *Lives of the Noble Greeks and Romans*, 25]

Sculptural and archaeological evidence points to the Gauls using long wooden shields about one-half to three-quarters the length of the body. These could be oval, round or geometric in shape, with iron bosses covering the handgrip, and, more rarely, iron edging strips. Parts of shields that have been discovered suggest they were made of a tough wood like oak, about 1.2m long and 1.2cm thick at the centre, with the addition of a thick wooden spine. Roman shields of this type date to about 300 years before the first Gallic examples, so it is likely that the Gauls adopted the shield form after their invasion of Italy in the fifth century BC. It is thought that in rare cases the fronts of Gallic shields were decorated in elaborately decorated bronze sheet with inlays. Although nothing like this has been found at Alesia, this is no surprise, as richly decorated shields would have been removed as booty. Most Gallic shields of the period had either round or 'butterfly' bosses, made from a single piece of beaten iron. Seventeen dome-shaped shield bosses were discovered at Alesia, all conforming to these descriptions. Although the wood does not survive, the iron shield bosses, nails, edging strips and ornamentation have been discovered. The bosses are typically Gallic, occurring in a wide circular form with large attachment nails and a butterfly form with small nails. We have no evidence of the colours that shields were painted, but sculptures hint they were very ornate, which seem to match the Gallic love of intricate design as manifest in their beautiful metalwork.

'The spears of the Gauls were not like javelins, but what the Romans called pila, four-sided, part wood and part iron, and not hard except at the pointed end.'

[Appian, *History of Rome: Gallic Wars*, 1]

Although the Gallic warrior is described by the ancient sources as predominantly a swordsman, for the poorer Gallic warrior the most fundamental part of his equipment was his spear. A warrior would be able to obtain a spear before a shield, sword or helmet. Spears tend to be split between the heavier forms and lighter throwing spears or javelins. The larger spears can range up to 2.5m long, the heads being almost 0.5m alone. Smaller spears are assumed to be throwing javelins. Almost 400 fragments of weapons have been found at Alesia, 140 of them being javelins and 180 being spears. The huge number of missile weapons discovered suggests that this form was the predominant weapon used at Alesia. Often the ends are bent and the edges are damaged by cut marks. Similarities in the manufacture of these weapons mean they could be Gallic, but they could also be Roman or German in origin. This is particularly the case with the leaf-shaped blades that are 15cm to 30cm in length. The larger acid-etched and wavy bladed spears are probably Gallic, although some of these may also be German in origin. The identifiably Gallic spears are of the long thrusting type, with a heavy median vein for strength. The concave section of the blades at the tip, along with many traces of cut marks, indicate that these weapons were used for thrusting as well as cutting. The majority of these larger blades have some form of acid etching, either circles, triangles, zigzags or lattice designs. With these decorated spearheads, comes a series of wavy edged spears, which would inflict particularly grievous wounds. Some spears also have cross guards towards their sockets. These guards led excavators working for Napoleon III to think of them as small stabbing swords. It is likely, however, that the cross guard was part of the offensive use of the spear, enabling a shield to be pulled down before the spear was thrust into its victim. As such, these are very similar to medieval spears of similar form. Pila have also been found at Alesia, and although usually attributed to Romans, some authors have suggested that they could also be of Gallic origin, as a few examples have been discovered in Gallic oppida. This is not too far-fetched, as it is known that the Germans at the time used a similar type of weapon, and so the Gauls may also have been employing related forms. The truth is that in a time of need, all forms of weaponry, whether indigenous or foreign, were put to use.

The Gauls were not famed for their archery but Caesar mentions Vercingetorix found archers for his army. Presumably these archers were made up from the lower classes of Gallic society, although their presence in the battle played a more significant role than this rank would suggest. More than forty examples of arrowheads have been recovered from Alesia, with either one or two barbs, and many can be paralleled by examples coming from other Gallic oppida. It is clear that the Gallic army also contained bands of slingers, but as yet evidence of their presence at Alesia is yet to come to light. This may be because their shot was usually simple rounded stones and so their presence elsewhere has usually only been confirmed by the occurrence of large piles of such material.

Opening Moves

------⇒»-○-«⇐------

Roman–Gallic Relations

The relationship between the Classical peoples of the Mediterranean region and their north-western neighbours is a long and complex one. Rome's attitude to the Gauls, in particular, was marked by the scars of numerous wars and invasions, and it is safe to say that they treated them like no other. Sometimes the relationship could be close, at other times it was fraught, but it was always one of mutual suspicion until Rome finally defeated Gaul and resolved the matter. The Roman affair with their Gallic neighbours had begun many centuries before Caesar and Vercingetorix's time. Southern France had been open to classical influence from Greek then later Roman traders since the seventh century BC. The derivation of the Gallic peoples from the wider 'Celtic' society of Europe is still much debated. The Celtic culture as a whole seems to have originated around southern Germany, from where it expanded across western Europe and the Atlantic isles by the fifth century BC. By this period the Italian peninsula was beginning to consolidate under Roman control. The once-divided and warring tribes of Italy, each with varying customs and alliances, had gradually come to recognize Rome as the most powerful of the Latin nations. After Rome defeated the Latin tribes at Lake Regillus in 499BC, a treaty was drawn up between Rome and the Latin tribes to provide equal legal rights to all members. This alliance was soon to be tested by a Gallic invasion that spilled over the Alps in Italy during the fourth century BC. From this point onwards Gaul's rocky relationship with her neighbours on the Italian peninsula grew. An initial incursion by the Gallic peoples was made by the *Insubres* tribe, who settled in the Po region of northern Italy. There then followed other tribes, progressively moving south until Rome itself was attacked by the *Senones* in 380BC. This act was a seminal moment in the history of Roman–Gallic affairs. The story of the sacking of Rome was retold down the generations; how only the Capitol held out whilst the Gallic invaders plundered the city and how one night, the Gauls preparing to attack the Capitol were only thwarted by the cackling of the sacred geese that raised the alarm. In the following days, the Romans decided to pay the Gauls to return home, and as the payment was being made the Roman army appeared and drove off the Gallic army. While the truth of the story may well be questionable (the Gallic warriors were just as likely to have finished their looting and decided to go home) this 'origin myth' embodied the Roman concept of themselves for the next 400 years. It reflected the difference between the ideal of Roman resolve and tenacity with Gallic capriciousness. This story more than any other set the backdrop to the action that took place between these two competing nations at the hill fort of Alesia.

The physical effects of the sacking of Rome are difficult to assess. What does appear clear is that this event seems to have galvanized Rome's efforts to expand its power throughout Italy, using a mixture of conflict, alliance and the granting of citizenship. By 272BC Rome had unified the whole peninsula under its rule, although it would take a further two centuries to assimilate the various ethnicities into a single Romanized culture.

This process seems to have been reinforced somewhat by the series of conflicts with Carthage. Throughout this episode, along with a growing self-image, the representation of the Gallic peoples as barbarians was no less reinforced. Hannibal's crushing defeat of Rome – followed by sixteen years of Carthaginian occupation – did nothing to help Rome's relationship with the Gauls; for Hannibal had used large numbers of Gallic allies in his conquest of Italy. At times up to 40 per cent of his army were Gauls. Ultimately, Hannibal's defeat at Zama (modern-day Tunisia) in 202BC, also meant a defeat for Carthage and removed the threat of war from Rome's doorstep for the time being.

The Carthaginian War had illuminated the continued weakness of Italy's northern border, as this was the route Hannibal took to invade Italy. Defeat in this region would always leave the way open for direct land invasion and the memories of the sacking of Rome, the Gallic incursions and Hannibal's scorched earth policy remained strong in the minds of the Roman public. These fears seem to have prompted Rome to institute the foundations for a militarized system, one that was to become the most predominant in Europe for the next 500 years. The result of this change was manifest in successive annexations of land during the following century. A commitment was made to strengthen Rome through a series of aggressive acquisitions of neighbouring territories. The northern borders of Roman territory were extended outwards and a connection was made along the Mediterranean coast, from Italy through the Spanish lands acquired from the Carthaginians. Spain was plundered and a series of rebellions there were finally settled when Numantia, the stronghold of the Celtiberians, fell in 133BC. 'The Province' was created in 123BC quickly followed by Transalpine Gaul in 121BC. These areas became trading centres that linked Rome's Spanish conquests with mainland Italy, thus providing safe harbours for Roman ships around the whole north-western end of the Mediterranean Sea. It was some of these provinces, newly taken and on the borders of the barbarian world that were shortly to come under the control of Julius Caesar.

By 113BC mainland Italy was under threat again, this time not from the Gauls but from German tribes – the *Cimbri* and the *Teutones*. After a disastrous Roman defeat at Noreia, courtesy of the Cimbri, the German threat dispersed, but fears were soon fanned again by more defeats in 109, 107 and 105BC. It appears that for all Rome's attempts to strengthen the Italian peninsula, it was still weak on its northern border. Feeling the effects of exposure to German attack, the Roman Senate placed all their hopes in Marius, who had recently been elected consul. Marius took the occasion to reform the army, revising its organization, its training and equipment, and thereby turning it into a well-organized and effective fighting force. Marius was re-elected on a rolling basis each year, until he defeated the Teutones in 102BC and the Cimbri in 101BC. Re-election in this form was contrary to law and precedent but reflected a pragmatic solution to increased threat developed during the Carthaginian War. This solution extended the command of successful generals beyond the statutory limit of one year.

If Italy's northern border was now safe for a time, then in this relative calm the Roman political elite set to fighting amongst themselves. The first century BC began with 'The Social War' (91–89BC), in which Rome's Italian allies forced the guarantee of citizenship to most of the tribes of Italy. Subsequently, attacks by the Persian King Mithridates in the east, brutal political strife in Rome, including senatorial uprisings, piratical attacks on the Mediterranean and Spartacus' Slave Revolt all had their effects on the consciousness of the Roman elite. Sulla finally set in place a senatorial oligarchy and an environment that ushered in the 'big men' that were to set the stage in the Alesia Campaign. The first of these was Pompey. An ally of Sulla, Pompey set about solving Rome's outstanding problems. After being granted sweeping powers and great resources, he swiftly solved the pirate problem and defeated Mithridates. On returning to Rome, Pompey made an alliance with Crassus and Caesar, known as the First Triumvirate. From this point on, Caesar's position in the fortunes of Rome was secure. With Pompey's popularity and Crassus' enormous wealth, Caesar was able to position himself for the future. Caesar became consul in 59BC, and was given special command in Illyricum and Gaul for five years, a time in which he could assault the old foes and carve for himself a place in the hearts of the *plebs urbana* – the commoners of Rome.

As the official governor of three provinces, Caesar took command of the

Caesar's Gallic Triumph

Roman territories that bordered the barbarians: Cisalpine Gaul (essentially northern Italy and the Alps), Transalpine Gaul – usually called 'The Province' (the south of France from the Pyrenees through modern-day Languedoc – Provence and part of the French Alps) and Illyricum (modern-day Slovenia, Croatia, Bosnia and Herzegovina). In the classical Roman mind the lands beyond these provinces were the fringes of the known world.

With the migration of the *Helvetii* from modern-day Switzerland to the Gallic territory of the Aedui in 58BC, Caesar saw his first opportunity to begin a process of self-aggrandisement. By refusing to allow the Helvetii to pass through Aedui territory to a location on the west coast of Gaul, Caesar placed himself in control of Gallic affairs. If Caesar had wanted a quick outcome to this problem, he could have allowed the migration under Roman supervision, which would have resolved the issue. By forcefully barring the progress of the Helvetii, Caesar was manifesting his aggressive tendencies – a behaviour that always seems to have brought him success in the short term. In order to bar the progress of the Helvetii, Caesar built a long bank and ditch, from lake Geneva to the Jura Mountains. This 19-mile barrier foreshadowed the defences he would build at Alesia. Undeterred, the Helvetii outflanked Caesar, who finally brought them to battle near Bibracte. Caesar adopted a defensive hilltop position and then, in an aggressive move, charged the Helvetii. Even though he was charged in return by further forces of *Boii* and *Tulingi* he ended victorious.

This success buoyed Caesar's ambitions and he seized on his next opportunity with vigour. Caesar was called in to restrain a German client king of the Romans, Ariovistus, who had also been expanding into and harassing the Gallic Aedui. Caesar immediately set out to defeat the German army, but his army suddenly became fearful of fighting Germans, a much worse prospect in their eyes than Gauls. Caesar managed to win the legionaries over with his rhetoric and after some initial difficulties managed to bring Ariovistus to battle. The battle didn't go entirely Caesar's way, but Roman tactics managed to turn the battle to a victory. As the year closed Caesar was able to return to Rome with two victories under his belt against two of Rome's traditional enemies.

The following year (57BC) Caesar undertook punitive measures, this time against the Belgic tribe, the *Belgae*, rumoured to be discontent with Caesar's behaviour. Caesar immediately marched to their homeland and dispersed their gatherings. The Belgae were made up of a group of tribes who lived in the north-east of Gaul and included of some of the most formidable warriors in Gaul. Caesar knew that if he could defeat the Belgae it would signal to the rest of Gaul that Rome was the most important power in the land, one that could make or break tribes as it saw fit. A Gallic victory would also have the benefit of increasing Caesar's standing in the eyes of Roman citizens and his influence amongst the wealthy elite. Caesar's pre-emptive action against the Belgic tribes was successful. Some of the tribes of the Belgae surrendered and were subjugated, but others retreated to the Somme region, defeated but not beaten. For the rest of Gaul these actions were clear enough. If they sided with Caesar they would benefit from Rome's military strength, but if they did not, then their fate would be the same as that of the Belgae.

After two years of success, in 56BC the Senate gave Caesar a further five years to complete his operations. Following the revolts in the north-east of Gaul, the tribes of north-west Gaul began to rebel. Caesar moved against the maritime tribes of Brittany, at the same time sending his best generals to the tribes in the south-west and north-east to quell any ideas of rebellion. Caesar had pre-planned the assault, building boats in preparation for the attack, and swiftly dealt with the revolt in Brittany. Caesar's retribution for the rebellion was quick and brutal – the first sign of things to come for the Gauls. Caesar finished the rest of the year putting down smaller revolts across northern Gaul.

After these successes Caesar now saw his position was secure enough to venture into areas unknown. The following year (55BC) Caesar expanded his influence outside Gaul, thwarting the expansion of German tribes across the Rhine, and venturing across the Channel to Britain. He returned to Britain again the next year (54BC), taking over half of his legions with him. Clearly this was more than a simple reconnaissance; it was, in fact, an attempt to increase Rome's – and more importantly Caesar's – sphere of influence. It was clear now to the Gauls and their neighbours that Caesar's actions betrayed more than simple policing actions, and were in fact indicative of an aggressive policy of political strategy and economic control.

This realization was to play out fully in the following three years. At the outset of the campaign of 53BC, Caesar was beginning to lay plans to defeat the Gauls. After five years' campaigning in Gaul this season was to be a decisive one. Caesar expected serious disturbances in Gaul and so set about levying extra troops and mobilizing them. In this way he hoped to go some way to pre-empting revolt through the overwhelming strength of Roman forces and reserves. Unbeknownst to Caesar, the tribes in the north were banding together with German tribes from across the Rhine. The Gauls were planning to attack the Roman legions before they could gather their forces. Caesar's position was undermined because he had been forced to spread his forces due to supply problems stemming from the poor harvests of the previous year, dividing and weakening his army. Interestingly, one of these attacks led to the Gauls using the Romans' own techniques, building siegeworks against them – not a usual form of Gallic warfare. By the end of the year Caesar had realized that this was going to be a longer and larger course of action than he had at first anticipated. He would now require more forces to quell the growing revolts within Gaul. Caesar raised and borrowed more legions, increasing the number in Gaul to eleven. At the end of the campaign of 53BC Caesar withdrew his army to a safe base at *Durocortorum* (modern-day Rheims). Here he convened a council of Gaul, bringing together the chiefs of the Gallic tribes.

In front of the gathered assembly he brought the lawsuit of the *Senones* against their neighbours the *Carnutes*. The principal instigator of the rebellion, a man named Acco, was ultimately condemned to death – *more maiorum*. According to old Roman custom, he was struck with rods then decapitated. For the Gauls, this sentence was an obvious demonstration by Rome that any further rebellion would be dealt with just as harshly. During the winter of 53BC Caesar placed the bulk of his army (six legions) in the centre of Gaul at *Agedincum* (modern-day Sens). A further two legions he wintered nearby in the territory of the Lingones, and a final two legions were wintered further to the north-east at Trier. Leaving his armies safely quartered Caesar left for Cisalpine Gaul to fulfil his duties as proconsul in Rome, in the safe assumption that his recent execution of Acco would guarantee quiet until he returned. Caesar was to be disappointed. During this period the Gallic chiefs wasted no time in meeting in secret and instigating plans to gather a great rising at their first opportunity.

Grand Coalition

In 52BC rumblings of Gallic discontent brought Caesar running back to Gaul to discover a young Averne prince, Vercingetorix, fomenting a general revolt. Caesar's fears over his control of Gaul were becoming a reality. At the head of the gathering of tribes, Vercingetorix was selected and proclaimed leader. Caesar, once warned of these events, moved to link up with his legions in Gaul. Pretending that the snow had forced him to travel through the Cevennes, Caesar drew Vercingetorix south, while all the time he planned to cross in the north through the Alps and back to the territory of the *Lingones*. Vercingetorix, aware of Caesar's success in Gaul and its neighbouring countries, decided that to be successful he would need a complete gathering of the Gallic tribes, otherwise he would be forced to wage merely a guerrilla war against Caesar. A scorched earth policy was instigated by Vercingetorix, to stall Caesar's advance. The Gauls refused to engage the Romans in open conflict and so forced Caesar to employ siege tactics against their occupied hill forts. After a series of successful encounters against the Gauls, Caesar's re-entry to Gaul was capped by a memorable siege and the capture of the Gallic oppidum of *Avaricum* (modern-day Bourges).

Thinking that he had broken the back of the Gallic revolt, Caesar moved with a reduced force of six legions to take Vercingetorix's own base, the tribal capital of the Arverni at Gergovia. The remaining four legions were sent with his best legate, Labienus, to capture Lutèce, the city of the *Parisii*. The Siege of Gergovia manifested some common traits of Caesar's tactics. Caesar first took control of the surrounding heights, setting up camps and cutting the Gauls off from their access to water resources. He then set about connecting these camps with a defensive barrier to provide easy, protected access. Following this, the Roman soldiers, overconfident in their previous successes, made a pre-emptive attack on the walls of Gergovia and were badly mauled. The attack against Gergovia ended in bloody failure, partly due to the rising of the surrounding tribes. However, Labienus' venture resulted in the effective elimination of the Parisii as a fighting force, which allowed him to rejoin with Caesar in the friendly territory of the Lingones at Agedincum (modern-day Sens).

A general assembly was called by the Gauls to bring together the chiefs of the rebel coalition at the Aeduian capital in the oppidum at Bibracte (modern-day Mont Beuvray). Vercingetorix was confirmed as the leader of the revolt, although from this time on he was compelled always to bear in mind the general assembly's opinions. Vercingetorix immediately attempted to capitalize on his success at Gergovia by ordering that the tribes closest to The Province, the previously pro-Roman Aedui in particular, launch attacks against Caesar.

Caesar was now faced with a dilemma, well aware that his position was complicated. So far, he had managed to use his army to attack the Gauls piecemeal, to divide and conquer. Presently, he was isolated in Gaul and his supplies were low. He knew that a combined army of Gauls could hit him with an overwhelming force in a single battle. His men had been fighting for months and his only reinforcements were available in Italy or The Province. On top of this the *Sequani* seem to have joined in the Gallic coalition, blocking his return through the Jura Mountains. One option open to him was to withdraw his armies from Gaul and return to the safety of Rome; but this would compromise both his career and his generalship. Any doubt about his martial effectiveness would call into question his ability and thereby affect his political credentials. Frequently one to go on the offensive, Caesar rejected a full-scale withdrawal and decided to attack. Ordering reinforcements from German allies from across the Rhine,

Caesar's Gallic Triumph

Caesar planned to force a way back to The Province. There he would have time to gather new reinforcements and supplies to attack again the following season. He would also have time to plead his case in Rome, against the threat of a combined Gallic force that could threaten Rome itself and gather much needed political and monetary support in this venture. Caesar therefore headed south, with the River Seine and its tributary the Armançon protecting his flank. Any attack on his march would be likely to come from the Aedui, but they would have to approach him from across the river, which would provide Caesar with an effective defence against ambush. His plan was simple: to return through the same gap he had first entered Gaul by six years earlier in 58BC.

Campaign Chronicle

---◈◈◈---

'The enemy often launches rapid ambushes or raids at river crossings.'

[Vegetius, *Epitome of Military Science*, 3.7]

Week 1, Day 1: Caesar Marches to The Province

'Caesar moved from those parts, and passed over the territory of the Lingones, wishing to join the Sequani, who were friends, and formed a bulwark in front of Italy against the rest of Gaul. There the enemy fell upon him and hemmed him in with many ten thousands, upon which Caesar resolved to fight a decisive battle against the combined forces, and after a great contest, he gained a victory at last, and with great slaughter, routed the barbarians . . .'

[Plutarch, *Fall of the Roman Republic: Six Lives*, III. 26]

After the reverse of Gergovia, Caesar withdraws towards the security of 'The Province' (modern-day Provence). Here he will be able to resupply and prepare for renewed hostilities against the Gauls in the coming year. By undertaking a wide sweep through Lingones territory, Caesar attempts to avoid encountering the hostile forces of the Aedui. He follows the ancient route running from the north-west to the south-east of Burgundy, and on reaching the River Armançon, an important watercourse in antiquity, he crosses at the Gué des Pierre, the 'Ford of Stones'. This ford is large, and its location on a slow-moving S-bend of the Armançon makes crossing here relatively easy. Travelling now along the southern bank of the Armançon, Caesar knows he will have to cross back to the north bank to progress towards Provence. Scouts and locals sympathetic to the Romans have brought to his attention another ford 25 miles or so further downstream, near modern Lézinnes. Today, the study of field names in this region tells us that this location probably represents the border of the territory of the Lingones and the *Mandubii*. Caesar crosses the river at this point and goes on to camp between Lézinnes and Aisy-sur-Armançon (approximately 10 miles from Montbard). Tomorrow he will begin his move through Mandubii territory towards Provence.

Caesar's Gallic Triumph

'Those who have made a careful study of the art of war assert that more dangers tend to arise on the march than in battle itself. For in battle everyone is armed, and they see the enemy at close quarters and come mentally prepared for fighting. On the march, the soldier is less armed and less alert; he is thrown into instant confusion by a sudden attack or concealed ambush.'

[Vegetius, *Epitome of Military Science*, 3.6]

The Roman army has undergone serious defeats on the march before and Caesar is well aware of the dangers as he sets forth to The Province. But he must balance these practical difficulties with the morale of his troops. Although he has had victories, he knows he must not let his withdrawal become – or even be seen as – a defeat. Although he is marching through enemy territory, the men are not formed as if expecting an attack. Five

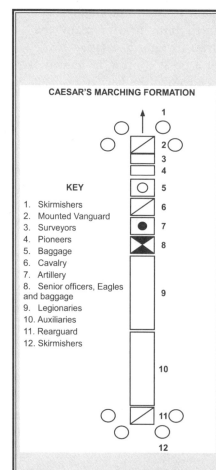

CAESAR'S MARCHING FORMATION

KEY

1. Skirmishers
2. Mounted Vanguard
3. Surveyors
4. Pioneers
5. Baggage
6. Cavalry
7. Artillery
8. Senior officers, Eagles and baggage
9. Legionaries
10. Auxiliaries
11. Rearguard
12. Skirmishers

Caesar's Army on the March

The Roman army on the march tended to move quite slowly, theoretically averaging about 20 Roman miles at normal speed (about 18 modern miles) and 24 Roman miles at the double (22 modern miles). Of course these were the distances given by military treatises but, in reality these would be hampered by weather, road conditions and impedimenta (baggage). Caesar was renowned for the speed of manoeuvre and he says that he was able to march his legions 25 miles a day when required. In *The Gallic War* he often describes his armies marching from base to base, to crush revolts or provide reinforcements. It is likely that these were exceptional events, using lightly equipped troops in extreme circumstances. Caesar's retreat to The Province may well have been undertaken in extremis but a prolonged

Week 1, Day 1: Caesar Marches to The Province

years previously, the *Nervii* had attacked Caesar on the march and he had set his column out in expectation of this. On that occasion he had, in his own words, formed his army as if 'approaching the enemy'. Against the Nervii Caesar had 'followed his usual practice' of leading his forces with six legions in light marching order, followed by the baggage train, with two inexperienced legions in the rear and cavalry on both flanks. On the march to The Province, Caesar has not drawn up his column in like fashion: rather he has drawn up his column in a more customary formation for marching. The cavalry ride at the head, with the baggage behind and legions and auxiliaries following. He is more concerned with the enemy in the rear than with any threat from the direction in which he is going.

'Vercingetorix encamped in three camps, about 10 miles from the Romans and having summoned the commanders of the cavalry to a

journey under such circumstances, when encumbered by baggage and moving through unfamiliar enemy territory, would have been achieved far more slowly and cautiously.

Caesar and his contemporaries were all of the opinion that appropriate marching formations should be used according to situation. These circumstances were mainly defined by tactical or topographical factors, although in Caesar's own accounts his approach seems to vary. When marching against the Nervii, Caesar had led with six legions, followed by their baggage, with two legions in the rear and cavalry on both flanks. Other authors such as Onasander, Polybius and Vegetius suggested that the army should march so as to form battle formation as quickly as possible. In this formation, cavalry would form the front and back of the column, with the legions in the centre and baggage spread between them. If attacked, the column could, in theory, turn to face the enemy in a line of battle, thus shortening the length of time the army was vulnerable. Skirmishers on the flanks of the column would provide a covering screen while the army made this manoeuvre. While Caesar usually used a formation with his strongest legions at the front and baggage at the rear, he does not seem to have used this formation on his retreat to Provence. This may have been because he was concerned that an attack would come from the direction of the enemy, from the rear. Therefore, Caesar seems to have used the more common line of march while moving to Provence. This form of column was described in detail by Josephus, and a simplified version can be seen in the illustration.

council, he showed that the time of victory was come; that the Romans were fleeing into The Province and leaving Gaul; that this was sufficient for obtaining immediate freedom; but was of little moment in acquiring peace and tranquillity for the future; for the Romans would return after assembling greater forces, and would not put an end to the war; therefore they should attack them on their march, when encumbered.'

[Caesar, *The Gallic War*, VII. 66]

Vercingetorix has scouts observing Caesar's progress, reporting back to him as necessary, and so Caesar's march towards Montbard is anticipated. The route leads Caesar towards a series of rolling hills that border the sides of the Armançon south of Montbard, the perfect location for an ambush. Vercingetorix senses that at this place he can give Caesar a defeat that will delay his ambitions in Gaul. Vercingetorix is aware of the political machinations ongoing in Rome and knows that if he can break Caesar's legions before they leave Gaul, Caesar might never regain sufficient backing to assemble further forces to invade again. The location near Montbard is an ideal spot for an ambush, as Vercingetorix's army can hide in the folds of the land, while his cavalry can observe Caesar's advance from the hilltops. The wide rolling hills will favour the hit-and-run of cavalry combat, a tactic Vercingetorix has begun to prefer in view of the Gauls' previous defeats in pitched battles. The Gallic troops encamp on the three hills to the east of the Armançon and Vercingetorix spends the night inspiring his troops for the coming clash.

'In addition to their trait of simplicity and high-spiritedness, that of witlessness and boastfulness is much in evidence . . .'

[Strabo, *Geography*, IV. 4. 5]

'[Vercingetorix went on] If the Roman infantry should relieve their cavalry, and be held back by doing so, the march could not be accomplished: if, abandoning their baggage, they should provide for their safety (which, he trusted, was more likely), they would lose both property and character. For as to the enemy's horse, they ought not to entertain a doubt that none of them would dare to advance beyond the main body. In order that they [the Gauls] may do so with greater spirit, he would marshal all their forces before the camp, and intimidate the enemy. The cavalry unanimously shout out, "That they ought to bind themselves by a most sacred oath, that he should not be received under a roof, nor have access to his children, parents, or wife . . . who shall not twice have ridden through the enemy's army." This proposal receiving general approbation, and all being forced to take the oath . . .'

[Caesar, *The Gallic War*, VII. 66–7]

That night, in Vercingetorix's camp, the Gauls think that success against the column will destroy Roman morale and bring the year's fighting to an end quickly. Vercingetorix has begun to develop a *guerrilla* style of fighting and is confident an ambush will break the Romans' spirit. He knows that the undulating folds of the landscape around Mont Reux will hide the awaiting Gallic army from the Roman column. Vercingetorix plans to break up the Roman column with an initial cavalry attack, thus scattering the Roman army and leaving them at a disadvantage. Then, with a feigned retreat, the Gallic cavalry will draw the Romans into an uncoordinated counter-attack that will lead them directly into the arms of the Gallic infantry waiting in the surrounding hills. But Vercingetorix has another motive. By allowing the cavalry to attack the Romans first, Vercingetorix will allow the nobles to show their mettle. He will give them an opportunity surprising to modern eyes: the chance to sacrifice themselves to the gods in battle. The Gallic cavalry are the aristocracy of the Gauls and they are required to show their prowess over the Romans, signalling their strength to their dependants and subordinates and allowing them to die a dignified warrior's death.

Week 1, Day 2: Vercingetorix Springs a Trap on Mont Reux

'Now although they are all fighters by nature, they are better as cavalry than as infantry; and the best cavalry-force the Romans have comes from these people.'

[Strabo, *Geography*, IV. 4. 2]

'On the next day the cavalry were divided into three parts, and two of these divisions made a demonstration on our two flanks; while one in front began to obstruct our march. On this circumstance being announced, Caesar orders his cavalry also to form three divisions and charge the enemy.'

[Caesar, *The Gallic War*, VII. 67]

The next morning Caesar encroaches into *Mandubii* territory. Shortly after beginning his crossing of the diminutive River Bornant, Caesar comes face to face with Vercingetorix's cavalry. A squadron of cavalry is drawn up in front of him in the depression near Fain-les-Moutiers, with another on the hill at Mont Reux, about a kilometre away to his left and a similar squadron on the foothills of Mont Reux to his right. Caesar becomes fully aware of the desperate circumstances of the situation by reports from his skirmishers screening the head of his column of march. Nevertheless, he must continue crossing the Bornant to avoid splitting his army in two on either side of the river. Immediately, he calls up his cavalry to deal with the Gallic horsemen. The right wing of the army is usually the most prestigious position and so the best troops are usually stationed there. Here Caesar places his Germanic mercenaries, a mixed cavalry and infantry unit he recruited shortly before this season's campaign began. The Germans have no love for the Gauls and have a reputation as fearsome warriors. The rest of the Roman cavalry take up positions on the left and in the middle of Caesar's line of attack. The two cavalry lines manoeuvre into the most advantageous position, then they engage. With the proud boasts of the night ringing in their ears the Gallic cavalry charge, although these words hang heavy as soon as they realize that after their initial onslaught, the Roman army is failing to break. A reckless desire for a warrior's death and recognition for bravery has resulted in an impulsive and unsupported Gallic attack. Again and again, the Gallic noblemen charge through the Roman lines in a courageous attempt to validate their boasts. On discovering that the attack will be no easy victory, a further disappointment is about to overcome the Gauls.

'Then the action commences simultaneously in every part: the main body halts; the baggage is received within the ranks of the legions. If our men seemed to be distressed, or hard-pressed in any quarter, Caesar usually ordered the troops to advance, and the army to wheel round in that quarter; which conduct retarded the enemy in the pursuit, and encouraged our men by the hope of support.'

[Caesar, *The Gallic War*, VII. 67]

After the initial cavalry charges of the Gauls, the legions move forward from their positions in the middle of the column to surround the baggage. Meanwhile the allied infantry take up defensive positions to the rear and sides of the Roman line in the event of an attack on the flanks or rear of the army. Thus it is that the thin Roman column begins to reform around the baggage into a line along the foot of the hills of Mont Reux facing the Gallic cavalry. Caesar knows that he has been outmanoeuvred, but by drawing his troops into a strong defensive position he can hold out for longer against an anticipated infantry attack. However, no such attack manifests itself. The Gallic infantry are ensconced along the River Armançon about 5km to the east and are of no immediate threat. As the situation unfolds on Mont Reux, it becomes apparent to Caesar that the initial Gallic cavalry attacks were engaged with no infantry support, allowing him to stabilize his position. At this point, Caesar's confidence in

Week 1, Day 2: Vercingetorix Springs a Trap on Mont Reux

his innate ability to change his misfortune to his advantage takes over. So much so, that he orders light Roman infantry detachments to move up in support of the already engaged cavalry. The skirmishers begin to protect the flanks of the legionaries by attacking the Gallic cavalry with defensive skirmish fire.

> 'And intercepting the Roman general [Caesar] . . . when he was among the Sequani, he [Vercingetorix] surrounded him, but did him no harm; on the contrary, he compelled the Romans to be brave through despair of safety, whereas he himself failed by reason of his numbers and audacity. His defeat was due in part to the Germans who were acting as allies of the Romans; for with their unquenchable enthusiasm and their mighty bodies which added strength to their daring they succeeded in breaking through the enclosing ranks.'

> [Cassius Dio, *Roman History*, 40.39]

> 'At length the Germans, on the right wing, having gained the top of the hill, dislodge the enemy from their position and pursue them even as far as the river at which Vercingetorix with the infantry was stationed, and slay several of them . . .'

> [Caesar, *The Gallic War*, VII. 67]

The first cracks in the Gallic assault begin to show on their left wing. The German cavalry, supported by the ever-present German infantry detachments, overcome the odds and, fighting uphill, defeat the Gallic cavalry on the slopes of Mont Reux. On reaching the heights, the Germans – now passionate with battle fury – charge down and slaughter many of

Battle on Mont Reux

The identification of the site of the first battle between Caesar and Vercingetorix is fraught with difficulty. Caesar gives no clue to the actual location of the battle and geographical detail is only mentioned in passing, *'the German cavalry gained the top of a ridge on the right'*. The only other clue to the location is the fact that Caesar marched to Alesia the next day. To these small details, we can add an understanding of the major road and river routes of Ancient Gaul, and place name evidence. This combination of evidence has led to the identification of Mont Reux as the most likely location of the battle. A closer examination of this location, with its valleys and ridges showing an 'M' profile, match Caesar's choice of the term *'iugum'* or 'cattle yoke' for his description of the ridge.

the Gallic cavalrymen, who are now fleeing back towards their camps on the eastern side of the River Armançon. From their vantage point on the ridge, the Germans can begin to see in the distance the bands of Gallic infantry drawn up along the banks of the river.

> 'the rest [of the Gauls], on observing this action, fearing lest they should be surrounded, betake themselves to flight. A slaughter ensues in every direction, and three of the noblest of the Aeudi are taken and brought to Caesar: Cotus, the commander of the cavalry, . . . Cavarillus, who had held the command of the infantry . . . and Eporedorix . . . [a leader of the Aedui]'

[Caesar, *The Gallic War*, VII. 67]

On seeing the left flank of the Gallic cavalry break, the rest of the Gallic cavalry likewise take flight. The Gallic right flank is sitting upon the largest hill in the area, this position being expected to be the strongest and least likely to be broken by the Romans. But at this very moment the Gauls on the Gallic right wing are likewise in trouble. In their position higher up the hill, they can easily see their left wing collapse and feel that it will only be a matter of time before they, too, will succumb. Although their initial Gallic bravado enabled them to fulfil their vow to ride through the enemy twice, they now feel the strength of Roman resistance. The Gauls therefore decide that a strategic withdrawal will not be seen as dishonourable. It will also allow them to link with their infantry and gather their strength, where they will pose a greater threat to the Romans again.

The reality for both flanks of the Gallic cavalry is anything but a controlled withdrawal, and their departure disintegrates into a massed flight. In the ensuing rout, the Roman army charges forward en masse, catching the retreating cavalry. The Gallic infantry waiting below on the banks of the Armançon are unaware of the events that are unfolding over the ridge before them. Soon, as the remnants of the Gallic cavalry charge down the ridge into their ranks, the infantry are rudely awoken to this defeat. Rather than stand, they endeavour to make a fighting withdrawal across the Armançon to their camps. At this point, Caesar decides not to attempt to take the battle any further. Making an unsupported crossing of a river in the face of the enemy, even a beaten one, would be suicidal. Caesar therefore makes the decision to restrain his cavalry after a welcome victory and sets about consolidating his position. This has been a significant success for Caesar because during the battle three leading Aedui leaders have been captured: Cotus, the commander of the Gallic cavalry, Cavarillus, commander of the Gallic infantry and Eporedorix, a chieftain of the Aedui. Along with these leaders, the strongest section of

Week 1, Day 2: Vercingetorix Springs a Trap on Mont Reux

Vercingetorix's army, the cavalry, has been badly mauled and his infantry has been shaken. The loss of these leaders will hit Vercingetorix hard in the coming weeks. Not for the first time Caesar reminds himself that he has managed to snatch victory from almost certain defeat – and it will not be the last time.

> 'All his cavalry being routed, Vercingetorix led back his troops in the same order as he had arranged them before the camp, and immediately began to march to Alesia, which is a town of the Mandubii; and ordered the baggage to be speedily brought forth from the camp, and follow him closely. Caesar, having conveyed his baggage to the nearest hill, and having left two legions to guard it, pursued as far as the time of day would permit, and after slaying about 3000 of the rear of the enemy, encamped at Alesia on the next day.'
>
> [Caesar, *The Gallic War*, VII. 67]

After seeing his army routed, Vercingetorix immediately withdraws what

---

Oppida

Caesar uses the Latin term *oppida* to refer both to fortified towns and collections of dwellings. The term is now generally applied to fortified settlements surrounded by natural or man-made fortifications across continental Europe. While many of these fortifications were occupied for hundreds of years before the Roman conquest, it is possible that some were created as a direct response to the conflict of the period. The Gallic oppida were often defended by imposing stone walls, termed by Julius Caesar as *murus gallicus* (Gallic walls). They were constructed from a wooden lattice of intersecting beams placed along the edge of the settlement, with long iron nails used to pin the beams together at each intersection. The open space within this wooden structure was then filled with earth or rubble, and layers were built in this way to the desired height. Finally, the wall was clad in close-fitting blocks of stone, through which the ends of the beams protruded. Oppida represent a significant stage in the development of urban settlement in Gaul and functioned on a number of levels – protecting strategic locations, serving as trade centres and acting as refuges in times of crisis. While these roles differed from region to region, in general the influence of the oppida came directly from the rich merchant nobles who lived there.

troops he can towards the safety of the oppidum at Alesia, modern-day Alise-Sainte-Reine, 15 miles to the south-east. Over the course of the remainder of the day and the following night, the remnants of the Gallic stragglers, along with their baggage, follow him. Caesar, on the other hand, after consolidating his position, decides to regain the initiative. He leaves two legions to protect the baggage, ordering them to set up camp for the night on Mont Reux, while he takes the cavalry and follows up his victory. By harassing the Gallic rearguard and slaughtering the remnants of Vercingetorix's ambush, Caesar is able to begin to weaken his enemy's forces and regain much needed morale for what he anticipates will be a series of imminent guerrilla assaults by Vercingetorix. For Vercingetorix the day has been a huge disappointment. Important commanders have been captured, and what should have been a turning point in his dealings with Caesar failed to materialize. Therefore, contrary to Caesar's expectations, Vercingetorix decides not to attempt an ambush again.

'However, the chief part of those who then escaped, fled with the King to the city of Alesia.'

[Plutarch, *Fall of the Roman Republic: Six Lives*, III. 27]

'The [Gallic] men did not give up, however, until they had arrayed themselves once more beside the very walls . . . along with the people from the city who came out to fight.'

[Cassius Dio, *Roman History*, 40.6]

Instead, Vercingetorix's response is to refuse further combat until he has regained the initiative; so he falls back to the hill fort at Alesia, an action he takes with some trepidation. While the oppidum will offer much needed resources and a place to consolidate his forces for a further attack, Vercingetorix is fully aware of Caesar's string of successful sieges against Gallic hill forts. Vercingetorix therefore broods over the possibility of entrapment and a prolonged siege by the Romans. This mood is somewhat alleviated by the memory of his recent success against Caesar at his tribal hill fort at Gergovia. At the end of the day, the opportunity to recover his army's composure in a protected environment with adequate supplies ultimately proves the more attractive option to Vercingetorix. Nevertheless, only fate will decide whether this is the better choice.

Week 1, Day 3: Caesar Marches on Alesia

'Having met with this good fortune, Caesar did not give ground, but shut up and besieged in Alesia such of the foe as escaped.'

[Cassius Dio, *Roman History*, 40.39]

Week 1, Day 3: Caesar Marches on Alesia

The following day, Caesar begins to capitalize on the Gallic defeat, turning his defensive response to the ambush of his troops into an aggressive attack on Vercingetorix's forces. Marching after Vercingetorix, Caesar plans to force the Gauls onto the back foot, not allowing them time to recover the situation. All the while he will be getting ever closer to his ultimate goal of returning to the safety of Provence. Consequently, Caesar follows Vercingetorix's path of retreat along the River Brenne, right up to the foot of the imposing oppidum at Alesia.

Alesia

The principal fortified town of the *Mandubii* tribe, Alesia is situated on the edge of Mont Auxois, a limestone plateau. Mont Auxois is an eroded diamond-shape, 2km long and 600m wide, sitting 400–420m above sea level. The hill has a continuous drop surrounding it, save in the west where a narrow ridge attaches it to the plateau of Mont Pennevelle. Two rivers border Mont Auxois; the Oze in the north and the Ozerain in the south, both of which are tributaries of the River Brenne that lies further to the west on the plain of Laumes.

Currently it is impossible to be precise about the fortification of the oppidum. This is due in part to settlement that has built up around the hill since Vercingetorix's time. Archaeological investigation has therefore focused on the Roman siege defences in the main. Some of the ramparts of the oppida have been identified but localized erosion means that their extent is not certain. Traces of gateways have also been uncovered at the eastern and western ends of the plateau. It is possible therefore, that the fortifications did not entirely surround the hill, but simply reinforced the natural defences where they were weakest. Excavations have revealed that the Gallic settlement was only modest, about 2 hectares in size and where the defences do occur they were built using the *murus gallicus* technique. Unfortunately, no traces of the additional defences made for Vercingetorix's cavalry have been found; it is likely that Vecingetorix's cavalry and troops were stationed in the remaining 95 hectares of the plateau outside the hill fort. Surprisingly, the oppidum was only founded a decade or so before the Gallic Wars. This has been interpreted as the result of the migration of the *Mandubii* tribe from the north-west of France. It may be the case that the force that made the Mandubii migrate was also the stimulus that later forced the Helvetii to migrate, the event that became the catalyst for the Gallic War.

Caesar's Gallic Triumph

'On reconnoitring the situation of the city, finding that the enemy were panic-stricken, because the cavalry in which they placed their chief reliance were beaten, he encouraged his men to endure the toil, and began to draw a line of circumvallation around Alesia.'

[Caesar, *The Gallic War*, VII. 67]

On arriving at the oppidum, Caesar is faced with a dilemma. His preferred option is to press on to The Province to rejuvenate his forces before beginning a new campaign the following year. Nevertheless, the prospect of another march is daunting and further days on the march would provide Vercingetorix with time to gather reinforcements, as well as opportunities for more ambushes. In this regard the prospect of a siege proves more attractive. The previous sieges that had taken place in the campaign had been, for the most part, successful. But this siege would be slightly different, for without supplies and reinforcements it could prove disastrous. Caesar's characteristic willingness to confront a situation head-on wins out and he takes this opportunity to deal with Vercingetorix once and for all. Caesar gathers up the engineers of the legion, the integral part of the army's entourage of road and camp builders, and reconnoitres the situation from the hills surrounding Alesia. From the brows of the surrounding hills, Mont Réa and Mont Bussy, Caesar can see the entirety of the hill fort of Alesia, along with the character of the landscape surrounding it and he formulates a plan. Alesia's location on the top of a large hill makes it clear to him that the steepness of the cliffs abutting the oppidum are too great for him to attack frontally without suffering huge casualties. The position of Alesia, with hills neighbouring it on nearly all sides, leaves him only one option: to encircle the town and starve Vercingetorix out.

Week 1, Day 4: Caesar Blockades Alesia

'The town itself was situated on the top of a hill, in a very lofty position, so that it did not appear likely to be taken, except by a regular siege. Two rivers, on two different sides, washed the foot of the hill. Before the town lay a plain of about 3 miles in length; on every other side hills at a moderate distance, and of an equal degree of height, surrounded the town. The army of the Gauls had filled all the space under the wall, comprising the part of the hill which looked to the rising sun, and had drawn in front a trench and a stone wall 6 feet high.'

[Caesar, *The Gallic War*, VII. 69]

After his defeat in battle on the Armançon, Vercingetorix waits in the

Week 1, Day 4: Caesar Blockades Alesia

fortified hill fort of Alesia. With him have come approximately 12,000 cavalry and 80,000 infantry. As the town is too small for all the troops of the Gallic army to be housed inside, most are forced to camp outside the fortifications. They do so mainly on the large unoccupied eastern side of the hill, although some, most notably the nobles, take refuge inside the walls of Alesia. Vercingetorix's force immediately sets to building a hastily arranged ditch and wall to protect the vulnerable western edges of the hilltop. The defences utilize the existing rocky terrain, providing the Gallic army with strong protection. Vercingetorix quickly realizes that he is quite secure in this defended position. Alesia provides the Gauls with the ability to resist a formal siege, and should Caesar attempt to break into Alesia, the Gauls can quickly sally out to attack down one of the hillsides. If Caesar recommences his march back to The Province, Vercingetorix will simply attack his rear.

Facing Vercingetorix, Caesar's forces are made up of between ten and twelve legions. However, given losses sustained in previous battles, including that on the Armançon, and some losses on the march, the actual fighting strength of these legions is depleted. Caesar's position after six years of fighting mean that the actual size of his legionary forces is perhaps as few as 27,000. With an equal or smaller number of men making up his allied contingent, Caesar had arrived at Alesia with around 60,000 men. Nevertheless, Caesar's army comprises well-armoured, battle-hardened veterans for the most part, so he is confident his force will be adequate to deal with Vercingetorix's horde of 90,000.

> 'The whole race which is now called both "Gallic" and "Galatic" is war-mad, and both high-spirited and quick for battle, although otherwise simple and not ill-mannered. And therefore, if roused, they come together all at once for the struggle, both openly and without circumspection, so that for those who wish to defeat them by stratagem they become easy to deal with . . .'
>
> [Strabo, *Geography*, IV. 4. 2]

Vercingetorix's unsuccessful cavalry attack that began the battle on the Armançon was not undertaken in the context of military strategy. It was part of a complex social ritual played out between Gallic chieftains and their followers. The cavalry were sent in first to show their prowess to the rest of the Gallic army. Had the attack been undertaken in conjunction with the infantry Caesar may well have been destroyed. With this in mind Caesar plans his strategy to approach Vercingetorix's army holed-up in Alesia. Although he has sufficient manpower, Caesar is still faced with a difficult situation. Vercingetorix's superior force is fresher than his and well defended in Alesia. Caesar is well aware that if he deploys for a traditional battle with the Gallic army on the open Plain of Laumes, the Gauls will most likely refuse combat. Even if they do commit to battle, it will not be a foregone conclusion and is likely to be a hotly contested and risky option. Equally, if Caesar now continues his march, he will have to face the events of the previous days over and over again, with the possibility of Vercingetorix getting the upper hand. Vercingetorix will not pass up an opportunity to capitalize on favourable circumstances. Vercingetorix can play the waiting game until the circumstances are right for him. Furthermore, Vercingetorix's vast numbers are daunting, especially as there is the ever-present danger that Gallic reinforcements will swell their number. Circumstances are such that an all-out assault on Alesia – such as those Caesar had undertaken at Gergovia or Avaricum previously – are out of the question. The cliffs of Mont Auxois are much larger than those at Gergovia or Avaricum, and the presence of huge numbers of defenders and cavalry always allows Vercingetorix the opportunity of a sally against Caesar's assault. The possibility of a blockade is therefore uppermost in Caesar's mind, as this will provide him with a fighting chance. Although time-consuming, defended siege lines will provide the Roman army with an effective counterbalance to Vercingetorix's defensive position and numbers. They will also have the effect of starving Vercingetorix's forces, possibly into submission, but definitely weakening their resolve for further combat in the coming months, thereby permitting Caesar to make a dash for The Province.

> 'Gaius Caesar used to say that he followed the same policy towards the enemy as did many doctors when dealing with the physical ailments, namely, that of conquering the foe by hunger rather than by steel.'

> [Frontinus, *The Strategemata*, VI. 7]

Caesar's plan has many stages. First he will have to ensconce his troops in well-defended bases around Alesia. This will hamper Vercingetorix's ability to gather supplies and reinforcements, and will also allow Caesar's men protected bases from which to work. Once these fortified camps are built, they can be connected with a barrier to close the gaps between them, completely enclosing Alesia in a fortified circumvallation. The circumvallation will be a physical barrier, presenting the Gauls with an earthen bank topped with wooden walls and towers. It will prevent the enemy not just from escaping, but also from foraging, being supplied or even communicating effectively with the outside world. In so doing, Caesar will deftly turn Vercingetorix's attack on his vulnerable Roman column into the corralling of the Gallic army. Thus Caesar will effectively be turning his isolation in enemy Gaul into Vercingetorix's isolation within Roman walls. This will also physically signal to Vercingetorix's army the Romans' intent not to leave until the job is finished, intimidating the besieged while protecting the besiegers from sallies against them.

Caesar knows that by creating a blockade as quickly as possible, fear will increase in Vercingetorix's army. The warriors holed up in Alesia are well aware of the massacres that have taken place after previous sieges. Earlier the same year at Avaricum (modern-day Bourges), Caesar had massacred nearly all of the 40,000 inhabitants of the town, including women and children. The Roman attackers had fought under the convention that up until the point that the first battering ram hit the walls of the city, mercy could be granted, but thereafter it was accepted that no quarter would be given. Earlier in the year, at the outset of Vercingetorix's rebellion, members of his army had murdered the Roman merchants at Canabum (modern-day Orléans) in what the Romans saw as Gallic treachery. The attack at Avaricum was therefore all the more savage due to the temperament of the soldiers, who did not fight for plunder, but to avenge what they saw as the murder of innocent Roman civilians. Before the Battle of Avaricum, 800 of the inhabitants slipped out of the town and so were spared the slaughter. These 800 were now part of Vercingetorix's army and their terrifying experiences were presently uppermost in the minds of many of his army. If Vercingetorix were to allow a circumvallation to be built, the fate of Avaricum might also become the fate of Alesia.

Week 1, Days 5–7: Caesar Begins Construction

'Domitius Corbulo used to say that the pick was the weapon with which to beat the enemy.'

[Frontinus, *The Strategemata*, VI. 7]

'The circuit of that fortification [Caesar's circumvallation], which was commenced by the Romans, comprised 11 miles. The camp was pitched in a strong position, and twenty-three redoubts were raised in it, in which sentinels were placed by day, lest any sally should be made suddenly; and by night the same were occupied by watches and strong guards.'

[Caesar, *The Gallic War*, VII. 69]

In total, Caesar's planned circumvallation is to be over 10 miles long. Its line of defences will follow the natural contours of the ground. The wall will be built closer to Alesia, where the topography is more difficult for the

Gauls, and further away, where it is more open. But before this can be built, a ring of defensible encampments around the oppidum is required to provide secure bases to begin the siegeworks. These camps will provide the Roman units working on the circumvallation with defensive bases and capabilities in the event of attack. Caesar's first action, therefore, is to ride around Alesia with his engineers, studying the topography and planning the blockade. The legions are broken up into vexillations (detachments) and are sent to occupy the most advantageous positions around the hill fort, setting up temporary camps in these locations. This procedure is familiar to the Roman legions, which are well versed in building temporary camps as part of their training for campaigning. It was usual for them to

North-East Door of Camp 'C'

The illustration (see Plates section, 25) is a reconstruction of the north-east door of camp 'C' on Mont Bussy, looking south-west. The reconstruction of the walls and defences are all based on archaeological evidence uncovered from the site. Similar defences would have been used at all of the Roman camps. The internal structure of the camps would have been strictly defined, allowing each man to draw a sense of security from the familiarity of the structure of the camp and enhancing their response during emergencies. The tents are conjectural but indicate the position of the camp. Note the curved wooden wall behind the double gates of the camp and the unusual trapezoid-shaped tower. In-turned C-shaped walls of this type are of the internal clavicular type, and are the commonest form of gateway defence. Gateways of this type force the attackers to expose their undefended right side to attack, should they manage to force entry into the camp. It is likely that all of the larger camps at Alesia would have had difficult defences like this one. It is interesting to contrast this camp's ditch and bank defences and cheval-de-frise, with the complex multilayer defences found on the plain of Laumes.

build camps with an area of about 7 hectares, enough for about 3,500–4,000 men. This number equates to an understrength legion, which after a summer of fighting Caesar's legions certainly were.

Four sizeable hills surround Alesia: Mont Réa to the north-west, Mont Bussy to the north-east, Mont Pennevelle to the east and Mont Flavigny to the south. Each has similar natural defences to those of Mont Auxois, on which the oppidum of Alesia is built – namely, slightly rounded tops with steep shelving edges down to the rivers below. Soon after setting up their temporary field camps, the legionaries begin to build their serious fortifications. Following the classical tradition, the fortifications follow the topography of the site using natural features to their best advantage and so appear as large amorphous shapes. Caesar requires that twenty-three camps be built in all. Some of these camps will later be attached to the circumvallation, whilst others will simply be enclosed within its walls.

Within the Roman camps, the soldiers do not build interior structures but rather, they rely upon the homes they bring with them on the march. Tents are carried by the Roman baggage train and are used for temporary accommodation whilst on the campaign. Caesar prefers to focus all of his construction resources on the defensive fortifications, leaving the legionaries to sleep in their tents within the defences. As part of these defences, Caesar is clear that the hills surrounding Alesia are extremely important locations. Almost all of the larger camps use the steepness of the hills on the sides of the camps as extensive defences, providing formidable ramparts in and of themselves. The camp system as a whole comprises a complex line of camps and forts that provide a series of bases at the strategically significant points along the hills surrounding Alesia. Each fort has a slightly differing building method and form, a result of the different legions constructing them and a feature that is emphasized by the terrain. Contact is made between the camps primarily with visual signals, the camps being located close enough for this to happen easily. The camps retain the security of the Roman position, without needlessly putting troops in harm's way before the circumvallation lines can be started. Similarly, signals pass across the valley without the requirement for cavalry to be sent into an area where they are vulnerable to attack by Gallic cavalry.

As befits his status as subcommander to Caesar himself, Labienus plans his camp to be one of the largest and most important at Alesia and measures about 7 hectares. The size of this camp will easily accommodate the Seventh Legion he commands plus a cavalry complement. The Romans chose the location of all their camps with great care and Labienus' camp is no different. It lies on the central crest of Mont Bussy, to the north-east of Alesia. The hill is slightly higher than Alesia by about 15m and so from this position Labienus directly monitors Vercingetorix's troops. Further camps either side of Labienus' camp (camps 15 and 18 – *see* map of Alesia's defences), provide an unhindered view of the Oze valley, where it butts up against the foot of Mont Auxois. Labienus' troops have an unobstructed view of the Oze valley from Pennevelle in the east to the foot of Mont Réa in the west and even part of the plain of Laumes. From Labienus' camp the Roman army can not only look across into Alesia, but also over to Caesar's camp (Camp B – *see* map), across the valley. From Mont Bussy Labienus has a commanding view of the entire northern defences of Alesia and should he come under attack, is in a position to signal Caesar in the opposite valley.

After selecting this impressive spot, Labienus' men quickly begin work on the construction of a simple ditch and bank to protect the camp. The legionaries attempt to construct this camp in the usual rectangular shape, but the south-eastern corner is forced to undulate along with the topography. A V-shaped ditch, 4m wide and 1m deep, is dug completely encircling the camp area. The soil from the ditch is then mounded up over a framework of wooden timbers and covered with turfs. This provides the camp with a high defensive bank, akin to the *murus gallicus* technique defined by Caesar as a Gallic defence. This technique shows that the Roman army is expecting the worst and is prepared for the long haul. During the occupation of Labienus' camp, the smithies begin to work on producing weapons, including lead slingshot. The Roman soldiers are proud of their handiwork and will want their enemies to know who it is

Slingshot

These Roman lead slingshot (see Plates section, 12 & 13) were found at Alesia and are notable in that they have clear inscriptions cast onto their sides. Although slingshot don't usually carry a message, inscribed examples show they were commonly used between the sixth century BC and the first century AD, the ones from Alesia are therefore not atypical. Sometimes these shot could have pictorial representations, as with one slingshot from Alesia that is said to have a thunderbolt decoration on it. One of the slingshot illustrated has the inscription TLABI on it suggesting that it belonged to a unit of slingers under the command of Titus LABIenus. Other slingshot have been discovered at Alesia with inscriptions, but the units to which they belonged have not been identified yet. Fragments of ingots of lead and waste castings from Alesia, show that slingshot were manufactured in the Roman camps. Large quantities of lead shot were found on Mont Réa, Mont Peneville and in Caesar's and Labienus' camps. All these sites are located overlooking the valleys around Alesia and so have good lines of sight for firing shot. Firing tests suggest distances of up to 240m could be possible on the flat, and although a range around 180m was probably more practical, with positions overlooking the enemy like those at Alesia, the longer range would certainly have been possible.

that has defeated them. When the shot is cast, the heavy missiles have the raised letters TLABI, confirming they belong to the army of Titus Labienus.

Towers and gates protect the two main entrances of Labienus' Camp C. The soldiers are acutely aware that the gate of any military camp tends to be most vulnerable to attack. The legionaries build a 6m-wide gateway on the north side of the camp, with two large, in-swinging doors. Over the door, a tall pentagonal tower is attached to the end of the rampart with a covered connecting passage. These strong defences mean that the soldiers on guard have complete control over the access to the camp. Additional defences in the front of the gate enhance security there. Caesar's army is accustomed to building camps with a complex series of ditches and banks that force the attacker to manoeuvre around them. The front of the gate and walls either side are protected by parallel pairs of ditches. These are filled with sharpened branches called *cippi* (gravestones). The ditches form a *titula*, a defensive ditch used to break up any direct assault on the gate and is commonly used in many Roman camps. Inside the gate, the legionaries build a semi-circular high palisade fence. Should the Gauls attempt to attack, this fence will force them to manoeuvre around it, turning their undefended side towards the Romans. The soldiers building these defences are trained in their construction and so Caesar's use of them is not unusual. In fact, Roman writers recommend this very form of protection be used when constructing gateways. In contrast, the southern or internal defences of the camp are less vulnerable to Gallic attack as they sit on the edge of the hill. It is planned that this area will be incorporated into the middle of the circumvallation, so no special defences are considered necessary in this area.

After Labienus' initial camp has been fortified, thoughts then turn to building the circumvallation. Ultimately, the walls of the circumvallation will be built right up to the camp, connecting it to the circumvallation with a door to allow access in and out of the defences. To either side of the main camp, smaller camps are also built to enhance the larger camp's capabilities. On the eastern edge of Mont Bussy, Fort Fifteen has a simple rounded form, with an area of only half a hectare, enough for perhaps half a cohort of men. Arrows discovered in the fort match the fort's location, directly overlooking the Oze valley, an ideal place to station units of archers. On the opposite end of the hill, Fort Eighteen on the western edge of Mont Bussy is built. Like Fort Fifteen, this fort has a rounded form and an area of 0.7 hectares and will perhaps also be used by a cohort of specialist troops.

As Labienus' camp proceeds to completion, on Mont Flavigny across the valley, another camp is being built. Like Labienus' camp it sits slightly overlooking Alesia, this time 18m higher than the oppidum. This camp belongs to Caesar himself, and it plays a significant role in the southern part of the defensive system. As with Labienus' camp, Caesar's Camp B is built on a limestone outcrop, in this case overlooking the Ozerain valley. Here Caesar is able to see almost the entire circumvallation, as well as into Alesia directly in front of him in the valley. Caesar's camp is located deliberately, with a magnificent position providing excellent opportunities for signalling to the other camps, which would otherwise only be contactable by courier. Caesar's camp, as befits his status, is large enough to fit an entire legion at 7.3 hectares. Like Labienus' camp, rather than the usual rectangular form Caesar's camp is elliptical in shape. The legionaries construct Caesar's camp with a single 6m-wide ditch around it and 3m-square towers along its walls. As with any army, rubbish is a problem and is disposed of in the usual ancient way, by placing it in especially dug pits. In some of these pits Caesar's legionaries throw away the broken tools they have, such as an entrenching mattock and grindstones for corn. Other pits are also dug by the legionaries, but with a more menacing intent. These pits are dug as traps, protecting vital areas outside the camp, and for further effect *tribuli* (spiked tripods) are strewn around as an ancient but effective, anti-personnel device.

Like Labienus' camp, Caesar's camp has slightly smaller camps on either side, providing it with support and communications along the valley. Lower down the hill and to the west of Caesar's camp, a smaller camp is constructed of only about 2.3ha in area. This camp is typical of the many that are used to house *vexillations* or detachments of men, perhaps a few cohorts numbering no more than about a thousand men. The soldiers use these camps as fortified bases, from which they can forage, maintain communications and, in the future, use as bases from which they will construct the circumvallation. Camp A is constructed in the shape of a bean, the result of following the contours of hills quite closely for maximum defence. The position of the camp, right on the edge of Mont Flavigny, means that soldiers stationed there have an uninterrupted view directly down into the Ozerain valley and across the Plain of Laumes. This means that it is an ideal lookout and signalling post for Caesar's camp nearby. Camp A is built with two gates, one in the north and one in the south. The northern entrance is protected by an internal clavicular defence, while the southern entrance is protected by a wide titular defence and two ditches like Labienus' camp. The legionaries who build this camp seem to be content that the complex double ditches of the southern side of the camp are sufficient to defend it and later the circumvallation, as they don't feel the need for additional anti-personnel obstacles. This may be due, in part, to the placement of artillery equipment in this camp, some of which they will leave behind in the form of stone artillery balls and slingshot. Artillery here is well placed to defend Caesar's camp and can also be used to fire stones into the valley below.

Along with these camps, smaller 'forts', such as Fort Eleven, provide fortified support bases. Initially these are to be used during the construction phases, and then later on they will become the sentry points for manning the circumvallation. The soldiers building Fort Eleven create an enclosed area of 0.9 hectares, but they also build even smaller forts surrounding it down the hill. All these forts combine to provide a complex series of interlinked in-depth defences on each of the hills that overlook Alesia.

Two more large camps are constructed on the Plain of Laumes, one on the River Oze and the other on the River Ozerain. Camp K, the more southerly of the two, lies at the foot of Mont Flavigny and is one of the forts that house Caesar's cavalry. The camp protects the southern plain and Brenne valley, along with controlling the Ozerain river and the slopes of Mont Flavigny. From here the cavalry can range across the Plain, ideal terrain for horses. The more northerly camp (Camp H) can also be used as a cavalry camp. It protects the northern plain and the River Oze. Between the two, a chain of smaller camps allows work to begin on the significant defences Caesar has planned for the Plain of Laumes. At the other end of Alesia, to the east, further forts complete the encirclement of the hill fort. A camp on the very tip of Mont Peneville in the east (Fort Thirteen) is located in a significant defensive position, guarding any exit from Alesia down both the Oze and Ozerain valleys. A final large camp is built in the northern Rabutin Valley (Camp G). Here it lies in a key position guarding the valley that runs north of Alesia and provides a link between Mont Bussy and Mont Réa. Nearby, two smaller camps are placed in this difficult to defend location, one at the summit and one at the foot of Mont Réa. Unbeknownst to the legionaries who defend it, this area is to become the most decisive area of the battle. Whilst the camp will be attached to the circumvallation, the defences here will soon prove to be inadequate.

Once built, this ring of forts provide secure bases for the Roman troops. But there is a secondary effect to this ring; by enclosing the oppidum in a chain of strongholds, Caesar has control over messages and signals sent from Alesia to the outside world. Thus Caesar is gradually tightening the noose around Vercingetorix's army. During the first few days of the construction Caesar has set about gathering all of the resources the area has to offer. Vercingetorix on the other hand, although a shrewd leader, has been slow to act and unable to halt Caesar's taking the initiative. If Vercingetorix had initially assumed that Caesar would attempt to march on to Provence, after a few days he is well aware that this is not what is taking place. He decides to send out his cavalry to make hit-and-run attacks on the Roman constructions in an attempt to hinder their works and supply-gathering.

Week 2, Day 1: Construction is Interrupted
'The work having been begun, a cavalry action ensues in that plain,

The Germanic Cavalry

[Caesar] sends across the Rhine into Germany to those states which he had subdued in the preceding campaigns, and summons from them cavalry and the light-armed infantry, who were accustomed to engage among them. On their arrival, as they were mounted on unserviceable horses, he takes horses from the military tribunes and the rest, nay, even from the Roman knights and veterans, and distributes them among the Germans.

[Caesar, *The Gallic War*, VII. 6. 65]

German cavalry were not so well provided with large horses as their Roman and Gallic counterparts. As a result of this, when they arrived at Caesar's camp before the Alesia Campaign, he replaced their horses with larger Roman ones. The German in the illustration (see Plates section, 14) is riding one of these larger horses and represents a reasonably wealthy individual. He wears his hair in an elaborate knot on the side of his head as a symbol of his tribal allegiance. The skull of a man from the first century AD, with a complete set of hair tied in a Suebian knot of this type, was discovered at Osterby, Schleswig-Holstein. The Germans were well known for these elaborate hairstyles and their usage continued for hundreds of years, the Franks still being identified by a topknot of hair in the fifth century AD. This cavalryman wears a heavy fringed cloak typical of tribes from the colder climes of northern Europe. Heavy cloaks of this type are mentioned by ancient writers and seen in many sculptural representations. Note that he rides without a saddle, and it is also likely that infantry may have held on to the horse's tail when charging into battle. The mixing of infantry skirmishers and cavalry may have enhanced the fighting ability of Caesar's German cavalry. Certainly by the first century AD Germanic cavalry units in the Roman army, such as the Batavi, were well regarded for their fighting prowess.

Week 2, Day 1: Construction is Interrupted

which we have already described as broken by hills, and extending three miles in length. The contest is maintained on both sides with the utmost vigour; Caesar sends the Germans to aid our troops when distressed, and draws up the legions in front of the camp, lest any sally should be suddenly made by the enemy's infantry. The courage of our men is increased by the additional support of the legions . . .'

[Caesar, *The Gallic War*, VII. 70]

The Plain of Laumes to the west of Alesia, comprises a wide, flat flood plain of the River Brenne and its two tributaries the Oze and Ozerain. A few days after Caesar has begun work on the camps, Vercingetorix can see that the Romans have plans to stay. Far from building temporary camps, and then moving on, the Romans are building large semi-permanent camps surrounding Alesia. He can see that it is only a matter of time before the chain of forts is completed. From the hill fort Vercingetorix can see camps being built in the Plain of Laumes blocking the route from the main gate of the oppidum and isolating Vercingetorix from the rest of Gaul. Vercingetorix decides that he has let Caesar take the initiative for far too long and so sets about planning an assault on the construction. By attacking the soldiers while working, he plans to harass them and slow their construction efforts. In a series of assaults, Vercingetorix resolves to let the Gallic cavalry pour forth from the hill fort and across the plain in an attempt to halt the construction.

At the appointed time, the first of these attacks sets out. Opening the doors of the oppidum, Vercingetorix watches his cavalry charge down the hill towards the Roman workers. On seeing their unarmed comrades in need, armed legionaries charge out of the nearby forts and draw themselves up in battle formation on the plain, while the troops engaged in construction make a hasty retreat to their rear. The Gallic cavalry continue their assault in an attempt to kill the unarmed workers. In response, the German cavalry likewise emerge from their camp at the foot of Mont Flavigny and suddenly the encounter changes course. The soldiers from the construction, emboldened by the stand made by their fellow legionaries, turn with shovels and mattocks raised. Meanwhile the Gallic cavalry, on seeing the legionaries prepared to fight and with the sudden realization that German cavalry is bearing down upon them, decide to draw back before they commit to a fight they might not win.

'the enemy being put to flight, hinder one another by their numbers, and as only the narrower gates were left open, are crowded together in them; then the Germans pursue them with vigour even to the fortifications. A great slaughter ensues; some leave their horses, and

69

endeavour to cross the ditch and climb the wall. Caesar orders the legions which he had drawn up in front of the rampart to advance a little. The Gauls, who were within the fortifications, were no less panic-stricken, thinking that the enemy were coming that moment against them, and unanimously shout "to arms"; some in their alarm rush into the town; Vercingetorix orders the gates to be shut, lest the camp should be left undefended. The Germans retreat, after slaying many and taking several horses.'

[Caesar, *The Gallic War*, VII. 70]

Too late, the Gauls realize that they are far too committed already. In their retreat back to their camp beside the hill fort of Alesia, they don't anticipate a continued attack by Caesar's German cavalry. As they approach the gates of the hill fort, they realize that the German cavalry at their heels are not about to withdraw. On the steep slope leading back up to the gate they have no opportunity to turn and fight, so their only option now is to continue their flight. But the gates back to their refuge prove too narrow to accommodate them all and so, as the Gallic cavalry attempts to crush through the gates, an inevitable panic ensues. Gallic cavalry fight with each other to gain entrance and the attempt to return to Alesia turns into disaster. As the Gauls endeavour by every means to gain refuge, they abandon their horses and clamber over the ditches and walls. In response, the Germans begin to hack away at their backs, slaughtering those who have been abandoned by their fellows.

On seeing the unexpected success of the German cavalry response, Caesar immediately recognizes an opening. Urging forward the legionaries already drawn up, it crosses his mind that this could be an unforeseen opportunity to break into the hill fort. No less aware of the situation, the Gauls inside Alesia who have been watching the raid turn into a rout begin to panic. Some rush to the town, calling for immediate arming of the warriors to forestall the attack, while others attempt to help their comrades back into the defences. Vercingetorix could not have feared a worse result. His attempt at harassing the construction and stalling its progress has, in fact, been turned against him. He calls for the gates to be closed. Those warriors left outside will have to look to their own defences, as his concern now is not to let the defeat become total. By closing the gates he will be able to protect those who are left. The ad hoc retreat will be a lesson to them all, that they must be more committed and plan more carefully in future if they are to defeat Caesar.

As the gates close, those left outside make frantic attempts to fight or flee. Some still try to break back into the defences while others turn and fight their German victors. Before long, seeing their objective as met, the Germans cease. With no opportunity to gain entry into the hill fort they collect any booty they can and ride back down the hill under a hail of missiles and insults from the Gauls. Once the danger has passed, the Gauls once again open the gates, this time to let in what remains of the Gallic cavalry. This has been a harsh lesson learnt by Vercingetorix, as twice now Caesar's German allies have defeated his cavalry. He will have to change his tactics to avoid further shame.

Week 2, Day 2: Vercingetorix Calls for Aid

'Vercingetorix adopts the design of sending away all his cavalry by night, before the fortifications should be completed by the Romans. He charges them when departing "that each of them should go to his respective state, and press for the war all who were old enough to bear arms; he states his own Merits, and conjures them to consider his safety, and not surrender him, who had deserved so well of the general freedom, to the enemy for torture; he points out to them that, if they should be remiss, 80,000 chosen men would perish with him; that, upon making a calculation, he had barely corn for thirty days, but could hold out a little longer by economy." After giving these instructions he silently dismisses the cavalry in the second watch, [on that side] where our works were not completed . . .'

[Caesar, *The Gallic War*, VII. 71]

'Now Vercingetorix had at first, before he had been entirely cut off by the wall, sent out the cavalry to get fodder for the horses, as there was none on hand, and in order to let them disperse, each to his native land, and bring thence provisions and assistance.'

[Cassius Dio, *Roman History*, 40.40]

When Caesar came to write these events in his *Gallic War*, he depicted Vercingetorix as weak, sending his cavalry out to beg for support, laying on them the guilt that 80,000 men will die if they are unsuccessful. His final act of silent dismissal portrays a broken man, pushed to act before it's too late. Caesar's circumvallation is nearing its completion. The Gauls know that the cavalry had no other option than to leave, as they had run out of food. With their access to foraging curtailed by the Roman blockade, the Gallic cavalry are a drain on the oppidum's resources, and therefore they are sent out to gather food, supplies and reinforcements.

The defeat at the gates of Alesia marks a turning point in Vercingetorix's mind. He realizes that the cavalry will no longer be of use once Caesar has finished his encirclement. At this point Vercingetorix resolves to remain in Alesia until the siege can be lifted. But his options are few: either break out with all of his men or await reinforcements. Vercingetorix is an astute warrior and he knows that the first option will place all of his men in the greatest of peril. His defeats over the previous days have cast a large shadow over this decision. Caesar appears to have the gods on his side, and tempting fate again with an attempt at breakout is not attractive. He has seen how the cavalry fared the previous day. If he does manage to breakout, he will still have to regroup his forces and gather new impetus to attack Caesar. In the meantime Caesar will have the opportunity to press further on to Provence and Vercingetorix's initiative would be lost. The best option left to him is to use his cavalry as messengers, taking the news of what has happened home to their tribal leaders. Vercingetorix and his men will hold out and in so doing keep Caesar in one place. By his actions, he hopes to shame the rest of the warriors of Gaul into coming to his aid, and defeat Caesar once and for all. Therefore, during the evening, Vercingetorix gathers all the remaining cavalry and briefs them on their mission. The cavalry will be sent out in groups, to break through the Roman defences in all parts, catching the Romans off guard. Once away from the Roman lines they will head home and gather an army the size of which has never before been seen in Gaul.

Week 2, Day 3: Vercingetorix Orders Rationing

'he orders all the corn to be brought to himself; he ordains capital punishment to such as should not obey; he distributes among them, man by man, the cattle, great quantities of which had been driven there by the Mandubii; he began to measure out the corn sparingly, and by little and little; he receives into the town all the forces which he had posted in front of it. In this manner he prepares to await the succours from Gaul, and carry on the war.'

[Caesar, *The Gallic War*, VII. 71]

The next day Vercingetorix calls a meeting of his warriors and the leaders of the Mandubii. He informs them that the cavalry have left to gather reinforcements the night before and tells them he is introducing a strict rationing of food. He gives instructions: all the food supplies are to be brought into a central place where they can be supervised by his men, and then he orders that any hoarding of food will be punishable by death. The food is distributed to his warriors with the warning that they will receive no more until the reinforcements and supplies he has called for arrive. With a heavy heart, the people of Alesia watch as they realize the consequences of these actions. The only result they can hope for now is victory, as all other actions will lead either to slavery or death. Not a few choose to sneak out during the night, in an attempt to break through the Roman lines and escape to their homes, but some are caught and their plans are betrayed.

Week 2, Day 4: Construction Continues Unabated

'Caesar, on learning these proceedings from the deserters and captives, adopted the following system of fortification; he dug a trench 20 feet deep, with perpendicular sides, in such a manner that the base of this trench should extend so far as the edges were apart at the top. He raised all his other works at a distance of 400 feet from that ditch; [he did] that with this intention, lest (since he necessarily embraced so extensive an area, and the whole works could not be easily surrounded by a line of soldiers) a large number of the enemy should suddenly, or by night, sally against the fortifications; or lest they should by day cast weapons against our men while occupied with the works.'

[Caesar, *The Gallic War*, VII. 72]

Once Caesar has gained knowledge of Vercingetorix's plans from the deserters he has caught, he resolves to begin the circumvallation. After the attack on the Plain of Laumes, Caesar can see that Vercingetorix is in no mood to sit back and allow him to gain an advantage. He has been lucky so far, but his vulnerabilities are also clear. Without an absolute barrier around Alesia, Vercingetorix will continue to attempt to gather support. A piecemeal string of camps will still leave areas vulnerable to attack both from the oppidum and possibly also from any Gallic forces in the surrounding area. Caesar needs to finalize the construction as soon as possible. Caesar's first action, therefore, is to provide a protective screen for his forces to continue the work on the circumvallation. At the foot of Mont Auxois, Caesar musters some of his troops in battle formation, behind which the rest of his army hastily dig a large trench, 20 feet wide by 20 feet deep, with near vertical walls. The workers dig the trench from the Oze to the Ozerain in a wide arc across the plain.

'The centurions measure the work with 10-foot rods, checking that no one's laziness has resulted in digging too little or making mistakes. The Tribunes also go around and, if they are conscientious, do not go away until it is completed in every part. However, to prevent a raid from being mounted on the men at work, all cavalry and that part of the infantry which through the privilege of rank does not labour, take position in front of the fosse in an armed cordon and repel any enemy attack.'

[Vegetius. *Epitome of Military Science*. 3.8]

Caesar's Gallic Triumph

The meticulous character of Roman engineering comes to the fore. An emphasis is placed upon the quality and speed of the entrenchment, especially in the face of the enemy. The soldiers are accustomed to digging defensive ditches of this type and proceed quickly. Once completed, the trench stretches for 2 miles across the plain, linking the rivers and blocking the access to and from Alesia. The ditch will now provide the legions with a preliminary defence while they finish working on the circumvallation in the plain. Like the ditch defences surrounding Roman camps, this impediment will break up any further Gallic attacks on the men and provide them with time either to retreat into their camps or for troops and cavalry to position themselves in their defence. In so doing, Caesar is continuing his integrated system of siegeworks, based on theories and practices stretching back to the earliest of classical times. As the ditch nears completion, Caesar recalls his Trojan ancestry and the ancient Greek text, the *Iliad*, which describes just such a ditch used by the Greeks to protect their camp on the plain before Troy. While he may not have to wait as long as the Greeks did for victory, in his mind it is inevitable that Alesia will suffer the same fate as Troy.

Week 3–4: Building the Circumvallation

'At this interval [400 paces], he drew two trenches 15 feet broad, and of the same depth; the innermost of them, being in low and level ground, he filled with water conveyed from the river. Behind these he raised a rampart and wall 12 feet high: to this he added a parapet and battlements, with large stakes cut like stags' horns, projecting from the junction of the parapet and battlements, to prevent the enemy from scaling it, and surrounded the entire work with turrets, which were 80 feet distant from one another.'

[Caesar, *The Gallic War*, VII. 72]

Once the ring of fortified camps surrounding the hill fort is complete, Caesar focuses his attention on creating an unbreakable fortified encirclement around Alesia. This he plans to do by connecting the camps together with high ramparts. Thus the camps and ramparts will form an unbreakable ring around Alesia. The larger camps sit furthest away, on the hills surrounding the town and off on the Plain. The smaller camps are now placed strategically, forming a ring around the base of the town. The plan is for work to proceed on building the circumvallation continuously. The walls of the circumvallation will be built in front of the camps providing them with a defensive screen. Caesar is aware that the weakest part in his siegeworks is the Plain of Laumes. Here his forces are not protected by steep cliffs and they are encamped in open ground vulnerable

74

Week 3–4: Building the Circumvallation

to attack from Alesia in the front, and from the rest of Gaul in the rear. Caesar decides, therefore, that the space between the circumvallation fortifications and the town will be increased where the land is flatter. Along with this increase in distance the provision of superior defences in these regions will permit extra time for the Roman army to react to any assault by Vercingetorix. Where the terrain is more hazardous to the Gauls, the Romans can afford to let the topography play a role in the defence of the circumvallation, requiring less defensive structures to the extent that in some places no significant ground defences will be constructed at all. In the river valleys of the Oze and Ozerain the wall is built close to them on the Roman side of the river. This makes the rivers, although small, another obstacle for the Gauls to deal with before they reach the walls. In contrast, where he is expecting the most serious assaults to come, on the flat Plain of Laumes, Caesar plans a wide area of complex and diverse defences in front of the circumvallation. In so doing, Caesar hopes that Vercingetorix's will to attempt to break through will be remorselessly crushed.

> 'Quintus Sartorial, when in Spain, was completely outmatched by the cavalry of the enemy, who in their excessive confidence advanced up to his very fortifications. Accordingly during the night he constructed trenches and drew up his line of battle in front of them. Then when the cavalry approached, as was their wont, he drew back his line. The enemy following close on his heels, fell into the trenches and thus were defeated.'
>
> [Frontinus, *The Strategemata*, II. 12]

Two more ditches are now excavated in a wide arc about a mile away from Alesia. These will be the first part of the series of defences protecting the circumvallation on the Plain of Laumes. The Roman legionaries dig the first ditch, closest to Alesia, with a flat bottom 5.5m wide and 1.3m deep. The ditch is connected to the two rivers, the Oze and the Ozerain at either end. Caesar demands that this ditch is filled with water, part of which comes from naturally occurring groundwater, the rest being topped up at either end by a sluice system which allows the water from the rivers to fill the ditch under controlled conditions. Once this water-filled ditch is finished the legionaries dig a second ditch behind it, this time slightly less wide at 4.5m. Unlike the first ditch, this one has a V-shaped bottom and, just like the common anti-personnel ditches surrounding the camps, is not filled with water. Caesar's engineers have thought carefully about the placement of these ditches, and have a plan for how they can be best employed in the event of an attack. The flat-bottomed, water-filled ditch will be easy enough to cross by even a mediocre swimmer, but for a Gaul encumbered by arms it will be a less easy proposition. Once across the first ditch, the now wet Gaul will enter the V-shaped ditch and find himself sliding into the bottom in muddy disarray. The V-shaped bottom will not allow the Gaul to get a purchase on the walls and he will have to struggle to pull himself up the slope on the other side. All the time the Gauls are attempting to cross these ditches they will be within the range of the artillery and archers placed on the Roman rampart. Although simple, these defences are only the prelude to what awaits any Gauls who attempt to press their attack further.

Following the digging of the two ditches, the Roman soldiers focus their attention on the construction of the main defences. A ditch and bank structure is built to the west of the ditches providing the main barrier against any Gauls who manage to cross the first obstacles. The bank is not unusual for Roman fortifications, being 3.5m (12 Roman feet) high and 3m wide at its base. A further ditch is dug at the foot of the bank facing Alesia, 2.5m wide and almost a metre deep, which effectively increases the height of the bank to be scaled to nearly 5m. The legionaries utilize the material from this, and the other ditches, in the construction of the rampart. Firstly, they shovel a layer of gravel onto the ground to form the base and core of the rampart. This provides a firm footing for the rampart and aides drainage. Over this, layers of earth and turf are built up to create height, with further turf being used on the outside face of the rampart. These turfs aid the consolidation of the rampart and make it more stable as the grass grows back. Across the top of the rampart the legionaries add a defensive wall of intertwined wooden strips forming a crenellated screen like a castle's battlements. At the base of the screen, sharpened wooden branches are fixed into the rampart to discourage attackers from scaling the bank. Further to this, Caesar has a series of towers added to the rampart. Initially, these will provide valuable lookout and signalling capabilities, keeping the officers informed of what is happening further along the ramparts and on either side of the circumvallation. The towers have four legs, are around 3.5m square and about the same height above the rampart. Each one is constructed about 15m apart (50 Roman feet) along the entire length of the circumvallation on the Plain of Laumes. During the upcoming siege these towers will prove vital platforms for launching projectiles; the increased fire position will allow them to aim directly into the zone between the outside defensive ditches and the rampart.

'It was necessary, at one and the same time, to procure timber [for the rampart], lay in supplies of corn, and raise also extensive fortifications, and the available troops were in consequence of this

Week 3–4: Building the Circumvallation

reduced in number, since they used to advance to some distance from the camp, and sometimes the Gauls endeavoured to attack our works, and to make a sally from the town by several gates and in great force.'

[Caesar, *The Gallic War*, VII. 73]

As well as the construction, the soldiers of Caesar's army are all engaged in a variety of other activities aimed at providing security and resources for the troops building the circumvallation. This is where the Roman war machine comes into its own. Although structured for fighting, the Roman army is a consummate organization. Each soldier is not only a trained warrior, but also trained as a tradesman or an administrator. The legionary soldiers tend to perform all the tasks of engineering work that are required to build the fortifications, under the supervision of their centurions. It is a desired qualification to be a legionary, that men have been previously skilled as a craftsman such as a carpenter or a smith. These skills will be put to good use at Alesia, cutting and fitting the wood required for the walls and towers or manufacturing the nails and tools used to secure them. The region around Alesia is well endowed with trees. Over the coming weeks, all of the wood required for the defences is gathered from the vicinity and brought to the siegeworks for the construction.

'Gaius Caesar, in one of his Gallic campaigns, deprived the city of the Cadurci of water, although it was surrounded by a river and abounded in springs; for he diverted the springs by subterranean channels, while his archers shut off all access to the river.'

[Frontinus, *The Strategemata*, III. 7]

The area surrounding Alesia is occupied by small farming communities cultivating corn and raising livestock under the protection of the nobles in Alesia. While their warriors are all trapped within the hill fort, the Gallic farmers have no protection and so it is an easy matter for the Roman army to appropriate goods at will. The auxiliary troops are sent out to gather in supplies and this is where the fortified Roman camps play a secondary role. Not only are they places of security for the troops, but they also perform a role as supply depots. Supplies that have been collected from the locality are stored at the larger camps under the security of the Roman control. The stores of food and supplies are housed at strategic positions around the circumvallation under the command of a Roman legate who then supervises their distribution.

As one can imagine, the large numbers of troops required to build the fortifications, collect supplies and generally run the whole process, leaves only a small percentage of troops to man the defences. Caesar dispatches his slingers, archers and artillery to cover the water sources in the vicinity of the town. He knows that Vercingetorix is struggling for food supplies. By preventing access to water he will also be reducing the Gauls' ability to fight while increasing his own. He places his missile-armed troops to shoot anyone attempting to use the springs, while at the same time he digs tunnels to redirect the water. Thus Caesar is able to avert an expensive attack on the oppidum while maintaining his offensive strategy against the town.

> 'Caesar thought that further additions should be made to these works, in order that the fortifications might be defensible by a small number of soldiers. Having, therefore, cut down the trunks of trees or very thick branches, and having stripped their tops of the bark, and sharpened them into a point, he drew a continued trench everywhere 5 feet deep. These stakes being sunk into this trench, and fastened firmly at the bottom, to prevent the possibility of their being torn up, had their branches only projecting from the ground. There were five rows in connection with, and intersecting each other; and whoever entered within them were likely to impale themselves on very sharp stakes. The soldiers called these "cippi".'

> [Caesar, *The Gallic War*, VII. 73]

The number of troops Caesar has, although large, is going to be insufficient to man the entire circuit of the defences and also gather supplies when needed. Therefore, Caesar sets about increasing the defences in the most vulnerable areas of the circumvallation to allow him more time to move his troops around the circuit in the event of an attack. What he requires is a 'defence in depth' – an approach that is directly inspired by his knowledge of earlier siege methods. In his works, Caesar rarely describes the details of his camps, so his descriptions of the siegeworks at Alesia are quite remarkable. We must conclude that he includes them because of their extraordinary character and that this is because he is faced with an extraordinary situation. Caesar decides that on the Plain of Laumes, the flat area between the twin ditches and the rampart of the circumvallation will need to be further enhanced with obstacles. The strip is 17m wide and completely within the range of his pila and lances on the ramparts and towers. If he can halt or slow the Gauls as they enter this area it will become a 'killing zone'. Caesar therefore plans a succession of anti-personnel traps in the area that will halt the Gauls in their tracks. He plans numerous and varied types of obstacle, some projecting from the ground and some set into the ground. This will stop the Gauls from quickly

Week 3–4: Building the Circumvallation

becoming familiar with the Romans' defensive scheme. Within these basic types of obstacles, the soldiers devise four main forms of anti-personnel device: *lilea* 'lillies', *stimuli* 'spurs', *tribuli* 'traps' and *cippi* 'tombstones'. These defences are designed as much to maim or disable, as they are to kill.

The simplicity of manufacturing anti-personnel devices in the field allows the Romans to use them throughout the defensive system. The defences are densest in the principal area of expected confrontation, on the Plain of Laumes. In front of the ramparts a series of five trenches is dug. During the construction of the camps, ramparts and towers, large amounts of offcut wood and branches are left as waste. These the soldiers put to good use, sharpening their ends and occasionally hardening them in fire. Sometimes they are simply buried in the ground, producing the effect of a spiky wooden barrier in the manner of a *cheval-de-frise*. Sometimes they are used in rows, sticking out along the top of the bank of the rampart and thus creating the same effect. In essence, they act as wooden 'barbed wire'. This type of defence is not new; it has been used for over a century. Caesar calls them tombstones ('cippi') doubtless because they will soon mark the death of many a Gallic warrior.

Caesar knows that during a siege, one of the most difficult problems for the defender is to feed his troops, and this is exactly what Vercingetorix is facing. Caesar will not prevail by killing Vercingetorix's men, because there are thousands more to take their places. On the other hand, if Caesar can disable the Gauls, his position will be strengthened. With reducing supplies, the warriors will be less able to fight, if at all, but more importantly, they will be a drain on Vercingetorix's resources and morale.

> 'Before these, which were arranged in oblique rows in the form of a quincunx, pits 3 feet deep were dug, which gradually diminished in depth to the bottom. In these pits tapering stakes, of the thickness of a man's thigh, sharpened at the top and hardened in the fire, were sunk in such a manner as to project from the ground not more than 4 inches; at the same time for the purpose of giving them strength and stability, they were each filled with trampled clay to the height of one foot from the bottom: the rest of the pit was covered over with osiers and twigs, to conceal the deceit. Eight rows of this kind were dug, and were 3 feet distant from each other. They called this a lily from its resemblance to that flower . . .'

> [Caesar, *The Gallic War*, VII. 73]

Two metres in front of the system of cippi, in the open space in front of the rampart, the Romans build a second set of defences – the so-called 'lilies'. The soldiers dig rows of deep, conical holes, laid out in a *quincunx* design, like the five spots on a die. After sharpening the thicker branches and hardening them in fire, they fit the stakes into the bottom of the hole, fastening them with rammed gravel. They then cover them with the scraps of branches and twigs left from the construction work to make them less obvious.

'Stakes a foot long, with iron hooks attached to them, were entirely sunk in the ground before these, and were planted in every place at small intervals; these they called spurs.'

[Caesar, *The Gallic War*, VII. 73]

In a variation of these defences, the legionaries dig a further six lines of smaller conical holes 20cm in diameter. Within these pits wooden stakes are hammered into the ground with iron spikes called 'stimuli' attached to their tops. Alesia is to be almost unique in France in having evidence of the use of these stimuli. There are at least four different Roman smithies working around the circumvallation, each one coming up with a novel way of attaching iron points to the wooden stake. One smithy makes simple barbed iron rods hammered into the ends of the stakes and then sharpened. Another smithy makes barbed iron rods that are bent into an S-shape to allow them to be hammered into the wood on the horizontal part of the shank. A further type is manufactured as a pointed iron bar with a ring attached which connects it to the wooden stake. A final version is produced that has a pointed iron tip and a spiral-like end that the soldiers screw into the buried wooden stakes. Whatever their form, all of these types perform the same function. Once fitted to the wooden stake, the iron spike protrudes between 5 and 10cm from the ground so as to impale or seriously injure an attacker. We can think of this form of defence as having the effect of an early landmine.

Along with these static defences, further, more flexible defences were designed. These were the tribuli, simple iron tripods manufactured by Roman smiths in such a way that they have four spikes. When thrown on the ground, they always rest upon a tripod of three of the points with the fourth spike sticking up. Like the stimuli, numerous different smithies are engaged in making these weapons. In general, two sizes of tribuli are made, one with spikes about 5cm long and other slightly larger with spikes about 7cm long. As with the stimuli these anti-personnel devices are to be used to disable Gallic infantry and horses. The tribuli are 'sown' on the ground around gateways and choke points of the defences before an attack, after which they can be recovered and the gateways opened up and used again as normal.

Thus far, the density of defences only applies to the circumvallation built on the Plain of Laumes. In other places along the circuit the defences are

Caesar.

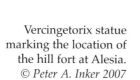

Vercingetorix statue
marking the location of
the hill fort at Alesia.
© *Peter A. Inker 2007*

Roman legionary of Caesar's army.
His equipment is reconstructed from
various archaeological and sculptural
sources dating to the First century BC.
© Peter A. Inker 2007

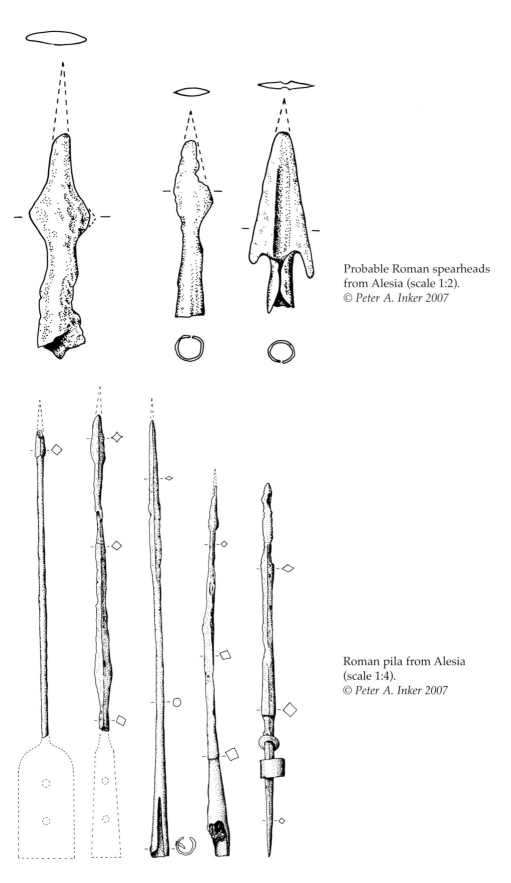

Probable Roman spearheads
from Alesia (scale 1:2).
© *Peter A. Inker 2007*

Roman pila from Alesia
(scale 1:4).
© *Peter A. Inker 2007*

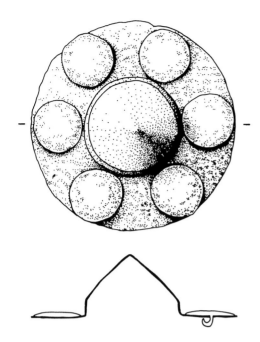

Circular Gallic shield boss from Alesia (scale 1:5).
© *Peter A. Inker 2007*

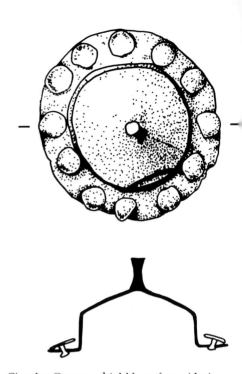

Circular German shield boss from Alesia
(scale 1:3). © *Peter A. Inker 2007*

Roman dagger from Alesia with reconstructed
handle (scale 1:3). © *Peter A. Inker 2007*

Roman ballista bolt and stimuli from Alesi
(scale 1:1). © *Peter A. Inker 2007*

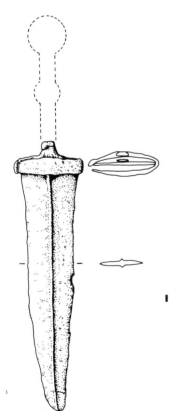

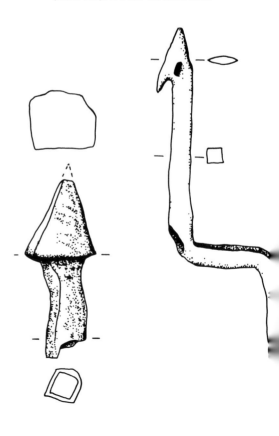

Gallic noble cavalryman. © *Peter A. Inker 2007*

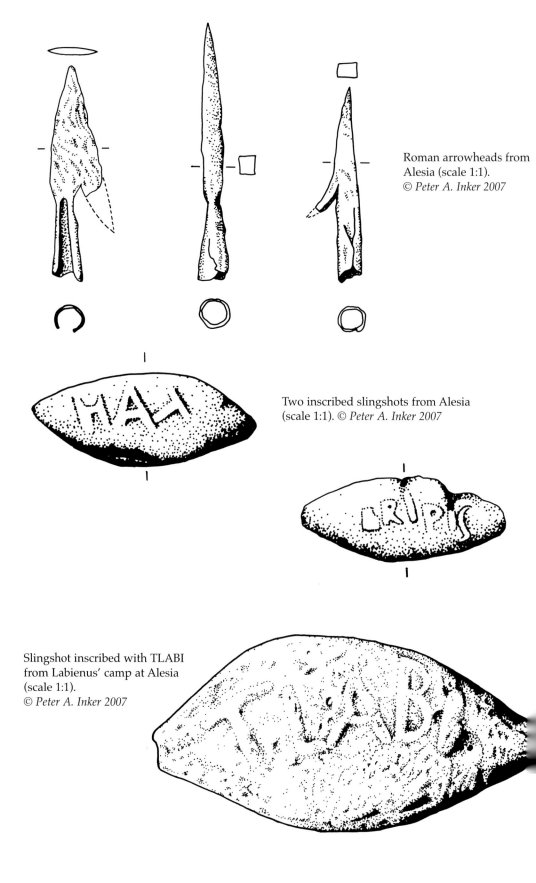

Roman arrowheads from Alesia (scale 1:1).
© Peter A. Inker 2007

Two inscribed slingshots from Alesia (scale 1:1). © Peter A. Inker 2007

Slingshot inscribed with TLABI from Labienus' camp at Alesia (scale 1:1).
© Peter A. Inker 2007

Germanic cavalryman. © Peter A. Inker 2007

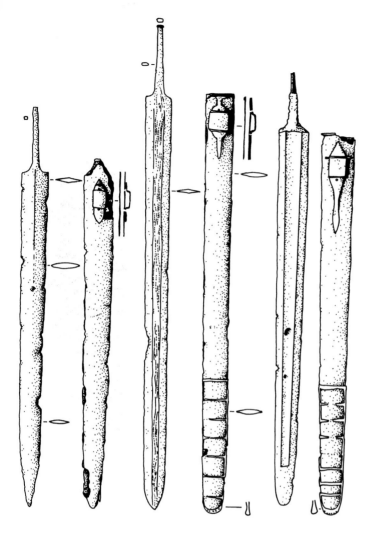

Three Gallic swords and
scabbards from Alesia (scale 1:8)
© *Peter A. Inker 2007*

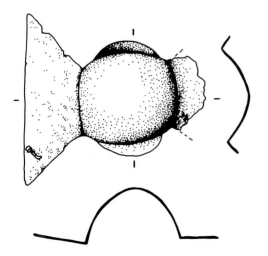

Gallic shield boss with wings from Alesia
(scale 1:4). © *Peter A. Inker 2007*

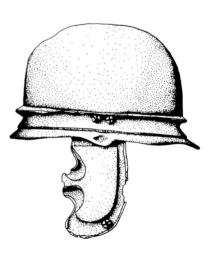

Gallic helmet from Alesia with reconstructed ch[e]
guards (scale 1:5). © *Peter A. Inker 2007*

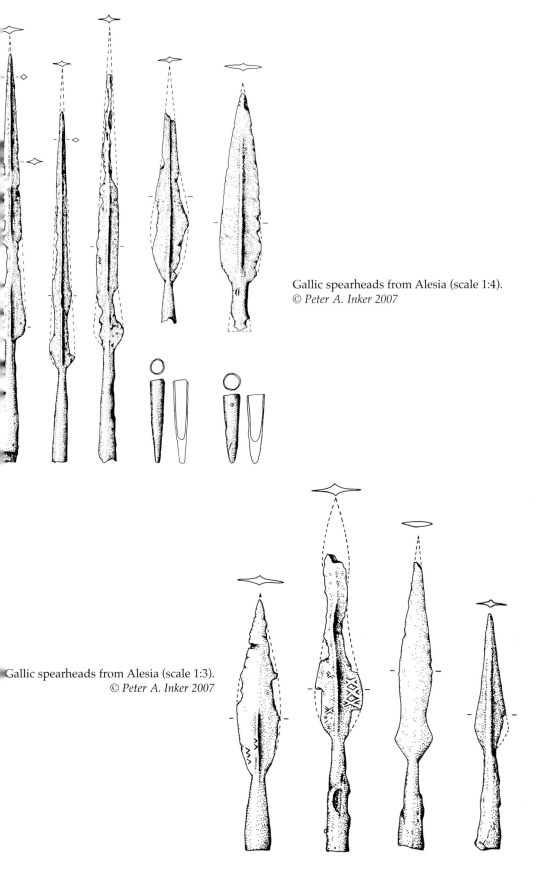

Gallic spearheads from Alesia (scale 1:4).
© Peter A. Inker 2007

Gallic spearheads from Alesia (scale 1:3).
© Peter A. Inker 2007

Gallic infantryman.
© Peter A. Inker 2007

Roman cavalryman.
© Peter A. Inker 2007

The Oze valley looking west to Mont Réa and showing the location of Camp D. The Plain of Grésigny is in the foreground. Vercassivellaunus' forces came over the ridge on the right of the picture. The lines of the circumvallation are marked in white.
© Peter A. Inker 2007

Close-up of the reconstructed wall at Bibracte showing the *murus gallicus* building technique.
© Peter A. Inker 2007

Cross-section through the defences on the plain of Laumes.

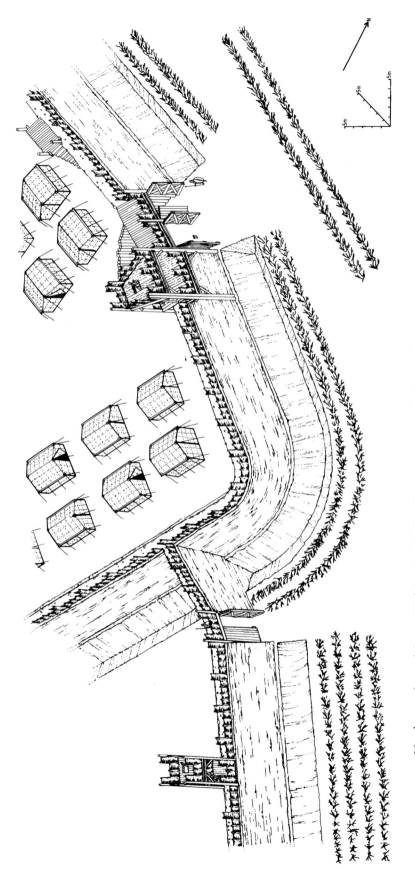

North-east door of Camp 'C' (after Reddé 96 with amendments). © Peter A. Inker 2007

The Oze valley looking west from within Caesar's defences on Mont Penneville. The lines of the circumvallation are marked in white. © *Peter A. Inker 2007*

Looking east towards Alesia from the Plain of Laumes. Caesar's fortifications ran through the cornfield in the foreground (marked in white). Note the level flat plain in contrast to the undulating valleys either side of Mont Auxois. © *Peter A. Inker 2007*

The Ozerain valley looking west from within Caesar's defences on Mont Penneville. The lines of t[he] circumvallation are marked in white. © *Peter A. Inker 2007*

This reconstructed gateway gives an impression of the kind of fortifications used in Caesar's circumvallation (Lunt Roman Fort, near Coventry, UK). © *Peter A. Inker 2007*

Reconstructed entrance to the hill fort at Bibracte. © *Peter A. Inker 2007*

Marcus Antonius.

Roman *testudo* or 'tortoise'. © *Peter A. Inker 2007*

Brutus.

Week 5: Building the Contravallation

not so intensive. To the north, on the Plain of Grésigny, an appreciably different system is used. The outer water-filled ditch found on the Plain of Laumes is not replicated; the Romans simply dig a basic 5m-wide flat-bottomed ditch. This is bordered on the inside by an 8m-wide strip of obstacles, half as narrow as the one used on the Plain of Laumes. In this region, the obstacles are made in a more haphazard fashion, being a mix of four lines of metal spikes (stimuli) and four to five rows of sharpened branches (cippi). The circumvallation rampart and ditch take the same form of construction as that used on the Plain of Laumes, although the towers are spread a couple of metres further apart. Although still fearsome, Caesar thinks that the Plain of Grésigny requires slightly less defence than the Plain of Laumes. This is to prove a serious misjudgement.

Week 5: Building the Contravallation

'After completing these works, having selected as level ground as he could, considering the nature of the country, and having enclosed an area of 14 miles, he constructed, against an external enemy, fortifications of the same kind in every respect, and separate from these, so that the guards of the fortifications could not be surrounded even by immense numbers, if such a circumstance should take place owing to the departure of the enemy's cavalry; and in order that the Roman soldiers might not be compelled to go out of the camp with great risk, he orders all to provide forage and corn for thirty days.'

[Caesar, *The Gallic War*, VII. 74]

After the unsuccessful attack on the Plain of Laumes, Vercingetorix has decided that his cavalry are of better use scouting for reinforcements. With this change in circumstance, Caesar is forced to adapt his strategy. The threat of attack from the rear is now very real, and Caesar cannot be certain that the Gallic cavalry will not return and attack his siege lines at any moment. Therefore, once the circumvallation of Alesia is complete, he deems it necessary to build a second line of defences to protect his army. Twin lines of circumvallation are not unusual in antiquity, but a significant investment of manpower is required. By ensconcing himself between these walls Caesar knows that he is here to stay, and ultimately this will become a decisive battle.

The contravallation is planned to be appreciably longer than the circumvallation. It will be built around the circumvallation, making it 3 miles longer (13 miles). Just as with the contravallation, the soldiers use their mattocks to cut 1-foot-square blocks from the clay soil and place them in two lines along the course of the contravallation rampart. These are tied together with timber beams and in-filled with earth and gravel from the underlying soil. As the wall height increases, the outsides are kept at a near vertical angle. Over time, the grass will grow back on the faces of the rampart, helping to solidify and weatherproof it, enhancing the cohesion of the bank and slowing erosion. On the Plain of Laumes the gap between the circumvallation and the contravallation narrows to only 100m, while on the hills it becomes a long strung-out defence line, in places almost a mile apart. On the hills surrounding Alesia the contravallation is able to utilize the topography of the region against a Gallic relief army, but there are places where the ground is too difficult, and even the Romans cannot construct the rampart fully. The larger camps are integrated into the contravallation itself, whereas the smaller camps sit within the two walls. In some cases, the small camps are extended after both walls of the circumvallation are built. By linking the camps to the front and back of the circumvallation, Caesar uses the camps as obstacles in what would otherwise be an uninterrupted open corridor formed from the two walls of the circumvallation and contravallation. Thus, if the Gauls breach the ramparts at any point, the invading force will not be able to swarm along the circumvallation without coming across further Roman defences. In essence, the circumvallation is broken down into cells that can be isolated and dealt with, and therefore the entire circumvallation cannot be weakened by a single breach.

Around the outer defences of the contravallation a shallow V-shaped ditch is dug. Then rows of cippi are fixed in front of the ditch, two rows on the Plain of Grésigny, and the same around the walls outside Labienus' and Caesar's camps. On the Plain of Laumes four rows of cippi are fixed in front of the ditch, with a further 5m-wide ditch and more lilea and stimuli, making the circumvallation comprehensively defended from within and without. However, on the Plain of Laumes, the defences are the most intensive within the circumvallation. Clearly, Caesar sees his greatest threat coming from Vercingetorix's 80,000 Gallic warriors trapped in Alesia.

In total, it takes over five weeks to build the entire defensive system. Once completed, the inner circumvallation is only 10 miles in circumference, but when combined with the outer contravallation and all of the inner works, the total extends to almost 30 miles of constructed defences. With this wooden ring of fortifications now in place Caesar prepares to starve the Gauls into submission. He gives orders for a month's rations to be stored inside the defences of the circumvallation. This will prevent the need to forage for food outside the defence lines when an attack comes. If Caesar's predictions are correct, starvation will force Vercingetorix to assault him. Caesar will need all the resources he can muster when this comes to pass. Every man will be required to fight the

Gauls and none, not even the slaves, will be spared to gather food. Neither would they want to. With Vercingetorix's cavalry camped outside the circumvallation, it is only a matter of time before they return to the attack.

Week 5: Gallic Council of War

'As for their might, it arises partly from their large physique and partly from their numbers. And on account of their trait of simplicity and straightforwardness they easily come together in great numbers, because they always share in the vexation of those of their neighbours whom they think wronged.'

Bibracte

Bibracte was mentioned by Julius Caesar in his chronicles of the Gallic war, but its location was unknown until relatively recently. The oppidum followed the topography of the three peaks of the hilltop of Mont Beuvray, comprising 200 hectares of land enclosed within 7km-long ramparts. The ramparts consisted of two pairs of ditch and bank defences made using the *murus gallicus* technique. The main gate of the hill fort was built twice as large as any other Gallic oppidum, with an entrance 19m wide (see Plates section, 30). The imposing size of this gateway represents the power and status of the hill fort, rather than being strictly defensive in nature. Bibracte's impressive proportions also reflect its function as the capital of one of the most powerful tribes in Gaul, the Aedui. This meant that it was the site where the Gallic armies were called to war councils during Vercingetorix's revolt, and it was here that Vercingetorix was proclaimed head of the Gallic armies. This significance was not lost on Caesar, as it was to Bibracte he retired to document the defeat of the Gauls in his Gallic Wars. Shortly afterwards, Bibracte's purpose had been lost, the hill fort was abandoned and a new town built along Roman lines was constructed at nearby Autun. Excavations at Bibracte now make it possible to confirm the hill fort was proto-urban in character, with huge amounts of amphora sherds indicating its role as a major importation crossroads. Bibracte specialized in the production of salt, pottery, glass and most importantly iron, and this, along with its central place in the territory, meant that by the mid-second century BC the oppidum was made the capital of the Aedui. Its pivotal position in the centre of Gaul ensured this relationship with Rome continued and even though they had sided with Vercingetorix during the revolt, they were restored as allies of Rome after the Alesia Campaign.

Caesar's Gallic Triumph

[Strabo, *Geography*, IV. 4. 2]

'Whilst those things are carried on at Alesia, the Gauls, having convened a council of their chief nobility, determine that all who could bear arms should not be called out, which was the opinion of Vercingetorix, but that a fixed number should be levied from each state; lest, when so great a multitude assembled together, they could neither govern nor distinguish their men, nor have the means of supplying them with corn . . .'

[Caesar, *The Gallic War*, VII. 75]

As Vercingetorix waits for support and Caesar finishes the circumvallation and contravallation, the Gallic cavalry ride to their homelands. Once there they inform their respective leaders of the fate that has befallen Vercingetorix and Alesia. As always before a major conflict, the war chieftains of the tribe gather together and convene an 'armed council'. But this time the leaders come not just from the local tribal groups, but from tribes across Gaul. They convene at the huge citadel at Bibracte, in the land of the Aedui, about 60 miles south of Alesia. Unfortunately for Vercingetorix, the council does not go as he had hoped. The war chiefs decide that Vercingetorix's demands are too onerous, so they do not follow his wishes. The council will not mobilize every available man, for they fear that they will not be able to govern, or even supply, such a multitude of men in the field. Unspoken fears also cross their minds: if every man is mustered then they will be leaving their homes and farmlands vulnerable to attack. It would be unwise to allow other Roman forces the opportunity to wage war at will behind their backs. Likewise, the Germans are ever watchful of Gallic affairs and always waiting to seize upon unprotected land when it is available. Therefore, if the leaders do not leave some troops behind in reserve, the consequences could be even worse than facing Caesar undermanned. It is therefore decided that each tribe will send a complement of men to Vercingetorix, the size of this complement being dependant on the tribe's capacity to provide warriors and their proximity to the conflict. Some, such as the Bellovaci chief, rebel against the imposition of demands, saying that it is up to them how they wage war against the Romans and that they will attack the Romans in their own way. It is only with soothing words and the reminder of old loyalties from Commius, the war leader of the *Atrebates*, that they commit men to the cause. Finally, with this temporary grand alliance, the numbers that will be required are drawn up and given to messengers who ride out across Gaul to gather the warriors from the various tribes.

Week 6: The Gallic Relief Army Arrives at Bibracte

Week 6: The Gallic Relief Army Arrives at Bibracte

'As for their former power, the Arverni hold out as a great proof
thereof the fact that they often times warred against the Romans
. . .'

[Strabo, *Geography*, IV. 2]

'Yet such was the unanimity of the Gauls in asserting their freedom,
and recovering their ancient renown in war, that they were
influenced neither by favours, nor by the recollection of private
friendship; and all earnestly directed their energies and resources to
that war, and collected 8,000 cavalry, and about 240,000 infantry.
These were reviewed in the country of the Aedui, and a calculation
was made of their numbers; commanders were appointed; the
supreme command is entrusted to Commius the Atrebates chief,
Viridomarus and Eporedorix the Aedui chiefs, and
Vercassivellaunus the Arverni chief, the cousin of Vercingetorix. To
them are assigned men selected from each state, by whose advice
the war should be conducted.'

[Caesar, *The Gallic War*, VII. 76]

Over the course of the next week, the Gallic war chiefs resolve to regain
their former glory and power by defeating Caesar and stopping the Roman
intrusion into Gaul. In nightly feasts they recall the sacking of Rome by
their ancestors, contrasting it with the humiliation that Caesar's invasion
and control of Gallic affairs has now brought them. The extreme nature of
the situation is reflected upon by the Atrebates chief, Commius, who has
rejected his old alliance with Caesar to side with his fellow Gauls. The
assembled council take a vote on who is to command the army. After
negotiations, it is decided that the command will be made up of four men:
Commius the noble of the Atrebates, Viridomarus and Eporedorix, nobles
of the Aedui, and Vercingetorix's cousin Vercassivellaunus, a noble of the
Arverni. All, bar Vercassivellaunus, have served as cavalry officers,
commanding Gallic auxiliaries in Caesar's army. They are all well aware of
the importance of the actions they must now take. They are familiar with
the quality and capability of the army they are up against and the
consequences should they fail. These men form the supreme command of
the Gallic army, under which the warriors are split into divisions led by
nobles from each of the tribes.

Nevertheless, the army is to be made up of such a collection of tribes that
even their hatred of Caesar does not completely mask old ambitions and
resentments that each has against the other. The tribal nobles will have to
provide advice on the direction of the campaign, and how best to motivate
and not alienate the men under their command. Within the week, almost

Caesar's Gallic Triumph

8,000 cavalry and 242,000 infantry are on their way to the Aedui capital at Bibracte. As the troops gather, their leaders assess their state of readiness for war. New weapons are prepared and displayed, and old weapons are rejuvenated. Rituals are performed where bravery is exalted. Warriors who have become fat or lack sufficient fighting spirit are punished. By humiliating the weakest, the crucial requirements for warrior status are maintained, courage is fostered, and the ties that will bind them in the upcoming fight are strengthened.

Week 7: At Alesia the Blockade Bites

'But those who were blockaded at Alesia, the day being past on which they had expected auxiliaries from their countrymen, and all their corn being consumed, ignorant of what was going on among the Aedui, convened an assembly and deliberated on the exigency of their situation . . .'

[Caesar, *The Gallic War*, VII. 77]

The moon has waxed and waned since Vercingetorix sent out the cavalry for reinforcements. With no help in sight for over a month, Vercingetorix convenes a council to decide on his next move. Clearly, the Gauls trapped in Alesia are in a difficult situation, as they appear to have no hope of reprieve and the food has run short. Thinking their relief army is not going to arrive, the assembly is forced to consider other ways of resolving the conflict. Some suggest that an all-out attempt at a break-out is made, while others suggest surrender before they all die. The idea of surrender is met with instant disapproval. It is made clear that this option is too disgraceful to consider for one who calls himself a Gallic citizen. On the other hand, almost certain death resulting from an all-out attempt at a break-out is seen as an easy way out for those lacking in honour to vindicate themselves.

'In the midst of evils expectation of rescue is very apt to persuade one to trust even in what is beyond reason.'

[Cassius Dio, *Roman History*, VII. 29]

One man is notable in his condemnation of any suicidal attempt to break out, an Arverni called *Critognatus*. He suggests that if the Gauls are butchered to a man, the effect on the morale of the whole of Gaul will be devastating. In such a situation, Caesar would certainly enslave the whole country. Critognatus suggests that it is better to bear honourably the deprivations of starvation, even if it includes cannibalization of those too old or too young to fight, than to be subject to Roman control. He says they need to give more time for the relief army to arrive. Critognatus goes

86

on to say that the Gauls must take their lead from the Romans, who have toiled night and day, bearing all deprivations with firm resolve. The fact that the Romans have built a contravallation is evidence that they expect the Gallic relief force to arrive at any time. Therefore, if the Romans believe that a relief army will arrive, then so should the Gauls in Alesia. Calls are made to remember times past, when German tribes had ravaged the land. The Gauls did not surrender then, rather, they retreated to their hill forts and although forced by starvation to eat the non-combatants, they came out with their lives, their lands and their liberty. Against this example, the neighbouring lands of Gaul, in The Province, are invoked as examples of what lies in store for the rest of Gaul if they are to fail – Roman despotism and oppression.

> 'But as these delayed and food supplies began to fail the besieged, he [Vercingetorix] thrust out the children and the women and the most useless among the rest, hoping either that the outcasts would be saved as booty by the Romans or else that those left in the town might survive by enjoying for a longer time the supplies that would have belonged to their companions.'

> [Cassius Dio, *Roman History*, 40.40]

> 'When different opinions were expressed, they determined that those who, owing to age or ill health, were unserviceable for war, should depart from the town, and that themselves should try every expedient before they had recourse to the advice of Critognatus. However, that they would rather adopt that design, if circumstances should compel them and their allies should delay, than accept any terms of a surrender or peace. The Mandubii, who had admitted them into the town, are compelled to go forth with their wives and children. When these came to the Roman fortifications, weeping, they begged of the soldiers by every entreaty to receive them as slaves and relieve them with food. But Caesar, placing guards on the rampart, forbade them to be admitted.'

> [Caesar, *The Gallic War*, VII. 78]

Although Critognatus' entreaty to wait the Romans out is heard with some sympathy, the majority of Vercingetorix's followers do not wish to be forced to commit the folly of their ancestors. The assembly therefore decides to force the old and infirm to leave the town before they resort to the unthinkable. As a result the townsfolk are ordered to an assembly where those of fighting ability are taken to one side and removed, while the rest told of their fate. The townsfolk are led to the main gate of Alesia and forcibly made to leave. With the crying of women and children in their ears, the Gallic warriors shut the doors to the town in steely silence. For Vercingetorix, these events mark yet another dismal turn. By ejecting the inhabitants of the town, he has reneged upon their welcome, and has repaid their generosity with mercilessness. The warriors left in Alesia are likewise dismayed, their hearts turning cold with the actions Caesar has forced upon them. A grim resolve fills the consciousness of the warriors, and where formerly thoughts of high-minded virtue ran, only hatred and fear reside.

> 'But he [Vercingetorix] hoped in vain, for Caesar did not have sufficient food himself to feed others; and believing, moreover, that by returning the expelled he could make the enemy's lack of food more severely felt (for he expected that they would of course be received again), he forced them all back. Now these perished most miserably between the city and the camp, because neither party would receive them.'

> [Cassius Dio, *Roman History*, 40.40]

The citizens of Alesia turn away from the Gallic warriors who have rejected them. Where once they thought to support the efforts of Vercingetorix to oust Caesar from Gaul, they now look to Caesar as their only chance of survival. Slowly they make their way down from the hill fort and up to the Roman lines. On seeing their enemies on the ramparts, the refugees forget all thoughts of Gallic citizenship and plead for help from their captors. The Romans on guard initially look favourably on this turn of events. Owning a few Gallic slaves is a good prospect; they will prove useful and may even be sold for gain later.

But Caesar quickly orders that no Gaul be allowed to enter the Roman lines. Caesar wants no distractions from the events ahead. If he allows one soldier to obtain a slave, all his troops will want the same. Even if he allows only a few in, he will be increasing the burdens on his own limited supplies. Equally, if the refugees are compliant now, under the threat of starvation, they may turn rebellious again, once they have food in their bellies. Caesar cannot conceivably let any enemy stay in his camp. He cannot even permit them to travel through his lines, as doing so will allow his enemies knowledge of his defences. Should they find succour with the neighbouring tribes, any information they pass on will be disadvantageous to the Romans. Caesar offers his soldiers a bargain: after the battle is won, he will award each soldier a slave of his own. The guarantee of booty seems to satisfy the troops, and in so doing Caesar has increased the focus the soldiers have on the task in hand. Caesar is determined that Vercingetorix will carry the burden of these civilians.

With no succour being given by the Romans, the refugees are forced back, once again, into the wilderness. The citizens of Alesia make their way back up to the gates of the hill fort, hoping against hope that the Roman refusal to let them enter their lines will change the minds of the warriors in Alesia. Vercingetorix, however, is as resolved on his course of action as Caesar is. The warriors on guard are instructed not to allow the civilians to enter. Thus, Alesia's citizens are left to their fate in the no-man's land between the Roman and Gallic forces. In desperation, the refugees from Alesia seek what measly food and shelter they can find on the slopes of the hill fort. The single-minded ruthlessness of both Caesar and Vercingetorix has sealed their fate: a slow and painful death from starvation and want.

Week 7: While Alesia Starves, the Relief Army Marches

> 'All march to Alesia, sanguine and full of confidence: nor was there a single individual who imagined that the Romans could withstand the sight of such an immense host: especially in an action carried on both in front and rear, when [on the inside] the besieged would sally from the town and attack the enemy, and on the outside so great forces of cavalry and infantry would be seen.'
>
> [Caesar, *The Gallic War*, VII. 79]

While the citizens of Alesia are cast out and left to their fate, the assembly at Bibracte draws to a close. The army that has collected is finally organized into groups and breaks up into separate units for the march to Alesia. Despite the individual differences between the tribes they are able to amass a huge and impressive army. Over the course of the next three days the 8,000 cavalry and 240,000 infantry split into smaller warbands. Each day the warbands gather their supplies, weapons and baggage and set out after their guides along the ancient routes north to Alesia. Towards the end of the week, as the last warband recedes into the distance, the people of Bibracte experience relief. The burden of hosting so many is lifted from them, certain that the sheer number of warriors will destroy Caesar and Rome's ambitions in Gaul for the foreseeable future. Confidence within the army is high: this is one of the largest gatherings of armed warriors that Gaul has ever raised. All are convinced that once they arrive at Alesia and join with their comrades in the town, the Romans will be unable to withstand their onslaught.

Week 8, Day 1: Arrival of the Gallic Relief Army

> 'In the meantime, Commius and the rest of the leaders, to whom the supreme command had been entrusted, came with all their forces to

Caesar's Gallic Triumph

Alesia, and having occupied the entire hill, encamp not more than a mile from our fortifications.'

[Caesar, The Gallic War, VII. 79]

During the course of the previous week, the Gallic relief army have made their way to the hill fort and rendezvous outside Alesia. As the troops arrive they make camp on the hills to the south and the west of modern-day Venarey-les-Laumes. From here the Gallic leaders look straight down the valley, across the Plain of Laumes to Alesia about 3 miles away.

Once the whole army is assembled, Commius and the rest of the commanders call a war council to meet and decide what to do. With such a sizeable army it will be impossible to remain in this place for long. While there is adequate water from the River Armançon, food is a more tricky matter. Supplying the army requires constant wagonloads of grain imported from far-off villages and there are none nearby because the Romans have already confiscated what they can and have burnt the rest. The Gallic commanders' first action therefore, is to send out scouts to gather information about nearby resources. The war council also needs to plan an assault and further scouts are sent out to gather information on Caesar's fortifications.

Once these scouts have returned, the Gallic war chiefs gather again to plan an attack. It is clear that the fortifications have been made in such a way that Caesar is expecting to be attacked both from within and without. The remnants of Vercingetorix's cavalry that fled from Alesia are also at the meeting. They make the Gallic chiefs aware that the threat from the German cavalry is particularly great. The Roman success at the Battle on the Armançon and the defeat Vercingetorix experienced on the Plain of Laumes make it clear that Caesar's cavalry must be dealt with first. This is because any army wishing to attack the Roman defences will first have to cross the Plain of Laumes and will therefore be vulnerable to attack from Roman cavalry based there. The chiefs therefore decide that their first aim must be to enable the Gallic cavalry to eliminate the Roman cavalry as a fighting force. This needs to be done before any further plans can be made to attack the defences.

Confident of victory, the leaders know that a battle of this sort will have the effect of allowing the Gallic nobles to show off their prowess to their assembled subordinates, thereby raising their spirits. It will also permit Roman trophies to be collected and sacrificed to the gods, in preparation for the more complicated matter of attacking Caesar's lines of defence.

> 'And while Caesar was besieging this city, which was considered to be impregnable by reason of the strength of the walls and the number of the defenders, there fell upon him from without a danger great

Week 8, Day 2 (Noon): Cavalry Battle on the Plain of Laumes

beyond all expectation. For the strength of all the nations in Gaul assembling in arms came against Alesia, to the number of 300,000; and the fighting men in the city were not fewer than 170,000; so that Caesar being caught between two such forces and blockaded, was compelled to form two walls for his protection, the one towards the city, and the other opposite those who had come upon him, since, if these forces should unite, his affairs would be entirely ruined.'

[Plutarch, *Fall of the Roman Republic: Six Lives*, III. 27]

On Mont Flavigny, Caesar is informed of the arrival of Gallic troops. Cavalry scouts are sent out to monitor the situation and over the course of the day, it becomes clear that the early reports of the Gallic relief force are underestimates and the host now massing to their west is huge. Caesar gathers his officers and outlines preparations for defence against a Gallic assault. He is certain it will come and given the Gallic desire for battle, it is likely to come sooner rather than later. Caesar also knows that the sheer size of the Gallic force, while impressive, will also work against it. Hemmed in by the sides of the valley, the warriors will not be able to surround the entire Roman defences. The most likely place that they will attack is on the Plain of Laumes. This is where Caesar has placed his most formidable defences and where he will gather his best troops and the bulk of his army. Caesar stresses that the biggest threat will come from a combined attack in the same location on both sides of his defences. With combatants fighting on two sides of the wall, it will take only the smallest breach in his defences to open the floodgates to a tide of Gallic warriors. At all costs, the Roman soldiers stationed at this point must not break. With this warning Caesar dismisses his officers and awaits the morning.

Week 8, Day 2 (Noon): Cavalry Battle on the Plain of Laumes

'The following day, having led forth their cavalry from the camp, they fill all that plain, which, we have related, extended 3 miles in length, and draw out their infantry a little from that place, and post them on the higher ground. The town Alesia commanded a view of the whole plain. The besieged run together when these auxiliaries were seen; mutual congratulations ensue, and the minds of all are elated with joy.'

[Caesar, *The Gallic War*, VII. 79]

The Gallic war chiefs supervise the gathering of the Gallic cavalry. The nobles ride their horses out onto the Plain of Laumes, but the progress is slow and takes most of the morning to organize and put into effect. Meanwhile, many of the infantry are sent to the hills west of the Plain, near modern-day Grignon. From here they anticipate they will witness the triumph of their noblemen and, should it be necessary, provide them with support. From the watchtowers of Alesia, Vercingetorix's warriors note the massing of men on the Plain of Laumes and know it can mean only one thing. The relief force has finally arrived. Ecstatic cries go out from the hill fort as the news of their arrival is passed between the warriors. The Gauls trapped in Alesia now feel that the tide of the campaign has turned their way. Surely Caesar's fortifications will not be able to withstand blows from two sides. Vercingetorix immediately gathers his leaders together and commences plans to attack the fortifications in conjunction with the relief force, certain of a swift victory.

Gallic Noble Cavalry

This warrior's appearance (see Plates section, 10) embodies the pinnacle of Gallic cavalrymen, and is representative of the leaders of the army at Alesia. Most of the equipment illustrated is reconstructed from types found at Alesia. The elaborate 'Agen' helmet and neck torc would mark him out as an important individual. Most Gallic horsemen present at Alesia would not have been so well armed. He wears a mail shirt and cape of typical Gallic style and carries a round shield for defence. In assault he could throw his two smaller javelins then use his long thrusting spear. Should the need arise, he also has a long sword for close combat. With this range of equipment a cavalryman could deal successfully with most situations. Note the Gallic-type saddle with prominent horns that hold the rider onto the horse and negate the use of stirrups.

'Caesar, having stationed his army on both sides of the fortifications, in order that, if occasion should arise, each should hold and know his own post, orders the cavalry to issue forth from the camp and commence action. There was a commanding view from the entire camp, which occupied a ridge of hills; and the minds of all the soldiers anxiously awaited the issue of the battle. The Gauls had scattered archers and light-armed infantry here and there, among their cavalry, to give relief to their retreating troops, and sustain the impetuosity of our cavalry. Several of our soldiers were unexpectedly wounded by these, and left the battle.'

[Caesar, *The Gallic War*, VII. 80]

Caesar's plans now go into execution. Legionaries and auxiliaries line both sides of the defences along the Plain of Laumes, each in their assigned position, with orders to hold. Along the ramparts, heavily armed legionaries collect their pila ready to throw. Auxiliaries likewise gather bundles of javelins and archers make final adjustments to their bows, gathering their arrows in useful locations. Slingers make little piles of shot near their posts ready to fire, and all along the fortifications the call goes up for attention to duty. Finally, the order is given and Roman cavalry pour forth from the camp in the corner of the plain.

Initially, the battle begins as a series of skirmishes. Separate squadrons of Roman cavalry engage with the clusters of Gallic cavalry, drawn up around their tribal leaders. The size of the plain is ideal for this type of cavalry engagement. The warriors fight in groups, skirmishing for a while then separating, and finally withdrawing to reorganize their troops and allow their blown horses to recover. The Gallic cavalry are not alone, they have brought with them small groups of archers. These lightly armed warriors are often the dependants of the nobles who ride before them. They stand back from the fray and wait for the fighting to cease, before moving in to shoot at the Roman cavalry. Once their superiors have disengaged fully, they then follow to protect their rear.

Gazing on from their vantage points on the hills overlooking the plain, the Gallic infantry eagerly watch the battle unfold. So too, does the Roman army. On the ramparts on the plain and from the hills above, all Roman eyes are focused on the ensuing combat, while in Alesia the hearts of the Gauls are raised by thoughts of Roman defeat and imminent relief. Throughout the afternoon, the cavalry battle continues with no real success coming to either side as each commander attempts to out manoeuvre the other. Then, as the Roman cavalry seems to be suffering from its accumulated injuries, events begin to turn.

'As for the relief looked for, the horsemen and the others they were bringing reached the barbarians before long, but these were then defeated in a cavalry battle . . . with the aid of the Germans . . .'

[Cassius Dio, *Roman History*, 40.4]

'When the Gauls were confident that their countrymen were the conquerors in the action, and beheld our men hard-pressed by numbers, both those who were hemmed in by the line of circumvallation and those who had come to aid them, supported the spirits of their men by shouts and yells from every quarter. As the action was carried on in sight of all, neither a brave nor cowardly act could be concealed; both the desire of praise and the fear of ignominy, urged on each party to valour. After fighting from noon almost to sunset, without victory inclining in favour of either, the

Caesar's Gallic Triumph

Germans, on one side, made a charge against the enemy in a compact body, and drove them back; and, when they were put to flight, the archers were surrounded and cut to pieces. In other parts, likewise, our men pursued to the camp the retreating enemy, and did not give them an opportunity of rallying. But those who had come forth from Alesia returned into the town dejected and almost despairing of success.'

[Caesar, *The Gallic War*, VII. 80]

The initial enthusiasm of midday has now given way to fatigue, both horses and men becoming exhausted. The only thing keeping the latter going is the fear of disgrace. Both sides know the importance of the battle and so do not want to been seen as unworthy in front of so many onlookers. Then, towards the late afternoon the battle begins to transform, Caesar's German mercenaries mass on the side of valley for one last assault. In a valiant charge, the German cavalrymen recall their victory at the Battle of Armançon and ride headlong at the Gauls. For some of the Gallic cavalry, fatigue has led them to be careless and so they are not fully prepared for this unexpected attack. Turning away from the assault, they hastily withdraw across the plain but in so doing, the archers who have for so long aided the Gallic attack, are left behind, unsupported in open ground. The Germans do not fail to realize the importance of this situation. Finally they can wreak vengeance on those who have tormented them all afternoon. In a single charge many of the archers are ridden down and slaughtered.

On seeing this triumph and buoyed up by memories of recent German victories against Vercingetorix, the rest of the Roman cavalry charge the retiring Gallic cavalry. Unexpectedly, a subtle change has taken place in the tone of the battle. Across the plain the Gallic cavalry begin to withdraw abandoning their skirmishers. This is a mistake. Now with no archers to protect them, the Gallic cavalry have no opportunity to rally, and so, are forced to flee back to their camps, followed closely by their Roman pursuers. What began as a tactical withdrawal becomes a rout. Within the hour, the Roman and German cavalry have taken the plain. The Gallic cavalry have fled back to their camps, leaving their subordinates to find what refuge they can from the slaughter. For the Gallic infantry in the hills nearby, this is an unfortunate turn of events and they return dispirited to their camps. In Alesia, the atmosphere is worse. Once again Caesar has bested the Gallic cavalry and once again Vercingetorix looks on, wondering what he has to do to defeat Caesar.

Week 8, Day 3: The Gallic Relief Army Prepares an Assault

Week 8, Day 3: The Gallic Relief Army Prepares an Assault

After the defeat on the Plain of Laumes, Commius and the other Gallic war chiefs are subdued. Their aim was to have the Gallic nobles eliminate the Roman cavalry in one decisive battle, but this has failed. Now they will have to press on with the assault against the contravallation in the knowledge that they have not expunged the threat of a Roman cavalry attack. A plan has to be devised that will remove the menace of the cavalry from the battle. The idea is proposed that the infantry attack the fortifications en masse during the night. The effectiveness of the Roman cavalry will therefore be removed, as the Roman cavalry will be less able to manoeuvre or anticipate the Gallic actions in the dark. In the Gallic camp over the course of the following day, preparations are made for the assault. Meanwhile in Alesia, all Vercingetorix can do is wait. He knows another attack is imminent, but with no communications with the relief army he does not know where or when it will come. All Vercingetorix can do is prepare his warriors so that when it does come he is ready.

> 'The Gauls, after the interval of a day, and after making, during that time, an immense number of hurdles, scaling-ladders, and iron hooks, silently went forth from the camp at midnight and approached the fortifications in the plain. Raising a shout suddenly, that by this intimation those who were besieged in the town might learn their arrival, they began to cast down hurdles and dislodge our men from the rampart by slings, arrows, and stones, and executed the other movements which are requisite in storming. At the same time, Vercingetorix having heard the shout, gives the signal to his troops by a trumpet, and leads them forth from the town.'
>
> [Caesar, *The Gallic War*, VII. 81]

Over the course of the day, the Gauls outside the Roman fortifications are tasked with overcoming the Romans' defences. From their positions surrounding the Plain of Laumes they can see that deep trenches and rows of sharpened branches protect the Roman lines. These will need to be neutralized. The Gallic war chiefs assign groups to collect wood from the surrounding forests. Some warriors simply gather vast quantities of branches and tie them into large bundles, or *fascines* that will be used to fill up the ditches. Other, more skilled Gauls are sent into the wood to harvest withies. These are the flexible young branches of trees such as hazel, ash and willow. Along with these, they collect thicker and harder branches, which are split along their length to form stakes. The stakes are hammered into the ground and once a length of stakes is formed, the withies are woven between them forming a strong wall of wood. These walls are lifted from the ground and carried back to the camp to be used as bridges across the ditches in the upcoming assault. Other warriors use trunks of small trees to manufacture crude wooden ladders using what basic tools they have. In the camp, the smiths are gathered to set up a rudimentary smithy. Here they take any spare weapons or metal and hammer them into large hooks, attaching them either to ropes or to long wooden handles. These hooks will be used to pull down the walls of the Roman ramparts. By the evening, all the siege paraphernalia is finished and it is gathered together in preparation for the attack. The Gallic war chiefs establish their tactics, drawing together groups of men and assigning them various tasks for the planned assault.

Week 8, Day 3 (Midnight): Gallic Night Attack

Just before midnight, the Gauls gather their equipment and make their way across the Plain of Laumes right up to the outer defences of the Roman contravallation. In the dark it is difficult to maintain coherency and the groups begin to intermingle, causing some confusion. Once they are in proximity to the Roman ramparts cohesion becomes academic. The Gauls, with their blood enraged, give a thunderous battle-cry, blow their war trumpets, and clash their weapons. The terrifying din has two purposes: to frighten the Romans, who are unaware of their presence, and to signal to Vercingetorix's army in Alesia that they are attacking. Howling and shrieking, the Gauls charge into the Roman defences shaking their shields and brandishing their spears.

> 'Thereupon they tried to enter the city by night through the wall of circumvallation, but met with dire disaster; for the Romans had dug secret pits in the places which were passable for horses and had fixed stakes in them, afterwards making the whole resemble on the surface the surrounding ground; thus horse and man, falling into them absolutely without warning, came to grief.'
>
> [Cassius Dio, *Roman History*, 40.5]

But the overconfident assault begins to falter at the first obstacle. The Gallic warriors are immediately caught up on the outer defences of the wall; the concealed lilea and stimuli are invisible to them in the darkness. The Gallic assault slows to a snail's pace as they carefully pick their way across the hidden traps. The commotion outside the Roman fortifications has drawn the attention of the guards inside Alesia, who race to inform Vercingetorix that the assault is under way. Vercingetorix immediately calls for the alarm to be sounded. On tall, monstrous animal-headed trumpets, the warriors inside Alesia respond to their comrades on the plain. The sound is at once harsh and heroic, calling the warriors inside Alesia to battle and informing their comrades they are coming. Outside the defences the Gauls continue their attack, acknowledging Vercingetorix's reply but proceeding cautiously. Throwing down the fascines and wattle hurdles they made earlier, the warriors attempt to cross the outer ditches. But as they cross, they are now in range of the Roman artillery and archers, and so they immediately come under a hail of fire from the Roman defences.

> 'Our troops, as each man's post had been assigned him some days before, man the fortifications; they intimidate the Gauls by slings, large stones, stakes which they had placed along the works, and bullets. All view being prevented by the darkness, many wounds are received on both sides; several missiles are thrown from the engines. But Marcus Antonius, and Caius Trebonius, the lieutenants, to whom the defence of these parts had been allotted, drafted troops from the redoubts which were more remote, and sent them to aid our troops, in whatever direction they understood that they were hard-pressed.'

> [Caesar, *The Gallic War*, VII. 81]

This is the moment the Roman defenders on the ramparts have been waiting for. After a month of hard work and waiting, the infantry have an opportunity to release their pent-up aggression. So far the cavalry has undertaken most of the combat. Now these hardy veterans take their opportunity to vent their fury on the Gauls. In a single action all of the slingers, archers and artillery open fire on the massed ranks of Gauls in front of them. Individual targets are hard to make out in the darkness, but the huge numbers of Gauls means that almost every shot will find a target. The Roman artillery trains its fire on the larger groups of warriors crossing the ditches and others constrained by the pit-traps. The slowness of the Gallic advance makes them easy targets to pick out in the shadows. Command of the Roman defences on the Plain of Laumes has been divided between two of Caesar's best generals, Marcus Antonius and Gaius Trebonius. These experienced generals have had the foresight to enlist more troops from the outer forts to use as a rapid reserve where necessary. Cohorts of legionaries wait in silence, listening to the sounds of combat in relative safety between the two ramparts. When ordered, they run along the line of defences, adding more firepower where needed, or supporting the sentries with hand-to-hand combat. In so doing, the areas of defences that are most vulnerable to attack are densely manned.

> 'Whilst the Gauls were at a distance from the fortification, they did more execution, owing to the immense number of their weapons; after they came nearer, they either unawares impaled themselves on

the spurs, or were pierced by the mural darts from the ramparts and towers, and thus perished. After receiving many wounds on all sides, and having forced no part of the works, when day drew nigh, fearing lest they should be surrounded by a sally made from the higher camp on the exposed flank, they retreated to their countrymen.'

[Caesar, *The Gallic War*, VII. 82]

The sheer weight of Gallic warriors means that even though the defenders are well protected, some Romans are inevitably injured by Gallic missile fire. Nevertheless, the Roman reserves manage to maintain the defences in good order. The same cannot be said of the Gallic warriors. With no cover to shelter in, they are extremely vulnerable to missile and artillery fire. Even though their attack is making progress, the numbers of dead are mounting and they have yet to penetrate the forest of sharp branches that protect the ramparts. After that they will still have to neutralize the rampart, either climbing up it with their ladders or pulling it down with their grappling hooks. The cover of night has brought only confusion to the attack and the Romans' deep defences and hidden traps have tamed the ferocity of the Gallic onslaught. With the dawn quickly approaching, the Gallic chiefs call the assault off. Thinking they would quickly breach the Roman defences, the Gallic chiefs have brought no cavalry support with them, as they would be of little use in the dark. Nevertheless, without this flexible defence, the Gallic leaders fear that once the sun has risen, Caesar's cavalry will be active again. They fear the Romans will ride out from their camp at the foot of Mont Flavigny and attack the undefended Gallic flanks and rear. Wearily, Commius calls for the trumpets – that once defiantly called for an assault – to sound a retreat. As he withdraws his men across the Plain of Laumes to his camps, Commius throws a defiant look back at the Roman defences. He is now beginning to experience the bitter taste of defeat that Vercingetorix knows all too well.

'But those within, whilst they bring forward those things which had been prepared by Vercingetorix for a sally, fill up the nearest trenches; having delayed a long time in executing these movements, they learned the retreat of their countrymen before they drew nigh to the fortifications. Thus they returned to the town without accomplishing their object.'

[Caesar, *The Gallic War*, VII. 82]

On the other side, within the Roman fortifications, Vercingetorix has emerged from Alesia and begun assaulting the Roman defences by filling in the outer Roman ditches. But the sound of Commius' trumpets

Week 8, Day 4: The Gallic Relief Army Plans Another Attack

signalling retreat plays across the plain and comes as a cruel blow to Vercingetorix's plans. He has not been sufficiently prepared for the assault, spending too much time gathering his men and organizing equipment to cross the Roman defences. Now, as Vercingetorix is in the process of neutralizing the Roman defences, his Gallic comrades on the other side are withdrawing. If he continues with his assault it will be unsupported by a concurrent attack on the other side of the defences. Thus it is that Vercingetorix is reluctantly forced to call off his attack, and once again he retreats back up the hill to the safety of Alesia.

Week 8, Day 4: The Gallic Relief Army Plans Another Attack
'The Gauls, having been twice repulsed with great loss, consult what they should do; they avail themselves of the information of those who were well acquainted with the country; from them they ascertain the position and fortification of the upper camp. There was, on the north side, a hill, which our men could not include in their works, on account of the extent of the circuit, and had necessarily made their camp in ground almost disadvantageous, and pretty steep. Gaius Antistius Reginus, and Gaius Caninius Rebilus, two of the lieutenants, with two legions, were in possession of this camp.'

[Caesar, *The Gallic War*, VII. 83]

After two consecutive failures, Commius calls the Gallic war chiefs to another council. In their camp overlooking the Plain of Laumes, the chiefs discuss revised plans of attack. The attack of the previous night has shown that weight of numbers is not enough to breach the unexpectedly complex defences on the plain. The Gauls need to revise their strategy altogether. They must identify a weakness in the Roman fortifications that they can exploit, and put in place a plan that covers all possibilities. With this in mind, Gallic scouts who have been studying the region around Alesia are called forth to a meeting. They describe the topography of the area and relay the details of the Roman fortifications to the chiefs.

It is clear that the Romans have been unable to enclose the circuit to the north of Alesia between the slopes of Mont Réa and the Plain of Grésigny. Here the slopes of Mont Réa are extremely steep. Caesar has attempted to run the fortifications up the side of the hill but has not been completely successful, determining that the topography provides enough of a defence in itself. At the foot of the hill a camp has been built, which is only strongly connected to the circumvallation on the eastern side, the south-western side being bounded by the River Oze. To its north, the steepness of the hill means that the contravallation cannot be built to cover the camp's rear.

This means the camp is only partially defended. The Gallic chiefs decide that this is the weak spot in Caesar's defences. If a sizeable force can break in here, the line of the defences will be smashed and Gauls from both inside and outside the circumvallation can join forces. The relief army will have to cause a diversion while another force attempts to breach the lines at this weak point. And so it is that the Gallic relief army once again plans an assault on Caesar's lines.

Week 8, Day 5: Commius' Plan Goes into Effect

'The leaders of the enemy, having reconnoitred the country by their scouts, select from the entire army 60,000 men; belonging to those states which bear the highest character for courage; they privately arrange among themselves what they wished to be done, and in what manner; they decide that the attack should take place when it should seem to be noon. They appoint over their forces Vercassivellaunus, the Arverni noble, one of the four generals, and a near relative of Vercingetorix. He, having issued from the camp at the first watch, and having almost completed his march a little before the dawn, hid himself behind the mountain, and ordered his soldiers to refresh themselves after their labour during the night.'

[Caesar, *The Gallic War*, VII. 83]

Over the course of the next day scouts are sent out with the local farmers to reconnoitre the route between the Gallic camp and the Roman camp on the foot of Mont Réa. A route is planned that will take the warriors in a wide loop north through the hills to the north-west of Alesia, ending on the back of Mont Réa. From here, when the time is right the Gallic force will pour over the hill and down the slope into the Roman defences. The council then agrees that the troops who will undertake this difficult task must be the most skilled and courageous. Picking only the most proficient of warriors from the most honoured tribes, 60,000 men are assembled and given their orders. The four war chiefs decide that given the attack's importance, command of this elite troop should be handled by one of their number. Therefore, due in part to his valour and in part to the fact that he is Vercingetorix's cousin, Vercassivellaunus is chosen for the role. It is seen as fitting that a member of Vercingetorix's family should be the one to bring him reprieve.

Just after midnight, the band of warriors leave camp under the cloak of darkness so the Roman sentries do not witness the manoeuvre. Following their local guides, the warriors march through the night along the small tracks that weave across the hills surrounding Alesia. As the sun begins to rise the Gauls arrive in their spot on the reverse side of Mont Réa. Here

Week 8, Day 5 (Noon to 3pm): The Battle of Alesia - Phase 1

they rest and regroup, while they wait until the allotted time of their assault.

Week 8, Day 5 (Noon to 3pm):
The Battle of Alesia, Phase 1 – Attack on Caesar's Weak Points

'The men [Gauls] did not give up, however, until they had arrayed themselves once more beside the very walls and had been defeated along with the people from the city who came out to fight.'

[Cassius Dio, *Roman History*, 40. 40]

'When noon now seemed to draw nigh, he marched hastily against that camp which we have mentioned before; and, at the same time, the cavalry began to approach the fortifications in the plain, and the rest of the forces to make a demonstration in front of the camp.'

[Caesar, *The Gallic War*, VII. 83]

When the sun is high in the sky, the Gallic relief army moves from the hills, down onto the Plain of Laumes. This, they plan, will be the decisive conclusion to Caesar's campaign in Gaul, and will result in his final expulsion from Gaul. Commius and the war chiefs have learnt the lessons of the previous days. This time they have organized a series of co-ordinated assaults that will stretch the Romans to breaking point. The first attack is planned to take effect on the plain. Here the Gallic war chiefs will make a concerted attempt to break into the Roman defences. Their hope is that the previous assault will have neutralized some of the Roman defences, making a second assault easier. They will attempt to break in at the same point, forcing their way through the anti-personnel obstacles with more siege equipment. This time the attack will be during the day, allowing the attackers to see the defences and improve their chances of killing the Roman defenders. However, they also know that the daylight will provide the Romans with more opportunities to defend themselves. The combat will be long, but Commius is determined that, this time, he will be victorious. The daylight will mean that the forces within Alesia will be more aware of the assault. A concerted effort from Commius and Vercingetorix should break through the Roman defences, and it will give Vercassivellaunus time to break through on Mont Réa. With a combined attack on both sides of the circumvallation, at the same point and with overwhelming numbers, the Roman defences should crumble.

'Vercingetorix, having beheld his countrymen from the citadel of Alesia, issues forth from the town; he brings forth from the camp long hooks, movable penthouses, mural hooks, and other things, which he had prepared for the purpose of making a sally. They

101

engage on all sides at once, and every expedient is adopted. They flocked to whatever part of the works seemed weakest. The army of the Romans is distributed along their extensive lines, and with difficulty meets the enemy in every quarter. The shouts which were raised by the combatants in their rear had a great tendency to intimidate our men, because they perceived that their danger rested on the valour of others; for generally all evils which are distant most powerfully alarm men's minds.'

[Caesar, *The Gallic War*, VII. 84]

On hearing the commotion on the plain and seeing the Gallic warriors' renewed assault on the Roman lines, Vercingetorix gathers his men once more. They have been busy since they last left the hill fort. Along with the devices made for the last effort, they have made further siege equipment. The most important addition to their paraphernalia are the penthouses. These portable defences are made of wood and wattle frames that can be easily carried by the Gauls. Under and behind these mobile defences the warriors of Vercingetorix's army are protected from all but the most effective artillery fire. The warriors also carry with them hooks attached to ropes and poles, their aim being to get close enough to the ramparts to pull down the wattle crenellations and leave the Romans undefended.

As the force approaches close to the Roman circumvallation, the bright midday sun allows them to see the Roman defences properly. Crossing the plain they are also able to see the remnants of the unsuccessful night assault. Men and siege equipment lie where they fell during the night's attack. Undaunted, Vercingetorix's army begins to split up, attacking the Roman lines at those points along the Plain of Laumes they think are the weakest. The troops make their way to the defences and begin to fill in the ditches and cover over the pit traps. As they do this, the Romans on the rampart once again use the opportunity to rain a deadly fire on the Gallic troops.

In response to the combined attack on both sides of their defences, Marcus Antonius and Gaius Trebonius order further vexillations of Roman soldiers to be drafted in from around the circumvallation. It seems clear that the Gauls have planned a combined attack on a widest part of the defences, in an attempt to weaken the Romans and stretch them to breaking point. With some difficulty, the legionaries manage to man the lines everywhere they are being attacked. But the fighting is demanding and the soldiers, even those hardened by campaign, cannot stop themselves from being apprehensive. The juxtaposition of the defences means that as the Romans defend to their front, they can hear the dread sounds of fighting on the walls to their rear. It is made clear to them that their lives

Week 8, Day 5 (Noon to 3pm): The Battle of Alesia - Phase 1

now depend on the abilities of the men fighting behind them, and without them in sight it is impossible to be confident of their victory.

> 'Caesar, having selected a commanding situation, sees distinctly whatever is going on in every quarter, and sends assistance to his troops when hard-pressed. The idea uppermost in the minds of both parties is that the present is the time in which they would have the fairest opportunity of making a struggle; the Gauls despairing of all safety, unless they should succeed in forcing the lines: the Romans expecting an end to all their labours if they should gain the day.'

[Caesar, *The Gallic War*, VII. 85]

From Caesar's commanding position on Mont Flavigny he can see the entire battle as it unfolds. From here he can control the battle by signalling down the lines or across to Labienus on the other side of Alesia. The soldiers in both armies instinctively know this is going to be the decisive battle. For the Gauls everything they have fought for thus far will be decided here. They are fighting for their autonomy, their homelands and families. Their victory at Gergovia now seems to be in the distant past. The string of defeats in the previous months means that they must win this battle or all will be lost. If the Gauls are defeated now, then so are the hopes for a Gallic alliance against the Romans. The relief army will return to their farms, Vercingetorix will be forsaken and each will have to deal with Caesar in their own way. In dread of this outcome, with one last defiant push, the Gauls hope to appease the gods with their valour and change the bad luck they have had so far into victory.

For the Romans the options are far more prosaic. They are professional soldiers, fighting only for their lives. If they lose here they will not return to The Province, as they will surely be slaughtered to a man where they stand. There have been too many massacres of Gallic men, women and children for the Gallic warriors before them to stay their hands when the time comes. But the veterans have been in this situation before, and they know their only hope is to keep fighting calmly and professionally until the bitter end. Hence, for the Romans, their choice is to fight or die.

> 'The principal struggle is at the upper lines, to which, we have said, Vercassivellaunus was sent. The least elevation of ground, added to a declivity, exercises a momentous influence. Some are casting missiles, others, forming a testudo, advance to the attack; fresh men by turns relieve the wearied. The earth, heaped up by all against the fortifications, gives the means of ascent to the Gauls, and covers those works which the Romans had concealed in the ground. Our men have no longer arms or strength.'

Caesar's Gallic Triumph

[Caesar, *The Gallic War*, VII. 85]

While the battle ensues on the Plain of Laumes, the more important Gallic assault prepares to the north, where Vercassivellaunus is about to attempt to break through the Roman lines. All at once, 60,000 men pour over the ridge of Mont Réa down the slopes onto the unprepared legionaries in camp below. The Roman position at the bottom of the hill means that the Gauls have the advantage. From the slopes above the Roman camp the Gauls throw javelins and fire arrows directly into the fortifications.

With the attack now under way across the western end of the circumvallation, the two legates Gaius Antistius Reginus, and Gaius Caninius Rebilus are left alone to attempt to defend the camp with only a legion each. This leaves the Romans at a real disadvantage, outnumbered as they are by more than ten to one. As the Romans come under increasingly intense missile fire from the slopes, the legionaries see that the Gauls have adopted a new tactic. Groups of Gauls have formed into the famous Roman *testudo* or tortoise. This siege technique is foreign to the Gallic way of war, but this extraordinary time requires extraordinary tactics. The Gallic warriors gather into large groups. The central members of the group raise their shields above their heads, while the members on the edges pull their shields in tight, locking them to their neighbours' shields and to the shields above. Thus, the Gauls produce an armoured body of men almost invulnerable to Roman missile fire. Moving slowly down the slope and aided by Gallic skirmish fire, numbers of Gallic 'tortoises' advance upon the Roman camp. Under the cover of these missile-proof formations, the Gauls fill in the ditches surrounding the camp, mounding up banks of earth and timber to surmount the defences. With their overwhelming numbers, the Gauls assail a wide length of the defences stretching the defenders to the limit. At the same time, more Gallic warriors provide missile cover or send in relief for the weary sappers. In so doing Vercassivellaunus slowly progresses towards the Roman ramparts and his warriors begin to neutralize the Roman obstacles ready, finally, to overwhelm their defences.

By the time the Gallic assault has reached the Roman ramparts the legionaries defending them have become exhausted with the constant fighting.

'Caesar, on observing these movements, sends Labienus with six cohorts to relieve his distressed soldiers. He orders him, if he should be unable to withstand them, to draw off the cohorts and make a sally; but not to do this except through necessity. Caesar himself goes to the rest, and exhorts them not to succumb to the toil; he shows them that the fruits of all former engagements depend on that day

Week 8, Day 5 (Noon to 3pm): The Battle of Alesia - Phase 1

and hour.'

[Caesar, *The Gallic War*, VII. 86]

From Mont Flavigny, Caesar can see the peril that the camp at the foot of Mont Réa is in. Caesar hurriedly sends a message to Labienus across the valley on Mont Bussy. Labienus is to rush to the aid of the legionaries with two cohorts, with the proviso that if he is unable to make any headway against the Gauls he should attempt to make a sally out of the circumvallation against their flanks. Immediately on receiving the message, Labienus gathers two cohorts and quickly marches them along the circumvallation and down the slope of Mont Bussy towards the besieged legionaries. Meanwhile, in an act now typical of Caesar, he too rides from his camp, this time down the slope of Mont Flavigny. With his hand-picked guard of men, Caesar rides along the defences of the circumvallation.

On arriving on the Plain of Laumes, Caesar halts to reconnoitre the position and takes charge himself. With an inspiring speech to his men and his personal presence among them, Caesar hopes to reinforce the spirits of his troops by encouraging them to resist the pressure of the Gallic attack on both sides. The legionaries respond well to this overture and inspired by his attendance, think that if Caesar is in their midst then their situation cannot be too calamitous. Each man is equally inspired by their leader's presence, encouraged to fight with greater vigour in an attempt to gain recognition for acts of bravery and thereby advancement in the ranks. Caesar awakens in the legionaries the awareness that all of their previous hard labour is now under threat, and that only by a supreme effort may they overturn the odds and their labours be justified with a great victory.

'The Gauls within, despairing of forcing the fortifications in the plains on account of the greatness of the works, attempt the places precipitous in ascent; hither they bring the engines which they had prepared; by the immense number of their missiles they dislodge the defenders from the turrets: they fill the ditches with clay and hurdles, then clear the way; they tear down the rampart and breast-work with hooks.'

[Caesar, *The Gallic War*, VII. 86]

Week 8, Day 5 (3pm to 6pm):
The Battle of Alesia, Phase 2 – Caesar Fights Back

Meanwhile, for Vercingetorix the situation inside the circumvallation seems to be one of unremitting failure. Although he has built equipment especially to break through the Roman defences, his goal is nonetheless unattainable. After many attempts have been made to neutralize the traps and obstacles on the Plain of Laumes, he finds it impossible to surmount the Roman ramparts. On seeing the Romans' renewed vigour, coming unbeknownst to him from Caesar's presence on the other side of the rampart, Vercingetorix revises his plan of attack. The Gallic army on the plain is withdrawn, out of the range of the Roman artillery and missile troops. At this point, he compliments the troops on their performance on the plain, counselling them that all is not lost. Their actions on the plain, although unsuccessful, were only defeated by the complexity of the Roman defences. If they attack the less well-defended places of the circumvallation they will be victorious. Choosing the defences on the slopes of Mont Flavigny, the Gallic warriors put their siege engines to renewed use. Under cover of their penthouses they fill in the ditches and cross the rivers in front of the Roman lines. Then, advancing further, their overwhelming numbers prove advantageous against the weakly defended ramparts.

The Roman defenders in this region have had their numbers depleted to reinforce the defences on the Plain of Laumes, so now they have to defend the ramparts with what limited forces they have. After a prolonged assault, the Gauls finally manage to get into a position where they can use their long grappling hooks and ropes to tear down the thin wattle ramparts made by the Romans. After the succession of failures against Caesar's troops, this success comes as a huge relief to Vercingetorix and his Gauls. Finally they are making headway against their enemy, the possibility of success spurring them on to further exploits.

> 'Caesar sends at first young Brutus, with six cohorts, and afterwards Gaius Fabius, his lieutenant, with seven others; finally, as they fought more obstinately, he leads up fresh men to the assistance of his soldiers himself.'
>
> [Caesar, *The Gallic War*, VII. 87]

The breach on Mont Flavigny is devastating to Caesar. Immediately he seizes on the dangers of the situation. If the Gauls manage to stabilize the breach they have made they will pour more troops into it, then the Roman line would be broken from within. Without delay, one of his young tribunes, Brutus, is sent with six cohorts to push Vercingetorix back. After further intense fighting, the Romans fail to halt the Gallic ingress, so Caesar is forced to send another seven cohorts to repel the Gauls. These are sent under the command of Gaius Fabius, an experienced legate who has been with Caesar since the start of the campaign. But even with these veteran legionaries he is still unable to halt the Gallic penetration. In a final burst of violence, it seems that Vercingetorix's warriors will take the Roman rampart. At this moment, Caesar himself is forced to make his presence felt. Taking troops from the already overstretched lines on the Plain of Laumes, Caesar rides back along the circumvallation to the aid of the beleaguered Roman defenders at the foot of Mont Flavigny. With his presence at their backs and the extra troops he brings adding to their ranks, the fading legionaries begin to fight with renewed vigour. In a cumulative push, the Romans finally manage to clear the ramparts of Gauls and recover the situation. For Vercingetorix's warriors, once they have failed to break the Roman defences, they know their tremendous exertions have failed and so they quickly begin to withdraw.

On seeing the threat is lifted, Caesar has no time to waste; he takes charge of the defences, reallocating the deployment of troops and solidifying the defences. With the Gallic threat in this area now removed, the legionaries are detailed to shore-up the broken defences in anticipation of renewed Gallic attacks.

'For skill contributes very largely to bravery, since when present it strengthens the power of men's resolutions and when wanting destroys the same more thoroughly by far than if they had never possessed it at all.'

[Cassius Dio, *Roman History*, VII. 25]

'After renewing the action, and repulsing the enemy, Caesar marches in the direction in which he had sent Labienus, drafts four cohorts from the nearest redoubt, and orders part of the cavalry to follow him, and part to make the circuit of the external fortifications and attack the enemy in the rear. Labienus, when neither the ramparts nor the ditches could check the onset of the enemy, informs Caesar by messengers of what he intended to do. Caesar hastens to share in the action.'

[Caesar, *The Gallic War*, VII. 87]

While the situation may be temporarily consolidated on Mont Flavigny, it is still not completely resolved for Caesar. He has managed to avert Vercingetorix's attacks inside the circumvallation from becoming successful on the Plain of Laumes and on the slopes of Mont Flavigny. But the soldiers on the plain are still engaged by the Gallic relief force outside the contravallation and now further bad new arrives. Labienus' relief force has been unsuccessful in supporting the camp at the foot of Mont Réa and at this moment is coming under renewed assault. From Mont Flavigny, Caesar can see what is happening across the valley on Mont Réa. Immediately he takes four cohorts of reserve troops from the remaining troops present and proceeds to Labienus' aid. Riding first to the cavalry camp on the Plain of Laumes, Caesar orders some of the reserve cavalry there to follow with him while the rest of the cavalrymen are ordered to ride counter-clockwise around the circumvallation to meet up with him and Labienus on Mont Réa. This will be a gruelling journey across the large hills of Mont Flavigny, Mont Penneville and Mont Bussy and will take a considerable amount of time. Caesar lets them know that he will endeavour to hold the enemy until they arrive.

> 'His arrival being known from the colour of his robe, and the troops of cavalry, and the cohorts which he had ordered to follow him being seen, as these low and sloping grounds were plainly visible from the eminences, the enemy join battle. A shout being raised by both sides, it was succeeded by a general shout along the ramparts and whole line of fortifications. Our troops, laying aside their javelins, carry on the engagement with their swords.'
>
> [Caesar, *The Gallic War*, VII. 88]

Week 8, Day 5 (6pm to 9pm):
The Battle of Alesia, Phase 3 – Gallic Withdrawal
Caesar now rides between the walls of the circumvallation surrounded by his bodyguard. Caesar always wears the traditional brightly-coloured robe of a general when in battle, its distinctive red hue marking him out from his companions. The arrival of Caesar at Mont Réa, with cavalry and infantry support, puts new heart into the defenders there. Labienus has managed to forestall the Gallic intrusion after they had breached the defences, but the Roman troops are under a constant threat of collapse.

As Caesar arrives, his troops immediately go into battle. The Gallic reserve on the hill carefully watch these events unfold, and seeing the arrival of Caesar realize the danger his presence can bring. And so, in anticipation of the rejuvenation of the Roman forces, Vercassivellaunus commits the last of his remaining forces to the attack. To counteract Caesar's presence, Vercassivellaunus himself charges down the hill into the fray, his presence stirring the Gauls on to further exploits. Both sides now raise a cheer of elation at the presence of their leaders. But the Gallic counter-offensive is too late. Caesar's presence, along with his reinforcements, is enough to shore up the legions already engaged in combat. The renewed Gallic assault shatters upon the reinforced Roman lines and so the fighting comes down to brutal hand-to-hand combat. The possibility of using projectiles has passed, as the two sides are engaged so closely it is difficult for the archers and slingers to pick their targets. Each combat now relies on the strength and the luck of the individual. Ultimately, this type of fighting favours the Roman style of combat. The

Week 8, Day 5 (6pm to 9pm): The Battle of Alesia - Phase 3

Gauls, with their long, slashing swords find it difficult to create adequate room to fight. The Romans, on the other hand, favour densely packed formations. Taking up a low stance behind their shields, they jab out with their stabbing swords. As the fighting progresses the balance of the battle swings slowly towards the Romans.

> 'The cavalry is suddenly seen in the rear of the Gauls; the other cohorts advance rapidly; the enemy turn their backs; the cavalry intercept them in their flight, and a great slaughter ensues.'
>
> [Caesar, *The Gallic War*, VII. 88]

With the battle at a critical stage, the fighting is swinging decisively the Romans' way. The dense fighting formations hold the Gallic forces back as they attempt to break through the Roman lines. As more support pushes forward from the rear, the Gallic assault surges forward under the pressure of numbers. At this crucial moment, fortune again favours the Romans. The cavalry that Caesar earlier sent around the circumvallation has finished its long journey. After crossing Mont Flavigny and Mont Pennevelle, the troopers reach Mont Bussy. Diverting now through the main gates of the contravallation they ride down into the Rabutin valley. The cavalry then charge across the slopes of Mont Réa onto the left flank and rear of the attacking Gauls. For Vercassivellaunus' army it is all too much. On seeing the encroaching cavalry on their flank, they realize the lines of the defences have now become a trap for them. Anticipating their own slaughter, they break and try to flee before it is too late. But as the Gauls take flight the Roman cavalry runs them down and the legionaries in the camp charge out against the retreating Gauls, massacring them as they flee. In the ensuing chaos, Vercassivellaunus is abandoned by his army and captured by the triumphant legionaries.

Caesar can now relax, as he has managed to avert two major breaches in his defences, and the Gauls are in retreat from both. The day is drawing to a close, and for Caesar, all that is left is to stabilize his troops and regroup within the circumvallation.

> 'Sedulius the General and Chief of the Lemovices is slain; Vercassivellaunus, the Arverni, is taken alive in the flight, seventy-four military standards are brought to Caesar, and few out of so great a number return safe to their camp. The besieged, beholding from the town the slaughter and flight of their countrymen, despairing of safety, lead back their troops from the fortifications.'
>
> [Caesar, *The Gallic War*, VII. 88]

It has clearly been another disastrous day for the Gauls. The attack on

Caesar's Gallic Triumph

Mont Réa, which at one time looked to have succeeded, has been repulsed by Roman bravery. The assault has ended in the death or capture of most of Vercassivellaunus' 60,000 warriors. The Lemovici chieftain Sedulius is slain and Vercassivellaunus, one of the Gallic war chiefs, has been captured. This is a bitter blow for the Gauls as now two chiefs of the Arverni are within Caesar's control, Vercassivellaunus is caught and Vercingetorix remains trapped within the Roman fortifications. The fighting on the Plain of Laumes has been too much and so the morale of the Gallic army begins to break.

With the cream of the Gallic army defeated on the slopes of Mont Réa, the rest of the army hold out little hope and withdraw from the contravallation. Anticipating a Roman follow-up they quickly return across the Plain of Laumes to their camps, more disconsolate than ever.

The Lemovicies are typical of many of the tribes, with no chief to lead them they are unlikely to fight again and are a clearly beaten force. Trapped inside Caesar's circumvallation, Vercingetorix's army, defeated twice today, has been made aware of the unsuccessful attempt to break through on Mont Réa. From Alesia the attack and rout has been followed with growing anguish. Now, on seeing the relief army in retreat, Vercingetorix's warriors retire into Alesia once more, utterly dispirited.

> '[The Gallic defeat] . . . was also unknown to the Romans who were guarding the wall towards the city. For they knew nothing of the victory till they heard the weeping of the men in Alesia and the wailing of the women, when they saw on the other side many shields adorned with silver and gold, and many breastplates smeared with blood, and also cups and Gallic tents conveyed by the Romans to their camp.'

> [Plutarch, *Fall of the Roman Republic: Six Lives*, III. 27]

> 'for they not only wear golden ornaments, but both chains round their necks and bracelets round their arms and wrists, and their dignitaries wear garments that are dyed in colours and sprinkled with gold.'

> [Strabo, *Geography*, IV. 4. 5]

> 'A flight of the Gauls from their camp immediately ensues on hearing of this disaster, and had not the soldiers been wearied by sending frequent reinforcements, and the labour of the entire day, all the enemy's forces could have been destroyed.'

> [Caesar, *The Gallic War*, VII. 88]

Week 8, Day 5 (6pm to 9pm): The Battle of Alesia - Phase 3

For the Romans on the circumvallation, the sight of Vercingetorix's troops retiring to the city and the relief army retiring across the plain, comes as a welcome relief. They have been fighting all afternoon and so an end to the hostilities means they can rest and recoup their losses.

Eventually, news of what has happened that day travels throughout the circumvallation. Along with these reports of victory, booty taken from the Gauls begins to make its appearance in the forts. The Roman soldiers see the loot as a legitimate acquisition. Unlike their Gallic counterparts – who would have to sacrifice to the gods any weapons or wealth obtained from the defeated enemy – the soldiers fighting for the Roman army have no such strictures. Once the enemy is defeated, the soldiers are sent out from the defences to mop up any stragglers and this is also when they take the opportunity to acquire what they can. As the soldiers make their way through the Gallic dead, they help themselves to trophies and treasures that will be sold when they return to The Province. Others left on the ramparts wearily gather what strength they can to rebuild the defences destroyed by the Gauls, in expectation of further onslaughts. Although they defeated the Gauls today, tomorrow may bring further attacks and they have to be prepared. The officers manning the Roman defences therefore decide to remain within their fortifications, renewing them and preparing for further Gallic assaults to come. Thus the Gallic army retreats back to its camp, unharassed by Caesar's forces.

> 'So quickly did so mighty a force, like a phantom or a dream, vanish out of sight and disperse, the greater part of the men having fallen in battle.'

> [Plutarch, *Fall of the Roman Republic: Six Lives*, III. 27]

The Gallic relief force, once a tough fusion of Gallic tribes forged in the face of the Roman army, is now a broken force. On returning to the camp it soon becomes clear that the objectives of the day have not been met. Meanwhile, the numbers of dead are gauged and the severe losses counted; added to which, Vercassivellaunus, leader of the army, is captured and seventy-four standards are lost. Sedulius, leader of the Lemovices, is dead, along with over a quarter of the army, including many of its best warriors.

This level of attrition is unbearable and conviction in the fragile union begins to crumble. Without any calling together of the war council of chiefs, tribal leaders independently decide to slip away. As Gallic warriors begin to leave, the news of the departure of tribes begins to spread from camp to camp. Soon the whole force, each fearing that they be left alone to the mercy of Roman troops, begins to disperse into the surrounding landscape and head home. The Gallic relief army, once a mighty force to be reckoned with, dissolves as quickly as it appeared.

Week 8, Day 5 (9pm to midnight):
The Battle of Alesia, Epilogue – Roman Cavalry Hunt the Survivors

'Immediately after midnight, the cavalry are sent out and overtake the rear, a great number are taken or cut to pieces, the rest by flight escape in different directions to their respective states.'

[Caesar, *The Gallic War*, VII. 88]

After its successful devastation of Vercassivellaunus' army on Mont Réa, the Roman cavalry returns to camp to recover and regroup. By the evening, Roman scouts and sentries begin passing news that large numbers of Gauls appear to be leaving the Gallic camp. It becomes clear the Gallic army, far from recovering its composure to fight again, has decided to cut its losses and run. For Caesar, this is an opportunity he cannot pass up. Gathering what groups of cavalry he can on the Plain of Laumes, he orders them to hunt down and destroy what Gallic forces they can discover. Over the course of the night, the Roman cavalry carry out their task with cruel pleasure. For them, the intensity of the fighting of the past days is vented through wholesale slaughter. As the morning sun begins to rise over the hill fort of Alesia, the Roman cavalry return after a night's concerted carnage. Their murderous task done, they have ensured the Gallic relief army is no longer a force to be reckoned with.

Week 8, Day 6: The Surrender of Vercingetorix

'Vercingetorix, having convened a council the following day, declares, "That he had undertaken that war, not on account of his own exigencies, but on account of the general freedom; and since he must yield to fortune, he offered himself to them for either purpose, whether they should wish to atone to the Romans by his death, or surrender him alive".'

[Caesar, *The Gallic War*, VII. 89]

Two months after his first attack on Caesar's column, Vercingetorix feels himself an utterly defeated man. He convenes a war council in the hill fort of Alesia. Gathering the leaders, he informs them that he holds all responsibility for the actions that have taken place over the intervening time. He had attempted to pull together the forces of Gaul in a unified army, in order to halt Roman expansion into the region. This he had done, not to promote his own interests in becoming King of the Gauls, but to maintain their freedom. While some may doubt the particulars of his speech, the constraints of the situation do not allow an opportunity to voice them. They are aware that the very name Vercingetorix means 'great

Week 8, Day 6: The Surrender of Vercingetorix

king of heroes' – how could he not want to exercise suzerainty over all Gallic tribes like his father had done? But all these dreams have now vanished. With no sign of the Gallic relief force returning and no prospect of ever breaking through Caesar's defences, Vercingetorix has only two options left open to him. If he surrenders, his people will live, if he doesn't they will starve and die. In either case the fate of Gaul outside Alesia has been decided. Whichever option Vercingetorix adopts, nothing will now stop Caesar's continued expansion into Gallic territory. In an attempt to pacify Caesar and reduce the ferocity of his response, Vercingetorix suggests that he be delivered to the Roman general on his own. Thereby, Vercingetorix planned to evoke the *devotio*, an explicit ritual understood by both the Romans and Gauls, in which the leader of an army sacrifices himself in the name of the war gods, and in so doing, attempts to save the rest of his army. Vercingetorix hopes that by sacrificing himself he may limit the revenge that Caesar will visit upon his fellow Gauls in Alesia.

'But those who held Alesia, after giving no small trouble to themselves and to Caesar, at last surrendered; and the leader of the whole war, Vercingetorix, putting on his best armour, and equipping his horse, came out through the gates, and riding round Caesar who was seated, and then leaping down from his horse, he threw off his complete armour, and seating himself at Caesar's feet, he remained there till he was delivered up to be kept for the Triumph.'

[Plutarch, *Fall of the Roman Republic: Six Lives*, III. 27]

'Ambassadors are sent to Caesar on this subject. He orders their arms to be surrendered, and their chieftains delivered up. He seated himself at the head of the lines in front of the camp, the Gallic chieftains are brought before him. They surrender Vercingetorix, and lay down their arms. Reserving the Aedui and Arverni, [to try] if he could gain over, through their influence, their respective states, he distributes one of the remaining captives to each soldier, throughout the entire army, as plunder.'

[Caesar, *The Gallic War*, VII. 89]

'Now Vercingetorix might have escaped, for he had not been captured and was unwounded; but he hoped, since he had once been on friendly terms with Caesar, that he might obtain pardon from him. So he came to him without any announcement by herald, but appeared before him suddenly, as Caesar was seated on the tribunal, and threw some who were present into alarm; for he was very tall to begin with, and in his armour he made an extremely imposing figure.

Caesar's Gallic Triumph

When quiet had been restored, he uttered not a word, but fell upon his knees, with hands clasped in an attitude of supplication. This inspired many with pity at remembrance of his former fortune and at the distressing state in which he now appeared. But Caesar reproached him in this very matter on which he most relied for his safety, and by setting over against his claim of former friendship his recent opposition, showed his offence to have been the more grievous. Therefore he did not pity him even at the time, but immediately confined him in bonds . . .'

[Cassius Dio, *Roman History*, 40. 41]

In due course, ambassadors are chosen from the Gallic leaders in Alesia, to take the news of Vercingetorix's surrender to Caesar. This comes as something of a surprise to Caesar, who is preparing for further hostilities against the hill fort. Once a truce has been established, Caesar convenes a meeting on the hilltop in front of his camp on Mont Flavigny. Caesar has his men set about arranging for him a *rostra*, an elevated seat around which his leading officers will convene. In so doing, he is recreating the Roman tribunal at which a magistrate decides on the fate of claimants in a trial. However, the ceremony is not for Vercingetorix's benefit, as his fate was sealed when he rebelled against Caesar. The ceremony is rather for the benefit of the Roman officers and legionaries present. Caesar is displaying his power and status and reflecting the strength of Rome, and its ability to decide the fate of the conquered.

Riding out from Alesia with his Gallic chiefs, Vercingetorix makes his way to Caesar's camp. Arriving at the Roman defences, the chieftains are taken aside and Vercingetorix is led to Caesar. At Caesar's tribunal, the Gaul creates something of a stir: he is tall and imposing, particularly so as he sits high in the saddle of his horse. Without descending from his mount as expected, Vercingetorix slowly rides once around the podium on which Caesar and his officers are sitting. Unbeknownst to Caesar, Vercingetorix is invoking a magical Gallic ritual in which his fate becomes bound up with that of Caesar's. Now descending from his horse, Vercingetorix removes his armour and offers himself up for sacrifice. Caesar, however, has other plans for Vercingetorix – he does not wish to give Vercingetorix any of a hero's trappings. He orders the Gallic chieftain to be swiftly bound and taken away under close guard.

Following this, Caesar orders the other Gallic chieftains forward, together with their followers. The Aedui and Arverni are put to one side – these are the powerful tribes and Caesar has plans to deal with them as a politician, for he will need their support to control Gaul. But the fate of the other warriors, from less important tribes, is different. With these Caesar

Week 8, Day 6: The Surrender of Vercingetorix

fulfils the oath he has given to his men and distributes one Gaul to each as booty. Because Vercingetorix has surrendered, he has avoided the sacking of Alesia. In so doing he has removed from his soldiers the prospect of razing Alesia and slaughtering its inhabitants. Caesar's actions, therefore, go some way towards reducing his soldiers' hostilities towards the Gauls.

Vercingetorix now reflects on his fate and that of his men. They are all to be held as slaves – a fate he now fears will be translated to the whole of Gaul.

Aftermath

---·—◦—·---

Death-Throes of the Revolt

'The whole of Gaul was now conquered.'

[Caesar, *The Gallic War*, VII. 1]

So begins the opening of the last chapter of Caesar's *Gallic War*. Although written after Caesar's death by Hirtius, the sentiment is clear: Alesia was the defining battle in the Gallic War. With the destruction of Vercingetorix's forces at Alesia, the impetus for rebellion in Gaul had all but dissolved. This was true to a point, but revolts were still taking place in the following year.

During December of 52BC Hirtius tells us that the Gauls reverted to their old tactics. Following the defeat at Alesia the Gauls had learnt that no matter how large their army, if it was concentrated in a single place the Romans' military tactics could defeat it. The Gauls resorted to hoping that if they rebelled in a series of locations, creating simultaneous havoc across Gaul, the Romans would have insufficient forces to subdue them all. In doing so they returned to the uncoordinated insurrection they had undertaken prior to Alesia, and in truth they had little choice, even though it had proved unsuccessful in previous years. Early discontent was displayed by the Bituriges. In response Caesar set out immediately to destroy the revolt before it had begun and thereby to stop the insurrection spreading to the tribe's allies. Caesar's sheer speed of reaction and unexpected arrival allowed him quickly to bring the Bituriges to heel. Caesar's subjugation of the Bituriges was followed swiftly by an attack by the Carnutes on the Bituriges, which was also summarily put down by Caesar. In so doing Caesar showed that he was in control of all Gallic affairs.

Meanwhile, events were beginning to develop in the north. The Remi, who had been loyal to Caesar in the past, were coming under threat from the Bellovaci. Led by their chieftain Correus, along with Commius (one of the leaders of the Gallic relief force at Alesia), the Bellovaci were mobilizing the Belgae to war. In the new year of 51BC Caesar took four legions, finally bringing the rebel tribes to battle on a mile-square plain enclosed by woods. The Gauls were confident that they could ambush Caesar, as they had placed their bravest troops on the plain and hidden the rest in the surrounding woods. Unfortunately for Correus, Caesar had discovered his plan and so approached the battle in expectation of a 'surprise' attack. Caesar had also gathered further reinforcements, so was confident of bringing overwhelming numbers to bear in the battle. After battle was engaged the legionaries held their position, strong in the knowledge that support was coming. Gradually, Gallic morale ebbed and confidence collapsed when they realized the woods that surrounded them would now hamper their escape. Correus and the best of the Gauls were killed and so the Bellovaci sued for peace. Caesar demanded hostages and the revolt was ended. But Commius, the veteran of Alesia was still alive. For Commius the war continued and an assassination attempt did not halt his desire to generate rebellion – a desire that continued until long after Caesar was dead.

With calm now descending over Gaul, Caesar set about exploiting the country's riches. In the wake of Caesar's victories many Gauls attempted to move away from Roman-controlled areas. Following shortly from Caesar's laying waste to northern Gaul, further rumblings of discontent were heard in the west. The final round of insurrection came to a head at the oppidum of the Carnutes, Uxellodunum (modern-day Puy d'Issolu in the Dordogne). The Roman General Caninius had surrounded two rebellious Gallic leaders, Drappes and Lucterius, who had retreated to the hill fort with their troops. Caninius set about repeating Caesar's triumph at Alesia, building camps and a wall around the stronghold. Learning from the mistakes of Alesia, the two Gallic leaders gathered all the corn they could so they wouldn't starve. Similarly, they took every opportunity to attack the Romans in an attempt to halt the progress of the circumvallation. Nevertheless, the Roman position increased in strength and during one of the Gallic foraging expeditions Caninius was able to destroy the Gallic force. Further Roman reinforcements only served to increase the pressure on the Gauls left in Uxellodunum. The final nail in the Gallic coffin came when Caesar himself arrived at the siege. Immediately Caesar set out to cut the water supply to the hill fort, undermining the spring that supplied the hill fort. Thinking it was a sign from the gods the Gauls quickly gave in and surrendered to Caesar. Once the Gauls had been rounded up, Caesar turned to terror tactics to halt any further rebellion. He ordered that any man who had carried weapons should have both his hands cut off, allowing them to leave after the mutilations so that they could pass on the horror of Caesar's actions to their fellow Gauls and thus subvert further insurrection.

The following year, 50BC passed relatively quietly, but if Gaul was now truly conquered, this was only the beginning of Caesar's triumphs. Caesar's troops were still billeted in Gaul but the country was now no longer seen as a problem. The threat of war in Parthia led to Caesar being instructed to hand back to Pompey the First Legion. This Caesar grudgingly did, even though Pompey had 'lent' it to him in the first place. Along with the First, Caesar lent the Fifteenth Legion to Pompey, his newest and least experienced legion. This event marked the opening of the events that began the following year and resulted in the Civil War. The war was ultimately won by Caesar's legions, no doubt in part due to his military genius. But also due to the skill of the seasoned veterans blooded in the battle for Gaul, and the Alesia Campaign in particular.

Consequences

'In Gaul Caesar pillaged shrines and temples of the gods filled with offerings, and more often sacked towns for the sake of plunder than for any fault. In consequence he had more gold than he knew what to do with . . .'

[Suetonius, *Lives of the Twelve Caesars*, 54]

The effects of Caesar's invasion of Gaul were long lasting, affecting both Gaul and Rome. Before Caesar's invasion Gallic warfare was limited to intertribal conflict that was often restricted in scale and intensity. Caesar's invasion brought with it a wholly new form of destruction that went beyond the internecine war of previous years. Caesar's approach was not only to subdue, but also to create opportunity for Roman exploitation. Roman warfare's goal was not simply the subjugation of rebellious tribes, but also the destruction of opponents for economic and political gain. If Caesar had simply set out to pacify Gaul in 57BC, he would have returned to the Roman provinces after settling the Helvetii problem. The reality was, of course, the opposite; Caesar not only stayed in Gaul but also invaded its neighbours, Britain and Germany, and thus his actions betrayed his real motivations.

The Gallic War expanded Roman influence and control over Gallic riches and resources, bringing them into the Mediterranean scope of exploitation. Caesar played the role of developing economic markets and creating supply routes into these under-exploited regions. Caesar states that the Alesia Campaign started when rebellious Gauls attacked the Roman merchants at the town of Cenabum, because the Gauls there rejected the sovereignty of Rome. But why did the Gauls attack a market town, when surely a blow against a military target would have been more inspiring? It is likely that this attack was not simply an attack on the unprotected merchants, but a direct attack on the source of their troubles – the exploitation of Gallic trade and resources by wealthy Roman

Aftermath

merchants installed in their midst by Caesar. Caesar had supported the position of Roman merchants by the force of arms and probably took a cut of the profits in return. The importance of the attack on Cenabum is shown by the fact that, on hearing of the assault, Caesar immediately headed for the region. In travelling to Cenabum he marched his army nearly 800 miles from Vienne (modern-day Vienna) to Agedincum (modern-day Sens). On the march Caesar passes up the opportunity to attack Vercingetorix's army just 60 miles to the south of Cenabum. The land of the Carnutes was recognized as the centre of Gallic religion and Cenabum was certainly one of its strongholds. Thus it may be the case that Caesar wanted to inflict a blow against the Gallic religious centre, demoralizing the Gauls. But Caesar says nothing of these motivations and surely a strategic military strike would have been more Caesar's style than an asymmetric assault on Gallic psychology? Without further evidence it is impossible to be certain of the actual reasoning behind Caesar's actions. But Caesar's actions against Cenabum betray more than simple revenge. Caesar actions throughout the Gallic War betray him as predominantly concerned with wealth and renown. Certainly, all of his military conquests resulted in the looting of towns and villages across Gaul and the creation of large numbers of slaves and precious metals as booty. This wealth brought fame and fortune to Caesar, so much so that he could position himself for an attempt to challenge Pompey for control of the entire Roman Empire.

> 'but at first it appears that he [Caesar] sustained some loss, and the Arverni show a dagger suspended in a temple, which they say was taken from Caesar. Caesar himself afterwards saw it, and smiled; and when his friends urged him to take it down, he would not, because he considered it consecrated.'

> [Plutarch, *Fall of the Roman Republic: Six Lives*, III. 26]

In the above quote, Plutarch gives reference to Caesar's first battle in the Alesia Campaign, the battle on the Armançon. Caesar was a religious man and his unwillingness to offend the gods by removing the dagger is not untypical. His smile of acknowledgement at seeing it shows us that he was also aware that the dagger served to represent yet another one of his great victories. However, for the people of Rome the dagger came to represent another event in Caesar's life, this time his downfall. In 43BC, less than ten years after Caesar's great triumph at Alesia, a coin was made with the inscription of EID MAR (the Ides of March) along with a dagger and a freed-slave's cap. These symbols implied that on the Ides of March, Caesar's assassination with a dagger had brought freedom to the people of

Caesar's Gallic Triumph

Rome. In the period between his success at Alesia and his assassination, Caesar had passed from enslaving the people of Gaul to enslaving the people of Rome. At the height of his success it was the people of Rome, with a growing feeling of enslavement, that brought about Caesar's downfall. With this in mind, Caesar would have done well to have heeded his own words at the opening of his commentaries on his war in Gaul:

'When the gods wish to take vengeance on humans for their crimes, they usually grant them, for a time, considerable success and quite a lengthy period of impunity, so that when their fortunes are reversed they will feel it more bitterly.'

[Caesar, *The Gallic War*, I. 14]

Alesia Today

Caesar presents us with numerous references to towns and locations where military actions took place during his campaigns over the course of eight years. Caesar sweeps us up in his drive through Gaul, and on to Britain and Germany, providing a unique insight into the campaign for Gaul. But even though he gives us this insight into the Alesia Campaign, his account is also frustrating for the lack of precise details on the locations in which these actions took place. Thus it is we turn to archaeology, with its analysis of the physical accumulation of human activity, to fill in these details. As such, the potential for archaeology should be quite great. Battlefield archaeology is a stimulating discipline because it presents us with the evidence of an event that took place over a short period of time, sometimes over the course of only a single day, but an event that often played a seminal role in history. Alesia presents us with all of these features in abundance.

During the nineteenth century, Napoleon III's interest was sparked by Caesar's works and the results of his search at Alesia form the basis for many modern studies of ancient France. But his and other subsequent research is often complicated by rushed conclusions or contradictions between evidence and desired results. More modern archaeological techniques have gone some way towards recovering this position.

Before we can excavate the battlefield we must first find it. This is more difficult than it sounds, because often the place only exists as a memory, without being specifically located. This is especially the case the further we go back in time. Although we have Caesar's recollections, disputes between scholars over the translation of different ancient authors, their interpretation and recounting of events and the various locations that can be extrapolated, present us with different sites for Alesia.

Aftermath

Until recently, three towns competed for the title of Vercingetorix's Alesia: Chaux-des-Crotenay in the Jura Mountains, Alaise in Franche-Comté and Alise-Sainte-Reine in Côte-d'Or. Alise-Sainte-Reine is currently the most likely of these places and most scholars confirm this. But even though there is compelling evidence of a Roman presence at Alise-Sainte-Reine, many details of Caesar's description have been used to argue against the archaeology. Contrasting Caesar's descriptions with the archaeology shows up a number of discrepancies in his description of the circum-vallation. Some argue that Alise-Sainte-Reine is too small for even a revised figure of 80,000–100,000 Gauls. But this is to suggest that only the oppidum of Alesia was occupied. The likelihood is that the entire 95 hectares of the top of Mont Auxois was occupied. In fact, Caesar states that when the Gauls arrived at Alesia:

'The army of the Gauls had filled all the space under the wall, comprising the part of the hill which looked to the rising sun, and had drawn in front a trench and a stone wall 6 feet high.'

[Caesar, *The Gallic War*, VII. 69]

This means that the majority of the army camped outside the walls ('under the wall') of the oppidum on the western unoccupied part of the hill. There it was necessary to build trenches and walls to defend themselves because up until then the area had been unoccupied. Other authors argue that the archaeology from Alise-Sainte-Reine did not match Caesar's description of two ditches that were part of the circumvallation. Archaeological excavation has shown that either one, two or three ditches were used in different places around the circumvallation. The obstacles he describes are sometimes in front of the ditches and sometimes between. The ditches have been found to be 50 feet wide rather than Caesar's 80 feet. Similarly, the towers have been found to be 50, 60 and 180 feet apart rather than Caesar's description of 80 feet apart. Although the variation in obstacles found contrasts with Caesar's precise description these details do not necessarily argue against Caesar's descriptions, and thereby the location of Alesia. What we need to realize is that the description Caesar gives is a general impression of the works. His audience would not want to know the mundanities of the individual make-up of each defensive system and its construction. They only required a general feeling of the defences and their structure, so Caesar was simply being economic with his words, and we should not take his words too literally.

Stoffel's excavations provide some of the most compelling evidence of the attribution of Alise-Sainte-Reine as Alesia. He dug half-metre-wide trenches, across interesting features or in areas where archaeology was expected. The results obtained led the nineteenth century excavators to distinguish two lines of defences, which were attributed to an inner circumvallation and an outer contravallation. Within this area different types of camp were also identified, including large fortified camps that they identified with a letter, and smaller forts within the lines of the circumvallation, which they identified with a number (*see* map section). Many of these labels were applied without any unequivocal archaeological investigation, and this was particularly so with regard to the smaller forts. Hence we must be cautious when using these classifications today.

Napoleon III thought he had located the twenty-three camps that Caesar mentions, but only a few of these have been confirmed using modern aerial photography or excavation. More recent excavations have mainly been used to clarify the nineteenth century findings, as Caesar doesn't provide us with any useful information on the exact location of any of the camps. Even though modern archaeological techniques are well in advance of those available to Stoffel, there are still limitations in an ability to understand the nature of the archaeological record. Agricultural practices, erosion, recent tree growth and urban development have all played a part in obscuring the remains of the siegeworks, often confusing or masking the evidence. The quality of the geology helps to clarify some of the archaeology as much of the soil is made up of light-coloured limestone. When this was dug into in antiquity, the unattended or dismantled ditches would consequently fill up with dark topsoil that makes their discovery much easier. But even with these clear indications to go by, mistakes can happen. During Stoffel's excavation of Camp C, the excavators dug two long trenches in hopes of finding the gate. Unfortunately these ran either side of the gate and so they missed the evidence they were looking for by mere centimetres. This area was excavated more widely in 1994 and excavations showed very interesting gate defences. Excavations by Stoffel at the base of Mont Réa were far more successful, recovering large amounts of weapons. This has led some to connect this area with the final decisive battle that took place at Alesia. In the wider context, the archaeological evidence from the site as a whole around Alise-Sainte-Reine displays all the hallmarks of its identification as Alesia, an attribution that is now generally accepted by most academics.

One could be forgiven for thinking that the statue of Vercingetorix that stands on Alesia today is also an accurate representation of the man. In some ways it is, but mainly because it reflects the Gallic ideal rather than the man. The actual image it portrays is the most accurate depiction that could be achieved when it was built in the nineteenth century. Today we

Aftermath

see the Gallic warriors of Vercingetorix's army very differently. The arms and armour depicted in the sculpture of Vercingetorix, whilst replicating actual items discovered in the vicinity of Alesia, are not of Vercingetorix's time, but are in fact from the Bronze Age. Similarly, the face depicted on the sculpture is not that of Vercingetorix, but that of the monument's creator, the French leader Napoleon III. Coins minted in the period with the face of Vercingetorix on them suggest he may not even have had a moustache.

The way in which we see Vercingetorix is inexorably linked with the fortunes of Napoleon the III, the last ruling monarch of France. A nephew of Napoleon I, Prince Louis-Napoléon Bonaparte grew up in exile after his uncle's defeat at Waterloo in 1815. After Napoleon II's death in exile in 1836, the Prince became Napoleon III, heir to the throne of France. That same year Napoleon III staged a failed coup against the Republic and as a result was exiled to the United States of America. From here in 1840 he tried again to regain his throne. This time he was caught and imprisoned in France, from where he later escaped to Britain to continue his attempts at French rule. In 1848 revolution overturned the French establishment and resulted in the creation of the Second Republic. Napoleon III immediately ran for office and won a seat in the assembly, ultimately winning the presidency by a landslide. Napoleon III's position as head of the government represented the restoration of order. The people of France linked him to his uncle in the hope of strong governance, social stability and the revival of military and national greatness. In this respect, the connection between the hopes placed by the Gauls in Vercingetorix and those placed by their descendants in Napoleon III seem to be aligned. Napoleon III's autocratic side was to come to the fore though after he was turned down by the assembly for an unconstitutional change to the restrictions on his presidency. After deciding to take what he had not been offered, on the anniversary of Napoleon I's coronation nearly half a century earlier Napoleon III staged a coup d'état and seized power in 1851. Napoleon applied himself to sidelining parliament and ushering in a Second French Empire. During the course of his rule, Napoleon III was forced to roll back some of his monarchy to mollify his opponents and, luckily for France, Napoleon's attempts to modernize coincided with an upturn in the economy and so a rapid period of development ensued.

The rude health of the economy consolidated Napoleon III's position and allowed him time to indulge his interests in the past. Napoleon III empathized with his Gallic forebears, particularly Vercingetorix, and so was favourable to archaeological work that searched for the location of Alesia. This culminated in the excavation of the works at Alise-Sainte-

Reine and the building of a statue to Vercingetorix.

In 1865 Napoleon III had erected a 7m-tall statue of Vercingetorix on a plinth at the peak of the hill at Alesia. Sculpted in bronze by Aimé Millet, unsurprisingly the image of Vercingetorix looks remarkably like Napoleon III himself. The monument was designed by Eugène Emmanuel Viollet-le-Duc, who was previously famed for his medieval restorations and for ushering in a Gothic revival in nineteenth-century France. Viollet-le-Duc continued this revival of the ancient sprit of France in an inscription on the base of the monument which reads:

> La Gaule unie
> Formant une seule nation
> Animée d'un même espirit
> Peut défier l'Univers.

> (A united Gaul/Formed into a single nation/Stirred by the same spirit/Can defy the World.)

This inscription was to ring hollow five years later when Napoleon III declared war on Prussia, thus beginning the Franco-Prussian War of 1870. After only a single year's fighting, France was facing defeat and Napoleon III was facing ruin. Two days after being captured at the Battle of Sedan, Napoleon III was deposed and the Third Republic was established, the war continuing without him into 1871.

Two years after France's defeat Napoleon III, like his hero Vercingetorix, died in exile, albeit in the much finer circumstances of rural England. In contrast to his rhetoric 'L'Empire, c'est la paix' (Empire means peace), Napoleon III's rule had involved France in a series of expansionist overseas wars that were to be the precursor to his final defeat. In most regards Napoleon III's circumstances were wholly unlike those of his Gallic hero, Napoleon's behaviour betraying far more of Caesar than of Vercingetorix.

Napoleon III's romantic idealization of the past is a familiar theme of the time and is visible in the large and dramatic sculptures and paintings of the nineteenth century. They portray dramatic scenes, inspired by the spectacular events of the Antique world. The depiction of Vercingetorix in these pictures is often most dramatic, tinged as they are with the melancholy of defeat. In Lionel-Noel Royer's 1899 painting, 'Vercingétorix jette ses armes devant César' (Vercingetorix throws down his weapons at Caesar's feet), a defiant Vercingetorix disdainfully approaches Caesar on his horse and, reining him in, throws his arms to the ground with a look of defiance. Here Vercingetorix is portrayed as the defiant leader, seemingly only defeated by circumstance and symbolizing the very essence of Gallic pride. This image of Vercingetorix as the defiant 'Celt' is still alive today.

Aftermath

A recent movie entitled *Vercingétorix: la légende du druide roi* ('Vercingetorix: the legend of the druid king'), released as 'The Druids' in English, portrayed Vercingetorix as a peaceful chieftain simply protecting his home and provoked into fighting by a sly Caesar. The film's tag line – 'His people made him a leader. The empire made him a renegade. History made him a hero' – continues the portrayal of Vercingetorix as a contemporary hero in the mould of many Hollywood icons. These images of Vercingetorix betray the hand of contemporary culture, rather than the balanced view of history. When we look at Vercingetorix we should not see him as a French folk-hero or hero of national independence or even, as some authors have gone so far as to suggest, as a stooge of Caesar's, put there to defeat the people of France. This perception of Vercingetorix is based on modern concepts infused with national ideologies, and stem from a modern viewpoint that has been imposed on an ancient context. If we are to understand Vercingetorix, and the Battle of Alesia, we need to discard any modern notions and see them within their contemporary world-view. The best place to experience the realities of the events of the Alesia Campaign are at the places themselves. The most important of these are Mont Beuvray and Alise-Sainte-Reine.

Visiting Bibracte: Modern-day Mont Beuvray

Bibracte is seen as a national treasure and lies within the 1,000 hectares of the Morvan Regional Natural Park, near Autun in Burgundy, France. Located on Mont Beuvray, the highest of a range of mountains in the region, this position can mean it is also extremely wet. The hill fort can be accessed by foot, although trees, the slope of the hill and its sheer size conceal the arduous nature of the task. Access is also given to vehicles and the use of a car allows easy movement between the most important spots. At the foot of the site is an interpretive museum, The Museum of Celtic Civilization. This modern building places Bibracte within the wider context of 'Celtic' culture in Europe. A permanent exhibition displays artefacts from the hill fort, along with pictures, audio-visual displays, models and life-size reproductions. Much of the display has English translations and an English audio guide to the museum and a guided tour of the hill fort itself are available.

Visiting Alesia: Modern-day Alise-Sainte-Reine

The oppidum of Alesia was located on the western tip of Mont Auxois, where modern-day Alise-Sainte-Reine is situated. The village lies 6km east of the town of Venarey-les-Laumes, about 60km north-west of Dijon and 14km south-east of Montbard, in Burgundy. At the time of writing there are few indications of the battle on the ground. The most important clue is the statue of Vercingetorix himself, which is placed on the tip of Mont Auxois, where the oppidum originally stood. Further across the hilltop lies the later Roman city, which was built on the hill after the Battle of Alesia. At present there is a museum providing some historical details of the battle, although it focuses mainly on the Roman town and its extensive ruins. A map of the battle is located on the D103 on the Plain of Laumes, but provides only limited information. The French government has put plans in place to rectify this sorry situation. In 2010 two new museums will be opened, built by Bernard Tschumi architects. One on the Plain of Laumes will be an interpretive centre with a reconstructed camp, ramparts and defences built nearby. The other will be a museum built on Mont Auxois itself, with a dominating view overlooking the defences. Along with these new centres, a guided driving route and walking paths will provide better access to the battlefield and a fuller experience of the events of 52BC.

Appendices

Vercingetorix's Commanders

The list of Gallic personalities given here is by no means representative of all the Gauls mentioned in Caesar's *Gallic War*, but includes characters that played a part in the Alesia Campaign.

Cavarillus

Put in command of the Aedui infantry before the Siege of Gergovia (modern-day Gergovie), Cavarillus was captured at the Battle of Mont Reux on the first day of the Alesia Campaign.

Commius

Set up by Caesar as a puppet ruler of the Atrebates in northern Gaul in 55BC, Commius acted as Caesar's intermediary in Britain the following year. In 53BC he was used by Caesar to control the Menapii and the Morini tribes, and was a loyal client through the revolts of the next two years. But at some point Commius' allegiances changed, because in 52BC he took supreme command of the forces against Caesar. Caesar himself says that Commius 'loathed Rome' and after Alesia he led another rebellion, this time in support of the Bellovaci. Following this unsuccessful revolt, Commius fled to the German tribes to ferment further revolt. Caesar tried unsuccessfully to get the Germans to release him, and so he finally resolved to have him assassinated. Caesar sent a Roman Centurion, Gaius Volusenus Quadratus, to do the job but Commius managed to escape with only a serious head wound. Within the year, he was back again in his home region of Belgium. The last we hear of Commius is when he sent envoys to Marcus Antonius saying he would submit, only requesting he would not be required to come into the presence of any Roman in the future. This request was granted and hostages were received.

Conconnetodumnus

One of the leaders of the Carnutes tribe from the Loire valley, Conconnetodumnus was involved in leading the surprise attack on *Cenabum* that sparked Vercingetorix's rebellion.

Convictolitavis

One of the contenders for Magistracy of the Aedui, Caesar gave in favour of Convictolitavis because his opponent, Cotus, was legally ineligible for the position. Immediately afterwards, the Aedui sided with Vercingetorix in the revolt against Rome. Caesar says that Vercingetorix bribed Convictolitavis, although

Caesar may just be covering up the fact that he chose the wrong man when he decided the election. Convictolitavis convened a tribal council at the Aedui capital Bibracte and he made a treaty of peace with Vercingetorix there.

Correus

Leader of the Bellovaci tribe during their revolt in 51BC, friend and ally of Commius.

Cotuatus

One of the leaders of the Carnutes involved in the surprise attack on Cenabum.

Cotus

Contender for Magistrate of the Aedui. Caesar made Cotus resign from the magistracy because his brother Valetiacus had held the post of magistrate of the Aedui the previous year; magistrates were not allowed to hold the office while a family member who had also held the office was alive. Caesar also said that his election was not official because it had been held in secret, did not call the whole assembly, and was not conducted at the proper time. Cotus was the commander of one of the Gallic cavalry units at the Battle of Mont Reux, and he was captured in the battle on the first day of the Alesia Campaign.

Critognatus

Arverni noble who gave a rallying oration that led to the expelling of the non-combatant Mandubii from Alesia.

Eporedorix (1)

Powerful young Aedui noble who originally sided with Caesar, Eporedorix successfully supported Convictolitavis as the Magistrate of the Aedui. Initially siding with Rome, Eporedorix managed to get Caesar to stop the Aedui siding with Vercingetorix, brought Litaviccus' treachery to Caesar's attention and supported Caesar with cavalry for his attack on Gergovia. Once the Aedui had been deceived into revolting against Caesar, Eporedorix was compelled to fight on Vercingetorix's side. Eporedorix was given supreme command of part of the Gallic relief army at the Battle of Alesia.

Eporedorix (2)

Another commander of the Aedui, this Eporedorix is not connected to the leader above. Eporedorix engaged in war against the Sequani before Caesar's arrival in Gaul. Eporedorix was part of Vercingetorix's army and was captured at the Battle of Mont Reux on the first day of the Alesia Campaign.

Gobannitio

Vercingetorix's uncle, who cast him out of Gergovia for beginning the uprising against Rome in 52BC.

Appendix II

Litaviccus

Aedui noble who was put in command of 10,000 men sent to aid Caesar, when he was besieging Gergovia in 52BC. On his way to Caesar, Litaviccus told his men that the Romans had destroyed the cavalry and their leaders, Eporedorix and Viridomarus, had been put to death. He got the infantry to agree to side with Vercingetorix's revolt, and messages were sent across the territory marking this change of sides. At Gergovia, once his deception was made evident, Litaviccus fled into the oppidum with only his aides.

Sedulius

General and Chief of the Lemovices, slain during the action on Mont Réa during the Battle of Alesia.

Teutomatus

King of the Nitiobriges tribe from Aquitania in south-west France. Prior to Alesia, his father Ollovico had been given the title 'friend of Senate'. At the beginning of 52BC Teutomatus joined Vercingetorix with a large number of cavalry from his home region of Aquitania. Teutomatus was nearly captured at Gergovia by Caesar's army.

Vercingetorix

Chieftain of the Arverni who led the forces of Gaul in revolt against the Romans during 52BC, events that led to the Battle of Alesia. His father was once the most powerful leader in Gaul, but was killed when he attempted to become its king. Vercingetorix was initially expelled by his uncle Gobannitio and other leaders of the tribe, for fomenting revolt. Vercingetorix found support amongst other Arverni outcasts and ultimately was hailed king by them. He took his fight against Caesar to the rest of Gaul and led a revolt through the tribes that ended in the final catastrophic battle at Alesia.

Viridomarus

Young Aedui of humble rank, whom Caesar raised to power. Viridomarus unsuccessfully supported Cotus as the Magistrate of the Aedui and supported Caesar with cavalry for his attack on Gergovia. After the revolt of the Aedui he was one of the supreme commanders of the Gallic Relief army. Once Litaviccus had tricked the Aedui into revolting against Caesar, Viridomarus was compelled to fight on Vercingetorix's side. Viridomarus was given supreme command of part of the Gallic relief army at the Battle of Alesia.

Appendix II:
The Gallic Tribes

Attempting to locate the tribes of Gaul in the period around 52BC is a complex and problematic proposition. Caesar provides us with the names of a number of tribes, but mostly these are simply passing mentions. Today the actual limits and size of the territories are still unclear. This is made worse by the fact that ancient authors often provide conflicting locations for a single tribe. Similarly, tribes often wandered from their original location or were amalgamated with, or absorbed by, other tribes. Given these factors, the modern French Departments are used below to locate the tribes with a modern reference point. Although these locations are close to their original locations, they should not be taken as literal translations of the original tribal territories.

Aedui

Occupied the modern-day departments of Saône-et-Loire, Loire, Rhône and Nièvre. The Aedui are said to have had a number of dependents, including the Segusiavi, Ambivareti, and Aulerci Brannovices. The Aedui had a long-standing association with Rome and were given the title of 'brothers and kinsmen' of the Roman people. Their electoral political system reflected some of this connection. Caesar considered the Aedui the most important tribe in Gaul and they had long struggled for supremacy with the Arverni tribe. In 52BC they asked Caesar to help with a political dispute between Cotus and Convictolitavis that had brought them to the edge of civil war. After this event, Caesar tells us that the Aedui were tricked into joining in Vercingetorix's revolt. Certainly after Vercingetorix was defeated, Caesar welcomed the Aedui back as a Roman client. The power base held at Bibracte was removed to a new Roman city nearby, at modern-day Autun. The Aedui had a number of client kingdoms under them, including Segusiavi, Ambivareti, Aulerci Brannovices and Blannovii.

Ambiani

Occupied the modern-day department of Somme. A Belgic people, they were one of the tribes that rebelled in the Belgic Campaign of 57BC. They also fought against Caesar at Alesia and again in the Bellovaci Campaign.

Andes

Occupied the southern part of the modern-day department of Mayenne on the upper Loire. Caesar stationed legions in their territory before the Alesia Campaign. The Andes subsequently sent men to fight at Alesia.

Aremoricae

Tribes coming under the term Aremoricae were said by Caesar to come from a region that equates to the modern regions of Basse-Normandie and Bretagne in north-west France. Caesar also said that these tribes spoke the same language. Included in these tribes were the Curisolites, Redones, Ambibarii, Caletes, Osismi, Lemovices, Veneti, and Venelli. The Aremoricae tribes were closely linked with similar tribes in south-west Britain, who to this day speak similar language dialects. In 57BC most of the tribes were forced to submit to Caesar, but the following year they revolted, probably as a result of understanding the onerous burdens that Roman rule placed upon them.

Appendix II

Arverni

Occupied an area in the modern-day department of Puy-de-Dôme. Their name was derived from the god Avernus and ultimately came to be applied to the region of the Auvergne. The Arverni capital was the important oppida of Gergovia (near modern-day Clermont-Ferrand). The Arverni had at least four clients, including dependants Eleuteti, Cadurci, Gabali, and Vellavii. Caesar says they were the most quarrelsome of peoples and records their long-standing dispute with the Aedui for power in Gaul. The Arverni certainly produced one of Gallic history's most quarrelsome of figures – Vercingetorix.

Atrebates

Occupied the modern-day department of Nord Pas-de-Calais. A Belgic people, they were one of the tribes that rebelled in the Belgic Campaign of 57BC. Their capital was at Nemetocenna, the modern-day city of Arras, where Caesar spent the winter of 51–50BC.

Aulerci

The Aulerci occupied the regions around the modern-day department of Sarthe in Pays-de-la-Loire. The Aulerci is an encompassing term that refers to a group of peoples, possibly coming from a single root ethnicity. Their name means 'Those who are far from their origins' and so may refer to a dispersion of peoples. There were four tribes that made up the confederation: the Aulerci Brannovices, Aulerci Cenomani, Aulerci Diablintes and Aulerci Eburovices. Of these, Caesar mentions all bar the Aulerci Diablintes as taking part in the Alesia Campaign. The name of the tribe Aulerci Brannovices means 'People of the Raven'. The capital of the Aulerci Cenomani was at *Vindinum*, modern-day Le Mans. The name of the tribe Aulerci Eburovices means 'People of the Yew'. Their position as a subtribe of the Aulerci is clear from the modern-day name for the Aulerci capital, Évreux, derived from the name Eburovices tribe. The Aulerci as a whole were brought under submission to Rome in 57BC, and were part of Sabinus' abortive attempt at revolt the following year.

Bellovaci

Occupied an area in the modern-day department of Oise, north of Paris. One of the strongest and most numerous tribes in northern Gaul, this tribe was conquered in 57BC as part of Caesar's actions against the Belgae. The Romans built a city in the territory called *Caesaromagus*, but its modern name Beauvais, is drawn from its original name, Bellovacum.

Bituriges

Occupied the modern-day departments of Indre and Creuse. Their capital was at Avaricum, modern-day Bourges. The name of their tribe means 'Kings of the world' which must refer to the power they once held, because by the time of Caesar's invasion the tribe was a dependant of the Aedui. This connection meant that Vercingetorix recruited them personally in the early part of the revolt of 52BC when the Aedui were still pro-Roman. Caesar attacked their oppidum of Noviodunum (modern-day Neung sur Beuvron) and Avaricum (modern-day Bourges), their largest and best-fortified oppidum during the first stages of the Gallic revolt. Caesar's actions prompted Vercingetorix to begin his scorched earth policy, burning twenty towns in the region.

Boii

Tribe that was associated with areas along the Alps and southern France, finally they were settled by Caesar in the territory of the Aedui and under their protection. At the beginning of the Alesia Campaign in 52BC, they sided with Caesar, which led to their oppidum at Gorgobina being besieged by Vercingetorix. After the Aedui sided with the rebels, they were obligated through their connection to fight with Vercingetorix.

Cadurci

Occupied the modern-day department of Tarn-et-Garonne in the west of Midi-Pyrénées.

Carnutes

Occupied land in part of the modern departments of Eure-et-Loir, Loiret and Loir-et-Cher, south-west of Paris. Their capital was at Autricum, modern-day Chartres, considered by Caesar to be the centre of Gallic religion. They were dependants of the Remi. The Carnutes were unhappy about Roman interference in their interests. In 56BC Caesar had placed a client king, Tasgetius, in control of the Carnutes. In 54BC the tribe had had enough and killed him as part of a widespread revolt in the north of Gaul that year. Further rumblings continued into 53BC and the next year the Carnutes were in revolt again, this time striking the first blow of the Gallic insurrection of 52BC. Led by two nobles, Cotuatus and Conconnetodumnus, the Carnutes attacked Roman merchants who were exploiting the town of Cenabum (modern-day Gien). This action ultimately led to widespread revolt across Gaul and to Caesar's Alesia Campaign. After Alesia, although the Carnutes supported further revolt, they were a broken force and finally submitted to Caesar for good, in 51BC.

Gabali

Occupied the modern-day department of Aveyron in the east of Midi-Pyrénées.

Helvetii

The Helvetii occupied an area of land that is modern-day Switzerland. Caesar says that the Helvetii wanted to gain more power and so they planned to invade Gaul, along with their neighbours the Raurici, Tulingi and the Latovici. Their route led them through the Roman Province of Transalpine Gaul and the Roman client kingdoms of the Sequani and Aedui. Caesar was determined to stop them, even building a wall across the route to do this. After a long chase through Gaul Caesar subdued the Helvetii, but this action led to Caesar's direct intervention in the politics of Gaul over the following eight years.

Lemovices

Occupied the modern-day departments of Haute-Vienne and Corrèze in Limousin. Their territory was rich in gold mines and they had a number of hill forts. One of the initial tribes recruited to Vercingetorix's revolt in the early part of 52BC, Sedulius a chief of the tribe, was killed at Alesia.

Lexovii

Occupied the modern-day department of Calvados in Basse-Normandie. Their capital was called *Civitas Lexoviorum* by the Romans and was located near Lisieux. The Lexovii took part in Sabinus' abortive attempt at revolt in the Maritime Provinces against the Romans in 56BC.

Mandubii

Occupied the modern-day department of Côte-d'Or in Burgundy. Their name probably means 'Horse people'. The tribe lived in the hill fort of Alesia and the surrounding vicinity.

Mediomatrices

Occupied the modern-day department of Vosges. Their name probably means 'Good kings of the middle lands', perhaps reflecting their location on the border between Gaul and Germany.

Morini

Occupied the modern-day department of Nord Pas-de-Calais. The tribal name probably means 'Coastal people' and they rebelled against Rome's Belgic Campaign of 57BC and Venetic Campaign of 56BC. In 55BC they appeared to submit to Caesar, allowing him to invade Britain. However, this was to be short-lived, as members of the tribe attacked Roman ships when they became separated from the main army. After these events Caesar felt it necessary to place a puppet ruler, Commius, in control of the Morini. This action did not have the desired effect. The following year, the Morini sent men to relieve Vercingetorix's army and Commius was at their head.

Nervii

Occupied an area that corresponds with the Scheldt region of modern-day Belgium and Netherlands. They were called by Caesar one of the most warlike of the Belgic tribes and their actions lived up to this reputation. They were the main tribe that rebelled in the Belgic Campaign of 57BC and were virtually wiped out. However, their forces had regained strength in the next few years and made further war in 54BC, 53BC and in the Alesia Campaign of 52BC.

Nitiobriges

Occupied the modern-day department of Lot-et-Garonne in south-east Aquitaine. Their capital, *Aginnon*, seems to be located near modern-day Agen and their name probably means 'Those who have their own country'.

Parisii

Lived on the banks of the Seine and gave their name to modern-day Paris. Their chief town was Lutetia Parisiorum, modern-day Paris. Although they were a small tribe they had importance beyond their size. The Parisii were closely connected with the Senones, with whom they had formed a single state. The Parisii were one of the initial tribes recruited to Vercingetorix's revolt in the early part of 52BC.

Petrocorii

Occupied the modern-day department of Dordogne. Their capital was named after the tribe and was located at the modern-day city of Périgueux. The tribal name Petrocorii means 'Four tribes' and so probably represents the conjoining of a number of tribes.

Pictones

Occupied the modern-day departments of Maine-et-Loire, Deux-Sèvres and Vendée on the Bay of Biscay. Their chief town *Lemonum* was located near modern-day Poitiers. Caesar noted that the Pictones were one of the more civilized tribes. They were instructed to supply Caesar with ships for the Venetic Campaign of 56BC, but after this experience the Pictones quickly sided with Vercingetorix in 52BC.

Rauraci

Occupied the region of modern-day Alsace. The Rauraci took part in the migration of the Helvetii in 58BC, after which they were made to return to their homes once Caesar succeeded in stopping their movements.

Ruteni

Occupied the modern-day department of Tarn in the south of Midi-Pyrénées. Their name means 'The red ones'. The Ruteni were included in the rebellion by Vercingetorix shortly after it began.

Santoni

Occupied the modern-day department of Charente-Maritime on the Bay of Biscay. Little is known about the Santones, although their capital was probably at the modern-day city of Saintes. Caesar tells us that the Helvetii were planning to migrate to the land of the Santoni in 58BC. During his campaign against the Veneti in 56BC, Caesar instructed the Santoni to supply him with ships for the campaign. This forced requisition, plus the actions of the Romans in Brittany, may have stoked resentment in the Santoni against Caesar, ultimately prompting them to side with Vercingetorix in the Alesia Campaign.

Senones

Occupied the modern-day departments of Seine-et-Marne, Loiret and Yonne, south-east of Paris, with their capital at *Agedincon* in modern-day Sens. The Senones were closely connected with the Parisii, with whom they had formed a single state. Caesar says that the Senones were powerful and influential. Even though they were one of the more rebellious tribes, the Senones originally allied with Caesar. But in 54BC, Caesar attempted to appoint a puppet king, Cavarinus, to rule over them and capitalize on their influence. This action backfired on Caesar, the Senones unsuccessfully attempted to kill Cavarinus and then went on to engage in hostilities with Rome in 53BC. Following Vercingetorix's revolt in the early part of 52BC, the Senones' oppida of Vellaunodunum (modern-day Trigueres) was besieged by Caesar and fell within three days. Much of the action prior to the Battle of Alesia took part in the territory of the Senones.

Sequani

Occupied a region that now includes Franche-Comte and parts of Burgundy. Their largest oppidum was at *Vesontio*, modern-day Besançon. During the migration of the Helvetii the Sequani helped, by allowing them to skirt Caesar's defences and travel through their land. The Sequani, along with the Arverni, were engaged in intertribal conflict against the Aedui before Caesar's invasion. As a result of this conflict they employed German mercenaries, which backfired upon them because the mercenaries refused to leave their territory and subjugated the Sequani. They requested Roman aid in removing the mercenaries, but Caesar simply replaced the Germans with his clients the Aedui, the tribe that the Sequani had been fighting originally. After this turn of events the Sequani had no affection for Caesar.

Suessiones

Occupied the modern-day department of Marne to the east of modern-day Paris. A Belgic people, they were one of the tribes that rebelled in the Belgic Campaign of 57BC. Caesar mentions a King Galba, and also a previous King Diviciacus, who were leaders of most of the Belgae and some tribes in Britain. Their capital was at Noviodunum, which is probably modern-day Soissons.

Turoni

Occupied the modern-day department of Indre-et-Loire. Their capital was probably at modern-day Tours. Caesar imposed his legions in Turoni territory to intimidate their neighbours, the Carnutes. Whether this was actually the case or because he didn't trust the Turoni, the result was the same: the Turoni became restless. As a result of these actions the Turoni were one of the initial tribes that sided with Vercingetorix early in the Alesia Campaign.

Veliocasses

Occupied the modern-day department of Seine-Maritime. Their main city, Rotomagus, is modern-day Rouen. The Veliocasses – not a numerous tribe – took part in the Belgic revolt in 56BC. Later they sent men to support Vercingetorix at Alesia in 52BC and the following year took part in the revolt of the Belgic peoples in 51BC.

Appendix III:
Caesar's Commanders

The list of Roman personalities listed here is by no means representative of all the Romans mentioned in Caesar's *Gallic War*. The Romans listed below are some of the characters who played a part in the Alesia Campaign. It is a shame that despite having so many names, we cannot as yet place them in direct relationship to the legions they commanded.

Antistius Reginus, Gaius

Legate who, along with Gaius Caninius Rebilus and two legions, defended the camp on Mont Réa that was attacked by Vercassivellaunus. After Alesia, during the winter of 52BC, he was placed in charge of the Ambivareti.

Antonius, Marcus

One of Caesar's legates, he was in control of the defences on the Plain of Laumes, along with Gaius Trebonius. After Alesia Caesar made him a *quaestor*, giving him automatic membership of the Senate. Marcus Antonius took part in the Bellovacian Campaign in 50BC and remained loyal to Caesar during the Civil War. After Caesar's assassination Marcus Antonius was one of the Triumvirate that ran Roman affairs. In 31BC he fell out with one of the Triumvirate, Octavian (later Emperor Augustus), a dispute that led to further civil war. His army was defeated at the Battle of Actium, after which Marcus Antonius took his own life, alongside his lover, Cleopatra, in Egypt the following year.

Aristius, Marcus

Tribune in charge of the oppidum of Cabillonum during the assault on Gergovia, during Vercingetorix's revolt. Aristius led the Roman soldiers and merchants out of the oppidum under the protection of the Aedui. Once they were in the open the Aedui surrounded and attacked the Roman column, later they repented their actions.

Caninius Rebilus, Gaius

Legate, who along with Gaius Antistius Reginus and two legions, defended the camp on Mont Réa that was attacked by Vercassivellaunus. In the winter of 52BC, after Alesia, he was in put charge of maintaining peace in the territory of the Ruteni. He was made consul in 45BC.

Fabius, Gaius

Legate in a command position throughout the Gallic Campaign. In 54BC he took a legion to control the Morini and Atrebates in northern Gaul. The following year he took part in the Treveri Campaign. During the revolt of the Aedui in 52BC, Gaius Fabius was left in charge of Caesar's camp at Gergovia when Caesar was away. At Alesia, he was sent with cohorts in the direction of Decimus Junius Brutus to deal with Vercingetorix's final assault on the circumvallation. After Alesia he was stationed with Lucius Minucius Basilus and two legions in the territory of the Remi to prevent an uprising by the Bellovaci. During the following year he took twenty-five cohorts and successfully brought the western tribes into line (probably the Santoni). He took over part of the siegeworks at Uxellodunum near modern-day Puy D'Issolu, finally being sent to the territory of the Aedui in 51BC.

Fabius, Lucius

Centurion of the Eighth Legion determined to be the first to climb the walls of Gergovia during the attack there. Ultimately, he was surrounded, hacked down and thrown from the defences.

Julius Caesar, Gaius

Leader of the Roman forces, it was at Caesar's behest that the Roman army permanently moved into Gaul. Using the grounds of shielding Gallic tribes under his protection from the intrusion of German tribes, Caesar spent the next eight years advancing Rome's political and territorial interests in Gaul. While his armies were thus engaged he also used the opportunity to make pre-emptive strikes into Germany and Britain. Although he states that his motivations were dominated by Gallic welfare, his actions betray the hand of a deft politician. When the Gauls rebelled against his presence and meddling in their affairs in 52BC, Caesar saw his opportunity to bring them to heel once and for all. Through the Alesia Campaign, Caesar was able to capitalize on the fluctuating fortunes of the war, finally crushing Vercingetorix's rebellion at Alesia. In Caesar's own words 'the whole of Gaul was now conquered' and so he went on to greater things, confident of a strong army behind him. The Gallic War had put him on a par with Pompey and Crassus, the two other Roman consuls of the Triumvirate. Things came to a head in 50BC when Pompey, through the Senate, ordered Caesar to step down, along with his armies. Fearing prosecution and marginalization, Caesar – ever the adventurer – took the aggressive decision to march his armies on Rome. On 9 January 49BC, in defiance of Roman law, Caesar crossed the Rubicon with the Fourteenth Legion. By this action he precipitated four years of civil war, although most of it took place outside the Italian peninsula. The war drew to a close in

Caesar's Gallic Triumph

47BC when Pompey fled to Egypt, where he was killed as a sop to Caesar. The war dragged on for another two years until Caesar finally defeated his old comrade, Labienus, at Munda in Spain. In 44BC Caesar was proclaimed dictator for life – a life that was to be cut short at the age of fifty-six by an assassin's blade.

Junius Brutus, Decimus

Legate commander of the Roman fleet in the war with the Veneti in 56BC. At Alesia he was commanded by Caesar to take six cohorts to deal with Vercingetorix's breach of the Roman defences, an action that proved unsuccessful. Brutus became one of Caesar's closest aides; in his will, Caesar named Brutus as his heir. But Brutus was one of the conspirators in Caesar's assassination, their intimacy resulting in his being selected to lead Caesar to his murder. (Not to be confused with Marcus Junius Brutus who took the lead role in the assassination and was immortalized by Shakespeare.)

Labienus, Titus

Chief legate of Caesar's army, he was regularly placed in charge of the army when Caesar was away, taking significant roles in the Helvetii Campaign, against the Nervii in 57BC and against the Treveri in 56BC. He remained in charge of Gaul while Caesar was in Britain in 55BC, and again in 54BC. The following year he was engaged in actions during the Treveri Campaign and at the beginning of the revolt of the Aedui he was in the control of the territory of the Senones and Parisii. At Alesia he was put in charge of the northern defences, his camp being placed in a highly significant position on Mont Bussy. On the last day of fighting he went with six cohorts to relieve his distressed soldiers in the fiercest fighting against Vercassivellaunus. After Alesia he fought in the campaign of the Bellovaci and attempted to assassinate the Gallic leader Commius. In 51BC Caesar made Labienus governor of Cisalpine Gaul. Even though Labienus fought loyally with Caesar's army, he turned against his general after Alesia. Labienus seems to have built up a deep resentment for Caesar during his experiences in Gaul, feeling he was never properly compensated for all the work he did on Caesar's behalf. Caesar came away with all the credit and Labienus had only a governorship, which finally pushed him to side with Pompey in the civil war against Caesar. Defeat ultimately came for Labienus in the final battle of the civil war, at Munda in Spain, where his army was overrun and he died in the fighting.

Minucius Basilus, Lucius

Legate who took part in the Treveri Campaign in 52BC.

Sempronius Rutilus, Marcus

Legate serving with Labienus after Alesia in the territory of the Sequani.

Sextius, Titus

Legate of the Thirteenth Legion at Gergovia who was in charge of the Bituriges after Alesia.

Appendix IV

Sulpicius Rufus, Publius

Legate in charge of the harbour when Caesar crossed to Britain in 55BC. After Alesia in 52BC he was in charge of the territory of Aedui.

Trebonius, Gaius

In 54BC he took part in the invasion of Britain and later commanded a legion in the territory of the Belgae. The following year he was again in action in the region, this time against the Aduatuci. In 52BC he was in charge of the siege against Vellaunodunum, the oppidum of the Senones. At Alesia he commanded the important defences on the Plain of Laumes, along with Marcus Antonius. In the winter of 52BC, Gaius Trebonius was placed in charge of Cenabum, the town that sparked Vercingetorix's revolt. Gaius Trebonius took part in the Bellovaci Campaign of 50BC and was made a consul in 45BC.

Tullius Cicero, Quintus

Well-connected legate, he took charge of a legion controlling the Nervii in 54BC. Once in winter quarters, the Nervii rose up and besieged his camp. After a long, courageous defence the camp was finally relieved some days later by Caesar's reinforcements. The next year he took part in the Treveri Campaign where he was put in charge of the Fourteenth Legion. Here, again, his camp came under assault by German forces and stout defence paid off, causing the Germans to retreat. After Alesia he was stationed with Publius Sulpicius in the territory of the Aedui.

Appendix IV:
Caesar's Legions

It is not a simple matter to elucidate the number and types of Roman troops involved in the Battle of Alesia. Caesar fails to provide us with even the basic information, let alone give specific mention to the legions involved. We are left, therefore, to supposition and speculation for the most part. Caesar mentions eleven legions specifically in his commentaries on the Gallic campaigns, namely: the First, Sixth, and Seventh to Fifteenth Legions. Suetonius provides another legion, the Fifth, which he says Caesar specifically raised for the battles in Gaul. The Fifth Legion seems to have replaced the First Legion during the Alesia campaign. Armies in Caesar's legions often had the bull as their emblem, although the adoption of individual emblems was also practised. The following is a brief summary of Caesar's legions known to have taken part in the Gallic campaigns, and an account of their more important later actions.

Legio V Alaudae – Fifth Legion ('The Larks')

This legion was founded in Transalpine Gaul in the 50s BC. Suetonius states that it was raised specifically for the Gallic campaigns. Paid for by Caesar himself, it was only recognized by the Senate afterwards.

'he added to the legions which he had received from the state others at his own cost, one actually composed of men of Transalpine Gaul and bearing a Gallic name too (for it was called Alauda), which he trained in the Roman tactics and equipped with Roman arms; and later on he gave every man of it citizenship.'

[Suetonius, *Lives of the Twelve Caesars*, 24]

By including provincials in a Roman legion, Caesar had begun the process of Romanization of the provinces, a practice that continued to the end of the Empire. By allowing provincial citizens to fight he was conferring on them the same rights as those of Roman citizens from mainland Italy. It is interesting to note that the nickname 'The Larks' has, at its root, a Gallic term and not a Latin one. This must have emphasized the provincial character of the unit to the rest of the army. The term has been associated with the wearing of feathers, sticking up on the helmet, reminiscent of the feathers on the head of the crested Lark. Then again, it may refer to Gallic-like wings or a crest on the helmet, or even to specifically pointed helmets. It is possible the legion was originally entitled the *V Gallica* and this might suggest that a distinctive physical characteristic of the legion may have led to a nickname that stuck. Whatever the physical manifestation of the cognomen, the unit certainly seems to have been conspicuous from the first. Following Alesia, the Fifth Legion fought well in the Civil Wars, its role being particularly noted at Thrapsus (Tunisia) in 45BC and Munda (Spain) the following year. The Fifth Legion fought across North Africa and the quality of the men of Caesar's Fifth Legion is evident from one quote from the battle at Thrapsus:

'And here we must not omit to notice the bravery of a veteran soldier of the Fifth Legion. For when an elephant which had been wounded and, roused to fury by the pain, ran against an unarmed camp follower, threw him under his feet, and kneeling on him with his whole weight, and brandishing his uplifted trunk, with hideous cries, crushed him to death, the soldier could not refrain from attacking the animal. The elephant, seeing him advance with his javelin in his hand, quitted the dead body of the camp follower, and seizing him with his trunk, wheeled him round in the air. But he, amid all the danger, preserving his presence of mind, ceased not with his sword to strike at the elephant's trunk, which enwrapped him, and the animal, at last overcome with the pain, quitted the soldier, and fled to the rest with hideous cries.'

[Caesar, *The African Wars*, 84]

It was this event that won the legion the emblem of the elephant. In the Civil Wars both Caesar's and Pompey's armies fought with prolonged lines of fortifications, each attempting to gain a better position to strike out at the other. On one such occasion men of the Fifth Legion are again mentioned. Caesar's forces were attacked while undertaking construction of the fortifications and so two centurions from the Fifth Legion made an attempt to stabilize the situation:

'two centurions of the Fifth Legion passed the river, and restored the battle; when, pressing upon the enemy with astonishing bravery, one of them fell overwhelmed by the multitude of darts discharged from above. The other continued the combat for some time, but seeing himself in danger of being surrounded, endeavoured to make good his retreat, but stumbled and fell. His death being known, the enemy crowded together in still greater numbers, upon which our cavalry passed the river, and drove them back to their entrenchments.'

[Caesar, *The Spanish Wars*, 23]

After the Civil Wars the Fifth Legion may have been disbanded, but it was reformed later under the control of Marcus Antonius in the 30s BC, possibly fighting at Actium. In the empire Augustus created in the wake of the Republic, the Fifth Legion fought in the Western Empire until their defeat and disbandment in the Batavian revolt of AD69.

Legio VI Ferrata – Sixth Legion ('Ironclad')

Another legion created for the Gallic War in 52BC, it was possibly raised in Cisalpine Gaul, although little is known about its origins. The title *Ferrata* refers to either the legion's iron will or some form of iron equipment. The term might be equated with the more modern term *Cuirassier*. Metallic armour of the period was usually mail links, so using the distinguishing term 'Ferrata' may have been a deliberate attempt to mark the unit out for its individualistic style of armour. Caesar mentions that the Sixth Legion was stationed at Saône, along with the Fourteenth, through the winter of 51BC, so its presence there means it was likely to have previously taken part in the Battle of Alesia. After the Gallic campaigns a 'Sixth Legion' is mentioned fighting in the Civil War on Pompey's side. In Africa this legion deserted to Caesar, along with the Fourth Legion, so may have been Caesar's old legion reverting to their old commander. Later, the Sixth Legion is identified as fighting in both Egypt and Syria. At Zela (now in modern-day Turkey) the Sixth Legion, although under strength from fighting in Egypt, fought well against a surprise attack by Pharnaces:

'After a sharp and obstinate conflict, victory began to declare for us on the right wing, where the Sixth Legion was posted. The enemy there were totally overthrown, but, in the centre and left, the battle was long and doubtful; however, with the assistance of the gods, we at last prevailed there also, and drove them with the utmost precipitation down the hill which they had so easily ascended before.'

[Caesar, *The Alexandrian War*, 76]

Caesar later ordered the Sixth Legion to return to Italy to receive the honours and rewards it had won. In the Spanish War the Sixth Legion was again caught in a surprise attack, this time from Pompey's forces:

'About nine at night, the besieged, according to custom, spent a considerable time in casting fire and darts upon our soldiers, and wounded a great number of men. At daybreak they sallied upon the Sixth Legion, while we were busy at the works, and began a sharp contest, in which, however, our men got the better, though the besieged had the advantage of the higher ground. Those who had begun the attack, being vigorously opposed on our side, notwithstanding all the inconveniences we fought under, were at length obliged to retire into the town, with many wounds.'

[Caesar, *The Spanish War*, 12]

After the Civil Wars the Sixth Legion remained in the east and was commanded by Marcus Antonius in the 30s BC. During the Empire the legion returned to the east, where it ended its days in the third century AD. The legion's emblem was the she-wolf and twins – symbolic of the Romulus and Remus myth.

Legio VII – Seventh Legion

Caesar often mentions the Seventh Legion, confirming its presence in the invasion of Gaul in 58BC, fighting against the Nervii in 57BC, again in the Veneti campaign of 56BC and also its involvement in both the British campaigns in 55BC and 54BC. During Vercingetorix's revolt the Seventh Legion fought under Labienus at Paris:

'But when the issue of the victory was still uncertain, and the circumstances which were taking place on the left wing were announced to the tribunes of the Seventh Legion, they faced about their legion to the enemy's rear and attacked it: not even then did any one retreat, but all were surrounded and slain.'

[Caesar, *The Gallic War*, VII. 62]

After the defeat of the Parisii, the remnants of the Seventh followed Labienus and united with Caesar before the march to Alesia. It is likely that they were in the heavy fighting with Labienus on the foot of Mont Réa. Following Alesia, the legion took part in the Bellovaci Campaign of 51BC, where Caesar marks it out along with the Eighth and Ninth Legions as having outstanding fighting ability. The legion went on to fight in the Civil War, being disbanded in 46BC. Reconstituted in 44BC by Augustus, the unit seems to have fought against Marcus Antonius. The Seventh Legion first won the title *Claudia Pia Fidelis* for being loyal to Claudius during Scribonianus' rebellion in AD42, finally winning it for a sixth time in the third century AD *Pia VI Fidelis VI* ('Six Times Faithful, Six Times Loyal'). The unit was still in existence in the fourth century AD on the middle Danube frontier. Its emblem was the Bull.

Legio VIII – Eighth Legion

This legion was raised around 59BC and fought in the Gallic War, where Caesar mentions it engaged in the fighting against the Nervii in 57BC and at Gergovia in 52BC. At Gergovia Caesar picks out the legion and cites the bravery of its centurions:

'Lucius Fabius, a centurion of the Eighth Legion, who, it was ascertained, had said that day among his fellow soldiers that he was excited by the plunder won at Bourges, and would not allow any one to mount the wall before him, finding three men of his own company, and being raised up by them, scaled the wall. He himself, in turn, taking hold of them one by one, drew them up to the wall.'

[Caesar, *The Gallic War*, VII. 47]

'Marcus Petreius, a centurion of the same legion, after attempting to hew down the gates, was overpowered by numbers, and, despairing of his safety, having already received many wounds, said to the soldiers of his own company who followed him: "Since I cannot save you as well as myself, I shall at least provide for your safety, since I allured by the love of glory, led you into this danger, do you save yourselves when an opportunity is given." At the same time he rushed into the midst of the enemy, and slaying two of them, drove back the rest a little from the gate. When his men attempted to aid him, in vain, he says, "you endeavour to procure my safety since blood and strength are now failing me, therefore leave this, while you have the opportunity, and retreat to the legion." Thus he fell fighting a few moments after, and saved his men by his own death.'

[Caesar, *The Gallic War*, VII. 50]

Given the legion was in Gaul, it is likely to have been one of those that fought at Alesia, particularly as it is mentioned in relation to the Bellovacan Campaign of 51BC. In that campaign Caesar again marks it out for comment, along with the Seventh and Ninth Legions, as having outstanding fighting ability. After the Gallic Campaign the legion was given the title *Gallica*, following which the Eighth Legion crossed into Italy with Caesar and continued to fight with him in the Civil War. The legion fought at Ilerda in Spain, in 49BC, where the fighting techniques of the Spanish were disconcerting for Caesar's troops:

'Almost the whole army being daunted at this, because it had occurred contrary to their expectations and custom, Caesar encouraged his men and led the Ninth Legion to their relief, and checked the insolent and eager pursuit of the enemy, and obliged them, in their turn, to show their backs, and retreat to Ilerda, and take post under the walls. But the soldiers of the Ninth Legion, being overzealous to repair the dishonour which had been sustained, having rashly pursued the fleeing enemy, advanced into disadvantageous ground and went up to the foot of the mountain on which the town Ilerda was built . . .'

[Caesar, *The Civil War*, I. 45]

Soon after Ilerda, the legion was commanded by Marcus Antonius at the battles of Dyrrachium (Albania) and Pharsalus (Greece) in 48BC. At Pharsalus the Eighth Legion, still under strength from the fighting previously at Dyrrachium, was placed alongside the Ninth on the left wing, in an attempt to bolster them both. This formation proved successful and was repeated again in Africa against Scipio's forces. Following its disbandment, after the Civil War, the legion was reconstituted in 44BC by Augustus, and fought with him against Marcus Antonius as the 'Gallic Augustan' legion. The legion went on to be attested along the Rhine–Danube frontier until the fourth century AD, and can possibly be identified as the '*Octaviani. Legio Palatina*' (derived from the conjoining of Augustus' original name Octavian and *Palatina*, denoting a senior unit) in the late fourth century AD manuscript the Notitia Dignitatum.

Legio IX (possibly titled 'Hispana') – Ninth Legion ('Spanish')

Probably raised by Caesar before 58BC, little is known of this legion, although given its cognomen it is likely to have been either constituted or stationed in Spain. It fought against the Nervii in 57BC and is likely to have also fought at Alesia. After Alesia the legion took part in the Bellovacan Campaign of 51BC, where Caesar remarked on its outstanding fighting ability, along with the Seventh and Eighth Legions. The Ninth Hispana fought on Caesar's side in the Civil War and was allied with the Eighth Legion on at least two occasions, in Africa and Greece. The Ninth is mentioned as coming under attack during the skirmishes around Dyrrachium (Albania) in 48BC. In response the Ninth replied bravely:

> 'The soldiers of the Ninth Legion suddenly closing their files, threw their javelins, and advancing impetuously from the low ground up the steep, drove Pompey's men precipitately before them, and obliged them to turn their backs; but their retreat was greatly impeded by the hurdles that lay in a long line before them, and the palisades which were in their way, and the trenches that were sunk. But our men being contented to retreat without injury, having killed several of the enemy, and lost but five of their own, very quietly retired, and having seized some other hills somewhat on this side of that place, completed their fortifications.'

> [Caesar, *The Civil War*, III. 46]

Later, Pompey tried again to break through the fortifications that were surrounding his camp and again he met with solid resistance from the Ninth Legion, only this time a multi-pronged attack led to success for Pompey:

> 'For when our cohorts of the Ninth Legion were on guard by the seaside, Pompey's army arrived suddenly by break of day, and their approach was a surprise to our men, and at the same time, the soldiers that came by sea, cast their darts on the front rampart; and the ditches were filled with fascines: and the legionary soldiers terrified those that defended the inner rampart, by applying the scaling-ladders, and by engines and weapons of all sorts, and a vast multitude of archers poured round upon them from every side. Besides, the coverings of osiers, which they had laid over their helmets, were a great security to them against the blows of stones that were the only weapons that our soldiers had. And therefore, when our men were oppressed in every manner, and were scarcely able to make resistance, the defect in our works was observed, and Pompey's soldiers, landing between the two ramparts, where the work was unfinished, attacked our men in the rear, and having

beat them from both sides of the fortification, obliged them to flee.'

[Caesar, *The Civil War*, III. 63]

Later that year, at Pharsalus, the Eighth Legion – still under strength from the fighting at Dyrrachium – was placed alongside the Ninth on the left wing, in an attempt to bolster them both. This formation was repeated again in Africa against Scipio's forces. The earlier valour of the Ninth Legion was not reflected by its behaviour at Placentia (Greece). Here its soldiers mutinied, saying they had served too long and demanding back pay. Caesar's response was swift: he threatened decimation (the execution of one in ten men). This threat seems to have worked, with Caesar ultimately conceding that only the twelve instigators should be executed. After the Civil War the legion was disbanded, but later reconstituted by Augustus in 41BC. The legion went on to fight in Germany and in the invasion of Britain in AD43. Up until recently, this legion was last attested in the historical record in second century AD Britain, the account of its destruction inspiring a number of books, such as Rosemary Sutcliff's *Eagle of the Ninth*. More recent evidence has shown its presence on the Danube frontier in the third century AD and so now it is thought that the legion may have been destroyed either there or during the Second Jewish War.

Legio X Equestris – Tenth Legion ('Mounted')

The Tenth *Equestris* was one of four legions Caesar inherited as governor of Cisalpine Gaul, and quickly rose to become one of Caesar's favourites. This legion was possibly raised in 61BC. Caesar mentions it in the Gallic campaigns, in the battle against the Nervii, taking part in the invasion of Britain and fighting at the Siege of Gergovia. It is very likely that this legion was at also Alesia, as Caesar singles it out a number of times, and on one occasion mentions that he placed his faith in the Tenth Legion.

'But that, if no one else should follow, yet he [Caesar] would go with only the Tenth Legion, of which he had no misgivings, and it should be his praetorian cohort. This legion Caesar had both greatly favoured, and in it, on account of its valour, placed the greatest confidence.'

[Caesar, *The Gallic War*, II. 40]

The legion went on to win the title 'Equestris', due to an unusual event from Caesar's conflict with Ariovistus, the so-called 'King of the Germans' in 58BC. Caesar had set out to stop Ariovistus' control of the Aedui and Sequani, a Roman client kingdom. Caesar openly writes that he was concerned that Ariovistus' intrusion into Gaul would end in the expansion of Germanic rule, and ultimately to the invasion of the Italian peninsula, as the Cimbri and Teutoni had previously done. Memories of Rome's failure when tested by the Germans galvanized Caesar to act. After lengthy negotiations, Caesar managed to bring Ariovistus to a meeting. Ariovistus had stipulated that no infantry attend the meeting, as he did not wish to be ambushed. Knowing Caesar had mainly Gallic cavalry, Ariovistus had tried to put Caesar on the back foot with this demand.

Caesar's Gallic Triumph

'Caesar, as he neither wished that the conference should, by an excuse thrown in the way, be set aside, nor durst trust his life to the cavalry of the Gauls, decided that it would be most expedient to take away from the Gallic cavalry all their horses, and thereon to mount the legionary soldiers of the Tenth Legion, in which he placed the greatest confidence; in order that he might have a bodyguard as trustworthy as possible, should there be any need for action. And when this was done, one of the soldiers of the Tenth Legion said, not without a touch of humour, that Caesar did more for them than he had promised; he had promised to have the Tenth Legion in place of his praetorian cohort; but he now converted them into knights . . .'

[Caesar, *The Gallic War*, II. 42]

The Tenth went on to fight with Caesar in the Civil War, taking the prestigious place on his right wing at Pharsalus in 48BC. The valour of one of its centurions prompted Caesar to comment:

'There was in Caesar's army, a volunteer of the name of Crastinus, who the year before had been first centurion of the Tenth Legion, a man of pre-eminent bravery. He, when the signal was given, says, "Follow me, my old comrades, and display such exertions in behalf of your general as you have determined to do: this is our last battle, and when it shall be won, he will recover his dignity, and we our liberty." At the same time he looked back to Caesar, and said, "General, I will act in such a manner today, that you will feel grateful to me living or dead." After uttering these words he charged first on the right wing, and about 120 chosen volunteers of the same century followed.'

[Caesar, *The Civil War*, III. 91]

Later that year the Tenth were in Africa and Caesar relates how they came into contact with one of Caesar's old generals, Labienus.

'Labienus, with his head uncovered, advanced on horseback to the front of the battle, sometimes encouraging his own men, sometimes addressing Caesar's legions thus: "So ho! You raw soldiers there!" says he, "Why so fierce? Has he infatuated you too with his words? Truly he has brought you into a fine condition! I pity you sincerely." Upon this, one of the soldiers said: "I am none of your raw warriors, Labienus, but a veteran of the Tenth Legion." "Where's your standard?" replied Labienus. "I'll soon make you sensible who I am," answered the soldier. Then pulling off his helmet, to discover himself, he threw a javelin, with all his strength at Labienus, which wounding his horse severely in the breast "Know, Labienus," says he, "that this dart was thrown by a soldier of the Tenth Legion . . ."'

[Caesar, *The African Wars*, 16]

Two years later the Tenth Legion mutinied, asking for discharge and back pay. To the legionaries' surprise, Caesar acknowledged their petition, granting them discharge and addressing them as ordinary citizens. After realizing they were now defenceless civilians the legionaries were soon asking to be taken back into service, fighting on Caesar's right wing at Munda in 45BC. Finally disbanded after the Civil War in 45BC, the Tenth Legion was later reconstituted by Augustus as the *X Gemina* ('Twin'). Well attested through the Roman Empire, the legion won the title *Pia VI Fidelis VI* ('Six Times Faithful, Six Times Loyal') in the third century AD and is finally mentioned as being stationed at *Vindobona* (Vienna) in the fourth century AD. The legion's emblem was the bull – typical of Caesar's legions.

Legio XI – Eleventh Legion

One of the two legions recruited specifically to fight against the Helvetii in 58BC, the Eleventh Legion also fought the Nervii in 57BC, at the Siege of Bourges in 52BC, after which it was likely to have followed Caesar to Alesia. In the Civil War the Eleventh was sent to Macedonia but no further information is forthcoming. Disbanded in 45BC, it was reconstituted by Augustus and is attested until the early fifth century AD. Reasonably well attested throughout the Roman Empire, the legion won the titles *Claudia Pia Fidelis* for being loyal to Claudius during Scribonianus' rebellion in AD42, and went on to be awarded the title for the sixth time in the third century AD *Pia VI Fidelis VI* ('Six Times Faithful, Six Times Loyal'). Vexillations (detachments of the legion) are attested around the Empire during the third century AD and the legion is last mentioned in the fifth century AD, guarding the lower Danube frontier at *Durostorum* (modern-day Silistra, Bulgaria). Its emblem seems to have been either the she-wolf and twins or the sea-god Neptune.

Legio XII Fulminata – Twelfth Legion ('Wielders of the Thunderbolt')

The second of the two legions recruited specifically to fight against the Helvetii in 58BC, the Twelfth Legion also fought against the Nervii in 57BC. In 56BC Caesar describes the Twelfth Legion as opening the route through the Alps under Servius Galba and encamping near Geneva. Suddenly the camp was overrun with a mixed army of Seduni and Veragri and for the under strength legion the onslaught was almost too much to bear:

'When they had now been fighting for more than six hours, without cessation, and not only strength, but even weapons were failing our men, and the enemy were pressing on more rigorously, and had begun to demolish the rampart and to fill up the trench, while our men were becoming exhausted, and the matter was now brought to the last extremity, P. Sextius Baculus, a centurion of the first rank, whom we have related to have been disabled by severe wounds in the engagement with the Nervii, and also Q. Volusenus, a tribune of the soldiers, a man of great skill and valour, hasten to Galba, and assure him that the only hope of safety lay in making a sally, and trying the last resource. Whereupon, assembling the centurions, he quickly gives orders to the soldiers to discontinue the fight a short time, and only collect the weapons flung [at them], and recruit themselves after their fatigue, and afterwards, upon the signal being given, sally forth from the camp, and place in their valour all their hope of safety.'

[Caesar, *The Gallic War*, III. 5]

'They do what they were ordered; and, making a sudden sally from all the gates [of the camp], leave the enemy the means neither of knowing what was taking place, nor of collecting themselves. Fortune thus taking a turn, [our men] surround on every side, and slay those who had entertained the hope of gaining the camp, and having killed more than the third part of an army of more than 30,000 men (which number of the barbarians it appeared certain had come up to our camp), put to flight the rest when panic-stricken, and do not suffer them to halt even upon the higher grounds. All the forces of the enemy being thus routed, and stripped of their arms, our men betake themselves to their camp and fortifications.'

[Caesar, *The Gallic War*, III. 6]

The Twelfth fought with Labienus against the Parisii in 52BC, where it was hard-pressed by the attacking Gauls.

'on the left wing, which position the Twelfth Legion held, although the first ranks fell transfixed by the javelins of the Romans, yet the rest resisted most bravely; nor did any one of them show the slightest intention of flying. Camulogenus, the general of the enemy, was present and encouraged his troops.'

[Caesar, *The Gallic War*, VII. 62]

The Twelfth held on until further legions could turn the assault. The legion's brave fighting at Paris meant it undoubtedly was with Caesar at Alesia. It is likely the Twelfth Legion was part of Labienus' tough fight on the foot of Mont Réa. In the year following Alesia the Twelfth Legion was given to Marcus Antonius, who commanded it under Caesar at the Siege of Uxellodunum. The legion went on to fight with Caesar in the Civil War and later with Marcus Antonius in the East from the 40s BC. From then on the Twelfth Legion saw all of its service in the East, finally being recorded guarding the banks of the Euphrates in the fifth century AD. With its service mainly in the East of the Empire, some authors even suggest that Legio XII has been mentioned as far from Rome as Azerbaijan. Although its emblem was Caesar's bull, it is thought that the thunderbolt was a more commonly used symbol.

Legio XIII Gemina – Thirteenth Legion ('Twin')

One of the two legions recruited specifically to fight against the Belgae in 57BC, hence its cognomen 'Twin'. It is also mentioned in the battle against the Nervii and at Gergovia and so we could expect it to be at Alesia. The following year it was at winter quarters in the territory of the Bituriges, after which it was summoned to Caesar for the Bellovacan Campaign of 51BC, where it took part in the Siege of Uxellodunum. In 55BC the legion was to be found protecting the north of Italy,

Appendix IV

and later it had the honour of crossing the Rubicon with Caesar in 49BC. The legion fought alongside Caesar during the Civil War, in Egypt, Tunisia and at Munda in Spain, after which it was disbanded. Reconstituted by Augustus as the *Legio XIII Gemina* ('Twin Legion'), it was celebrated on coins at least twice during the third century, finally being attested in the fifth century AD in Egypt. The emblem of the legion was the lion, symbol of Jupiter.

Legio XIIII – Fourteenth Legion

Possibly the second of the two legions recruited specifically to fight against the Belgae, there is no mention of the cognomen 'Gemina' at this date but if the Fourteenth was recruited along with the Thirteenth, then the 'Twin' nickname might be appropriate. Caesar refers to the legion in Gaul in 53BC, during his conflict with Ambiorix and the Sugambri.

> 'Then, having divided his forces into three parts, he sent the baggage of all the legions to Aduatuca. That is the name of a fort. This is nearly in the middle of the Eburones, where Titurius and Aurunculeius had been quartered for the purpose of wintering. This place he selected as well on other accounts as because the fortifications of the previous year remained, in order that he might relieve the labour of the soldiers. He left the Fourteenth Legion as a guard for the baggage, one of those three which he had lately raised in Italy and brought over.'
>
> [Caesar, *The Gallic War*, VI. 32]

Given Caesar's seeming lack of confidence in the fresh unit, its place at the Battle of Alesia may have been marginalized somewhat in favour of other veteran legions. There seems no doubt that the legion was at Alesia, as the Fourteenth is mentioned as being stationed with the Sixth, on the Saône, through the following winter. The legion fought in the Civil War with Caesar and was fighting at Thrapsus in 46BC. The Fourteenth fought with particular note in Spain, at Ilerda.

> 'In the first encounter about seventy of our men fell: among them Quintus Fulgenius, first centurion of the second line of the Fourteenth Legion, who, for his extraordinary valour, had been promoted from the lower ranks to that post.'
>
> [Caesar, *The Civil War*, I. 45]

Caesar once more recounted the bravery of the officers of the Fourteenth Legion, this time in the African Wars. A group of Caesar's soldiers had been captured, and Scipio had them brought to him and asked them to join him against Caesar:

> 'Scipio having ended his speech, and expecting a thankful return to so gracious an offer, permitted them to reply; one of their number, a centurion of the Fourteenth Legion, thus addressed him: "Scipio," says he "for I cannot give you the appellation of general. I return you my hearty thanks for the good treatment you are willing to show to prisoners of war; and

perhaps I might accept of your kindness were it not to be purchased at the expense of a horrible crime. What! Shall I carry arms, and fight against Caesar, my general, under whom I have served as centurion; and against his victorious army, to whose renown I have for more than thirty-six years endeavoured to contribute by my valour? It is what I will never do, and even advise you not to push the war any further. You know not what troops you have to deal with, nor the difference betwixt them and yours: of which, if you please, I will give you an indisputable instance. Do you pick out the best cohort you have in your army, and give me only ten of my comrades, who are now your prisoners, to engage them: you shall see by the success, what you are to expect from your soldiers.'"

[Caesar, *The African Wars*, 45]

'When the centurion had courageously made this reply, Scipio, incensed at his boldness, and resenting the affront, made a sign to some of his officers to kill him on the spot, which was immediately put in execution.'

[Caesar, *The African Wars*, 45–6]

The legion went on to fight in Tunisia, and after the Civil War the Fourteenth Legion seems likely to have been reconstituted, together with another legion as the Legio XIIII Gemina ('Twin') in the 40s BC. The legion was given the titles *Martia Victrix* (Victorious in Battle) by Nero after its victory over Boudicca in AD61. The legion then passed on to be stationed along the Rhine–Danube frontier, where it is attested in the fourth century at Carnuntum (in lower Austria). The emblem of the later legion was the Capricorn, like many of Augustus' legions, although it may be anticipated that the emblem of the legion at Alesia was Caesar's bull.

Legio XV – Fifteenth Legion

Little is known about this legion. It is possible that the legion fought at Alesia with Caesar. It did not serve in the Siege of Uxellodunum, Caesar preferring to send it to protect the Roman colonies in northern Italy. Subsequently, in 55BC, when Caesar was ordered by the Senate to send a legion to the conflict in Parthia, it was the Fifteenth he chose. It is possible that he chose the weakest of his units, as the rest of his legions were left to protect Gaul, which he had high personal interest in retaining. The Fifteenth Legion went on to become embroiled in Caesar's dispute with Pompey. On returning to Italy he discovered the Fifteenth still in Italy. The legion, along with the First (another of Caesar's legions), had not been sent to Parthia, but had been handed to Pompey and kept in Italy. At this point Caesar's fears over the political wrangling that had gone on in Rome while he campaigned in Gaul had come to fruition. At the Battle of Pharsalus in 48BC, Pompey used Caesar's old legions, the Fifteenth (now numbered the Third) and First, against him. These should have been some of Pompey's most experienced units in the battle, but they faced Caesar's favourite, the Tenth Legion. Whether because they lacked fighting ability or had split loyalties, Pompey's legions fought nowhere near as effectively as Caesar's. The result was a rout and disaster for Pompey. Caesar permitted the legionaries to surrender but the auxiliaries were slaughtered. It is likely the unit was reconstituted after the Civil War by Augustus (in 40BC) as the *Legio XV Apollinaris* ('Devoted to Apollo'), although there is no direct connection between the two units and the Augustan unit may simply have taken the number of a legion that had previously been disbanded. The Fifteenth Legion is attested throughout the Empire and seems to have finished in the east at Satala (Turkey).

Appendix V:
Orders of Battle

Vercingetorix's Forces

Caesar provides us with only small glimpses of Vercingetorix's army, and the rest has to be pieced together from fleeting mentions in his commentaries. The numbers below reflect Caesar's descriptions, which he goes out of the way to mention, and so should be reasonably accurate as far as they go.

ARMY OF VERCINGETORIX'S REVOLT (WINTER 53–52BC)

Unit	Leader	Number
Arverni	Commanding the Eleuteti Cadurci, Gabali, and Velauni	
	Vercingetorix (Supreme commander)	–
Aulerci	–	?
Andes	Dumnacus	?
Bituriges	–	?
Cadurci	–	?
Carnutes	Gutruatus ?	?
Gabali	–	?
Lemovicis	–	?
Nitiobriges	Teutomatos	?
Parisii	Camulogenus ?	?
Pictones	–	?
Ruteni	–	?
Senones	–	?
Turoni	–	?

STATES WHICH BORDER ON THE ATLANTIC

Curisolites, Rhedones, Ambibari, Caltes, Osismii, Lemovices, Veneti, and Unelli	–	–
Survivors of Avaricum	–	800
Total		more than 800

Caesar's Gallic Triumph

Vercingetorix's Gallic Army for the Alesia Campaign (Summer 52BC)

Unit	Leader	Number
	Aedui Cavarillus (infantry commander captured at Mont Reux)	
	Cotus (cavalry commander captured at Mont Reux)	
	Litaviccus Eporedorix (2) (infantry commander captured at Mont Reux)	
		10,000
		15,000
		–
		300
Arverni	Vercingetorix (Supreme commander)	
	Critognatus (infantry commander)	?
Nitiobriges	Teutomatus (cavalry commander)	?
Mandubii	–	?

Total (Actual total stated by Caesar)	(65,000 infantry & 15,000 cavalry) 80,000

The Gallic Relief Army

Unit	Leader	Number
Aedui including dependants Aulerci Brannovices and Blannovii	Eporedorix (1) (Supreme commander) Viridomarus (Supreme commander) Convictolitavis	35,000
Arverni including dependants Eleuteti, Cadurci, Gabali, and Vellavii	Vercassivellaunus (Supreme commander)	35,000

Appendix V

States which border on the Atlantic

Curisolites, Redones, Ambibarii, Caletes, Osismi, Lemovices, Veneti, and Venelli	–	30,000
Bituriges	–	12,000
Carnutes	Conconnetodumnus Cotuatus	12,000
Ruteni	–	12,000
Santoni	–	12,000
Senones	–	12,000
Sequani	–	12,000
Lemovices	Sedulius	10,000
Helvii	–	8,000
Parisii	Camulogenus?	8,000
Pictones	–	8,000
Turoni	–	8,000
Ambiani	–	5,000
Aulerci Cenomani	–	5,000
Petrocorii	–	5,000
Mediomatrices	–	5,000
Morini	–	5,000
Nitiobriges	Teutomatos?	5,000
Nervii	Boduognatus?	5,000
Suessiones	–	5,000
Atrebates	Commius (Supreme commander)	4,000
Aulerci Eburovices	–	3,000
Lexovii	–	3,000
Veliocasses	–	3,000
Bellovaci	Correus?	2,000
Boii	–	2,000
Rauraci	–	2,000
Total requested		273,000
Actual total stated by Caesar		(240,000 infantry & 8,000 cavalry) 248,000

Caesar's Gallic Triumph

Caesar's Forces

At the outset of hostilities in 52BC, Caesar had eleven legions available, equating to a total paper-strength of about 48,000 men. The actual number of fighting men was likely to be significantly lower than this. Caesar had had armies fighting in Gaul for the previous four years and the impact of this would have taken its toll on the legions' fighting ability. For instance, during the assault on Gergovia prior to Alesia, Caesar had lost 700 men, including forty-six centurions, precious resources indeed. Numbers were increased by levies of more soldiers during the winter months, and also the employment of significant numbers of mercenaries and client troops. Over the course of Vercingetorix's revolt, Caesar was still recruiting to his army, adding 400 German cavalry, with 10,000 Aedui allies due to be added before their revolt. The numbers involved on Caesar's side were constantly fluctuating, and absent a document giving their numbers, at present we are unable to calculate the true strength of his army. Therefore, the numbers below that are given for the legions are paper strengths, and as such should be seen as the likely maximum.

Appendix V

Unit	Leader	Number
Supreme commander	Gaius Julius Caesar	–
Senior legate	Titus Labienus (Chief legate)	–
Legate?	Decimus Junius Brutus	–
Legate?	Gaius Caninius Rebilus	–
Legate?	Gaius Antistius Reginus	–
Legate?	Gaius Trebonius	–
Legate?	Marcus Antonius	–
Legate?	Marcus Aristius	–
Legate?	Marcus Sempronius Rutilus	–
Legate?	Minucius Basilus	–
Legate?	Publius Sulpicius	–
Legio V Alaudae	–	4,800
Legio VI Ferrata	–	4,800
Legio VII	Titus Labienus?	4,800
Legio VIII	Titus Sextius (legate?)	
	Lucius Fabius (centurion)	
	Marcus Petronius (centurion)	4,800
Legio VIIII	Quintus Tullius Cicero (legate)	4,800
Legio X Equestris	–	4,800
Legio XI	–	4,800
Legio XII Fulminata	Publius Sextius Baclus (Chief centurion)	
	Gaius Volusenus Quadratus (tribune)	4,800
Legio XIII Gemina	Titus Sextius (legate)	4,800
Legio XIIII	–	4,800
Legio XV	–	4,800
Total		52,800

Caesar's Gallic Triumph

Appendix VI:
Campaign Glossary

Acid etching The technique by which acid is used to eat away the surface of a piece of metal so as to decorate it. At Alesia swords and spears were etched with circles, triangles, zigzags and lattice designs.

Agen-Port Name given to a variety of helmet types that developed in the late La Tène period (first century BC). The helmet was made of iron and became the forerunner to the Roman imperial Gallic helmet that was popular for the next 200 years. Agen-type helmets had wide strengthening brims while the Port-type had corrugated reinforcements.

Alae Literally 'the wings', the term was used to describe allied soldiers who usually took up position on either side of the legionary force.

Baggage Generally refers to the equipment that was carried along with the army, including personal effects, tents and equipment. It could also include slaves, non-combatants and supplies of food.

Ballista A static torsion catapult that used two twisted skeins of hair or tendons to provide energy for a string that fired projectiles. These skeins were mounted within a frame with arms protruding from either side. A cord was strung between the arms that could be pulled back under tension to fire a projectile. The ballista was built in various sizes that fired anything from small crossbow-sized bolts to large cannonball-sized stones.

Carroballista A form of mobile Ballista mounted on wheels or in a cart that allowed it to be relocated more readily than the standard Ballista.

Centurion Officer in charge of a century.

Century The basic building block of the legion, a century was an eighty man unit. Six centuries formed a cohort.

Cheval-de-frise Literally a 'Friesian horse', the term applies to a type of barrier used since antiquity. The origin of the name seems uncertain but probably comes from the Dutch Wars of the seventeenth century. A cheval-de-frise consists of a moveable wooden construction, often simply a log, fitted with sharpened wooden spikes that was principally a anti-cavalry device. Mainly they were used to block openings where access was required such as gateways.

Cippi Literally 'tombstones', the term was used to describe sharpened wooden stakes, often simply branches with sharpened ends. These stakes were buried in the ground along vulnerable areas and had the effect of primitive barbed wire.

Circumvallation A line of fortifications built by an attacking force around a besieged fortification. These fortifications would face towards the enemy fortification, and often comprised a ring of strong points connected by a wall of some form. From these defences the attacker would contain the besieged and control their communications and supplies. Assaults could be launched from the line of circumvallation and further defences could be extended towards the besieged.

Cisalpine Gaul The nearest province to the Italian peninsula, Cisalpine Gaul contained parts of northern Italy and the Alps.

Clavicular Roman fortifications often utilized elaborate entrance defences to protect them. In a clavicular defence the ramparts of the fort were extended in a C-shape in front of the gateway, either inside or outside the line of the wall. This form of defence forced the attacker to turn his unprotected right side to the defenders of the camp, thus making the attacker vulnerable. Clavicular defences were often used in conjunction with titular defences.

Cohort A cohort was a flexible fighting unit made up of six centuries, totalling 480 men. Ten cohorts would form a legion.

Consul During the Republic, a consul served in the highest civil and military role. Two consuls were usually elected each year, serving as a pair overseeing each other's actions, and each with the power to veto the other's actions should it be necessary. At times of conflict, a consul would command an army of at least two legions, with tribunes acting as subcommanders and a quaestor in charge of finances.

Contravallation Once a circumvallation was made around a besieged fortification, further lines of defences could be made. Defences which faced outwards, away from the fortification and towards the open country were called a contravallation. These were built so the rear of the besieging army would be protected from surprise attacks.

Coolus A type of helmet worn by Roman soldiers. Made of a copper alloy (such as bronze), it was manufactured as a simple dome with a short neck guard and simple cheek guards. The Coolus form was named after the place where the first example was discovered (in the Marne region of France) and was a direct descendent of Gallic forms of helmet.

Devotio Literally a 'self-sacrifice', it was a formal religious act practiced in many ancient religions. As part of the act the individual usually prayed to the gods to save his country or his comrades and then went forth to sacrifice himself to the gods. There are many recorded acts of *devotio* in Roman literature during battle and many of the rash acts attributed to barbarians must be seen in the light of the devotio. The act was formalized to the extent that there was a specific altar, the *lacus curtius*, established for this rite in the Roman Forum.

Donativa Literally a 'distribution of money to the army', the *donativa* was used as a form of gratitude to recognize the actions of the army. More often it was used as a form of bribe or benefit to encourage the army to remain loyal to a general.

Caesar's Gallic Triumph

Equites Literally 'horsemen' or 'knights', the term refers to one of the wealthier classes of Roman individuals. The term refers back to early Rome and the wealthier individuals who could afford horses.

Fascines Literally a 'bundle', usually of wooden sticks. At Alesia these were used by the Gauls to fill the ditches of the Roman defences.

Framea The name given to light spears or javelins with small heads, used by German warriors during the first century BC.

Hill fort Usually a fortified refuge or settlement. Hill forts were located in advantageous positions, usually hills, using the topography of the land to provide a defence from attackers. Often these natural defences were improved with walls or ditches.

Hoplite A form of heavy infantryman originating in Greece and named after the shield the soldier carried called a Hoplon (literally a 'tool of war'). Hoplite warfare relied upon dense formation of warriors' shields locked together to protect their comrades. This formation tended to be very rigid in the field and soon became superseded by looser formations.

Late La Tène A European Iron Age culture characterized by a very elaborate, flowing, decorative style of art. It was named after the archaeological site of La Tène on Lake Neuchâtel in Switzerland.

Legate The overall commander of the legion, usually drawn from the senatorial class. Each legate had six military tribunes to carry out administrative duties.

Legion A large body of heavily armed Roman soldiers with a paper strength of 4,800 men. The term legion is derived from the Latin *legio*, literally a 'levying'. Legions were subdivided into ten cohorts during the Republic; these cohorts could be used as individual fighting units when the larger body of men was inappropriate, such as manning the individual forts at Alesia.

Lilea Literally 'lillies', the term refers to defences used by the Romans to protect the ramparts of forts and circumvallations. Lilea were formed from digging conical pits in long rows and laid out in a design like the five spots on a dice. Once dug, thick wooden stakes were buried in their bottoms, often hardened in fire, and fastened with rammed gravel. Afterwards the pits were camouflaged with the scraps of branches and twigs left from the construction.

Maniple Literally a 'handful', a maniple was a subdivision of the legion containing 120 men and was the forerunner to the cohort.

Marius' Mules The requirement that legionaries carry all of their equipment is attributed to Marius, hence the term Marius' mules, intimating that the soldiers themselves were used as baggage animals. The likelihood is, however, that this is a misattribution. The soldiers had always been required to carry their equipment, a regulation that was regularly flouted. It is likely that Marius simply reinforced a standing regulation in an attempt to make the soldiers more self-reliant and less reliant on a baggage train, part of creating a professional army. Vegetius suggests up to 60 pounds of equipment should be carried during training and Josephus claims each soldier carried a saw, a basket, an axe, a pick, a strap, a billhook, a length of chain and three days' rations.

Montefortino A type of helmet worn by Roman soldiers. Made of a copper alloy (such as bronze), it was manufactured as a tall dome with a small neck guard. There now appear to be five different versions of this form of helmet, but the type as a whole is named after a cemetery in Montefortino, Italy where they were first identified.

Murus gallicus During his campaigns across Gaul, Julius Caesar mentions a specific form of defensive wall he terms *murus gallicus* (literally 'Gallic wall'). These walls were constructed from a wooden lattice of intersecting beams placed along the edge of the settlement, with long iron nails used to pin the beams together at each intersection. The open space within this wooden structure was then filled with earth or rubble, and layers were built in this way to the desired height. Finally, the wall was clad in close-fitting blocks of stone, through which the ends of the beams protruded.

Oppidum Caesar uses the Latin term *oppidum* to refer both to fortified towns and collections of dwellings. The term is now generally applied to fortified settlements surrounded by natural or man-made fortifications across continental Europe. While many of these fortifications were occupied for hundreds of years before the Roman conquest, it is possible that some were created as a direct response to the conflict of the period. The Gallic oppida were often defended by imposing stone walls, termed, *murus gallicus*. Oppida represent a significant stage in the development of urban settlement in Gaul and functioned on a number of levels – protecting strategic locations, serving as trade centres and acting as refuges in times of crisis. While these roles differed from region to region, in general the influence of the oppida came directly from the rich merchant nobles who lived there.

Ossuary A building that serves as a place where human bones were deposited. In Gaul, community ossuaries are known where dismembered bodies were laid on the ground and skulls detached and treated ritually. These practices may be connected with a cultic behaviour, as much of the evidence from these skeletons is of wounds that do not suggest a natural death. One ancient author, Nicander of Colophon, noted that the Celts practiced a form of divination at tombs of dead warriors. In the south of France, a whole range of stone sculptures from sanctuaries reveals that the development of a hero cult was widespread in the centuries before the Roman invasion. Entremont, Roquepertuse and Glanum, all in Provence, are some of the best-known

Caesar's Gallic Triumph

Celtic sanctuaries in the world, due mainly to the cult of the head found at these places.

Phalanx From the Greek word *phalangos* meaning finger, a phalanx was a body of heavy infantry in very close formation. Usually the warriors used large shields which they overlapped, with their spears protruding above them. The point of the formation was to create a nearly impenetrable forest of spears. This formation required strict discipline to retain and was awkward to manoeuvre on the battlefield.

Pilum A pilum (plural *pila*) was a Roman form of spear with a long thin metal shaft and a small pointed head. Although pila are a Roman invention, examples of similar types of weapons were also developed in Gallic and German contexts. After being thrown, pila would bend on impact, thus either disabling an individual or his shield; or if they missed their target, they would be unusable by the enemy. After a battle pila could be recovered and simply remade.

Province, The Refers to southern Gaul down, including the Rhone valley and Mediterranean coast, today called 'Provence'. This was originally a Greek trading colony and later played a significant role in trading between Gaul and Rome.

Quaestor During the Roman Republic quaestors were elected officials who were in charge of the treasury and financial affairs of the State, its armies and its officers.

Rostra From the Latin *rostrum*, or curved prow of a ship, the rostra was a podium in the forum decorated with ships' prows. A rostra was a term applied to a chair on a raised dais in which a magistrate would preside over official functions.

Senate The Senate was the leading council of state. Originally 100 advisers selected by Romulus, by the late Republic the Senate had increased to 400 elected officials. A senator wore a distinctive tunic with a broad purple stripe to indicate his status.

Sesterces During the late Republic, sesterces (singular *sestercius* literally 'two and a half') were small, high-value, silver coins only occasionally issued. Originally they were worth two and a half *asses* (another form of roman coin).

Slingshot The term slingshot is usually applied to a weapon used to throw a heavy projectile, manufactured as a cup or pocket with two cords attached. A heavy missile would be placed into the pocket and the slinger would hold the ends of the cords, spinning the missile around his head until it had gathered enough momentum to be released. The missiles that were thrown are often also called slingshot.

Stimuli Literally 'spurs' or 'goads', stimuli were metal spikes attached to the tops of buried wooden stakes, used to disable enemy infantry and cavalry.

Testudo Literally a 'tortoise', a testudo was a defensive formation made up of a body of men using their shields as a defensive 'shell'. The formation worked by each man on the outside of the formation crouching behind his shield, with the men in the centre of the formation raising their shields above their heads. This created an impenetrable defensive formation for attacking defended positions.

Titula A titula defence comprises a ditch and bank placed directly opposite the entrance to a Roman fort. The aim of the defence was to stop a direct assault on the fort, forcing the attacker to manoeuvre around it. Titula defences were often used in conjunction with clavicular defences.

Transalpine Gaul Transalpine Gaul became a province of Roman Gaul in 121BC and by Caesar's time included the land south of Gaul along the Mediterranean coast from Spain to the Alps.

Tribuli A simple iron device manufactured in such a way that they had four spikes. When thrown on the ground, they always rest upon a tripod of three of the points with the fourth spike sticking up. Tribuli were anti-personnel devices used to disable Gallic infantry and horses. Tribuli (or caltrops) were 'sown' on the ground around gateways and choke points of the defences before an attack. Afterwards they were recovered and the gateways opened up and used again as normal.

Tribune Young upper-class officer under the command of a legate. These officers tended to have no military experience and often used the position to develop their political career.

Triplex acies Literally 'threefold points', the Roman battle line that consisted of four cohorts in front, with two lines of three cohorts behind. This formation was something of a compromise between being wide enough to form a broad frontage and deep enough to have reserves. The middle cohorts were the reserve for the front cohorts, while the rear cohorts could be used for outflanking the enemy or if the legion was attacked in the rear.

Triumph A specific event that was both a civil ceremony and a religious rite. The Triumph was held in Rome to honour the military commander for a successful foreign campaign. The event consisted of a grand parade with specific requirements that displayed captives and booty taken during the conquest.

Vergobret An elected Gallic magistrate who functioned in the role of king, compatible with a Roman consul but with more power. Sometimes he was elected by the Druids and was neither allowed outside the tribal boundaries nor to control the army.

Vexillation A subdivision of the legion, usually a detachment selected for a specific purpose.

Bibliography

The titles listed here either contain essential source material, detailed recent research, or provide a general background to the Alesia Campaign.

Primary Sources

Appian, *History of Rome*.

Caesar, *The Gallic War*.

Cassius Dio, *Roman History*.

Diodorus Siculus, *Library*.

Diodorus Siculus, *World History*.

Frontinus, *The Strategemata*.

Paterculus, *History of Rome*.

Plutarch, *Fall of the Roman Republic: Six Lives*.

Plutarch, *Lives of the Noble Greeks and Romans*.

Plutarch, *The Parallel Lives*.

Strabo, *Geography*.

Suetonius, *Lives of the Twelve Caesars*.

Tacitus, *Germania*.

Vegetius, *Epitome of Military Science*.

Velleius Paterculus, *Roman History*.

Virgil, *Aeneid*.

Secondary Sources

Anonymous, *Vercingétorix et Alésia: Saint-Germain-en-Laye, Musée des Antiquités nationales, 29 mars-18 juillet 1994*, Editions de la Réunion des Musées nationaux.

Berresford Ellis, P., *A Brief History of the Celts*, Robinson.

Bishop, M. C. and Coulston, J. C. N., *Roman Military Equipment*, Batsford.

Bonaparte III, N., *Histoire de Jules César,* Imprimerie Impériale.

Bromwich, J., *The Roman Remains of Northern and Eastern France; A Guidebook*, Routledge.

Caesar's Gallic Triumph

Brouquier-Reddé, V., 'L'équipement militaire d'Alésia d'après les nouvelles recherches (prospections et fouilles)', pp. 277–88 in M. Feugère (ed.), *Journal of Military Equipment Studies*, Volume 8 (1997).

Brunaux, J. L., *The Celtic Gauls: Gods, Rites and Sanctuaries*, B. A. Seaby.

Cornell, T. and Matthews, J., *Atlas of the Roman World*, Facts on File.

Eluère, C., *The Celts First Masters of Europe*, Thames and Hudson.

Feugère, M., 'L'équipement militaire d'époque républicaine en Gaule', pp. 3–23 in C. van Driel-Murray (ed.), *Journal of Military Equipment Studies*, Volume 5 (1994).

Feugère, M., *Weapons of the Romans*, Tempus.

Fuller, J., *Julius Caesar: Man, Soldier and Tyrant*, London.

Le Gall, J., *La bataille d'Alésia*, Histoire Ancienne et Médiévale – 58, Université de Paris I-Panthéon Sorbonne.

Gilliver, K., *The Roman Art of War*, Tempus.

Gilliver, K., Goldsworthy, A. and Whitby, M., *Rome at War: Caesar and His Legacy*, Osprey.

Goldsworthy, A., *Roman Warfare*, Cassell.

Goldsworthy, A., *Caesar, The Life of a Colossus*, Weidenfeld and Nicolson.

Goudineau, C., Guichard, V., Reddé, M., Sievers, S. and Soulhol, H., *Caesar und Vercingetorix*, Phillip von Zabern.

Green, M. J., *The Celtic World*, Routledge.

Keppie, L., *The Making of the Roman Army*, Routledge.

Powell, T.G.E., *The Celts*, Thames and Hudson.

Reddé, M (ed.), *L'Armée Romaine en Gaule*, Editions Errance.

Reddé, M., *Alesia: Das erste Schlachtfeld Galliens*, Verlag Phillip von Zabern.

Sievers, S., 'Alesia und Osuna: Bemerkungen zur Normierung der spätrepublikanischen Bewaffnung und Ausrüstung', pp. 271–276 in M. Feugère (ed.), *Journal of Military Equipment Studies*, Volume 8 (1997).

Welch, K. and Powell, A. (eds), *Julius Caesar as Artful Reporter: The War Commentaries as Political Instruments*, Duckworth, with The Classical Press of Wales.

Wiseman A. and Wiseman P., *Julius Caesar: The Battle for Gaul*, Chatto and Windus.

Index